The Long Fix

Also by Stephen Graf

In this book, you will find easy-to-follow instructions for making your own American Longbow from scratch and advice on how to shoot it. It will take you through the entire process of building a bow, from design to construction. In addition, it explores both the philosophical and concrete reasons making your bow will add to the story of your good life. If you've ever thought about making your own bow, this book is an excellent place to start.

Reviews

Make no mistake, this book will provide both novice and experienced bowyers plenty of practical, perhaps even inspired, information about how to build the American Semi-Longbow, and he explains this as well as I've ever seen it done. But Graf's ability to integrate the goal of his labor into the environment he inhabits—reminiscent of Aldo Leopold—makes this book stand out from all the rest.

E.DONNALL THOMAS JR.,
Coeditor of *Traditional Bowhunter Magazine*

I have built several wood bows, but the specialized skills required to craft a fiberglass-backed bow have always remained a mystery to me until now. This book is a joy to read.

DAVID PETERSEN,
Conservationist and author of *Hunting for the Natural Life*

At last! A real treasure for us who are enamored with the simple longbow.

FRED ANDERSON,
Professional bowyer and author of *The Traditional Way*

The Long Fix

a Methodical Path
to Natural Shooting

-Methods and Exercises-

by

Stephen Graf

All proceeds from the sale of this book are assigned to the Theodore Roosevelt Conservation Partnership. The Partnership works to preserve wild places, whether public or private, so that we may always have somewhere to go a'roving.

An investment in the land is an investment in the good life.

IN DEDICATION

I have spent more hours and days shooting bows and arrows with my friend Harry Angel than I care to count. He was a natural and always (stubbornly) outshot me.

His steady good humor and friendly competition brightened my days and sharpened my aim.

My desire to be a better shot has been motivated by my desire to even the score. I don't guess I ever will now. But I owe Harry a big thank you for keeping me motivated when my shooting went south.

This book is dedicated to boon companions, friendly competition, roving the countryside on a crisp autumn day, and most especially to the memory of my friend Harry Angel.

TABLE OF CONTENTS

THANK YOU

Somebody once said, "The first draft is always shit." I think it's safe to say that was the case for this book. Getting the book to its final form took more work than writing it. These revisions would not have been possible without a lot of help.

I'd like to thank Dr. Art Spell for his critique and insight that helped me work through my understanding of how the human nervous system works to learn automatic fluid motions like those demonstrated in the swing-draw. He is, of course, not responsible for the hypothesis I proposed, whether it turns out to be true or false.

I'd like to thank my daughter, Anne Graf, for all her time and effort spent cleaning up the pictures in this book. She is a wiz with Photoshop.

I'd like to thank my fellow archers David Tetzlaff, Greg Ragan, and Chuck Cote for their feedback on the first draft. Based on their ideas, the manuscript got a significant rewrite.

I'd like to thank Nate Steen for his guidance in learning the swing-draw. He spent many hours schooling me in the way of the swing-draw and many more patient hours giving me feedback as this book took shape. Thank you, my friend.

I'd like to thank my sister-in-law Shannon McConnell for reviewing the manuscript and helping to make it more interesting and less pedantic. In addition, my mom, Mary Graf, carefully read the manuscript, which resulted in some nice improvements. My thanks to both of you.

THANK YOU

I would like to thank the team at JETLAUNCH Publishing. Chris O'Byrne edited the manuscript and tightened up the language nicely. Debbie O'Byrne designed an excellent cover, and Teri Kojetin kept the whole project on track.

Finally, I'd like to thank my wife. Jacqueline was the first to read these chapters, and she read them many times over. Her patience, critique, and support made this book possible. Thank you, my wife.

FOREWORD TO "THE LONG FIX"

As I sit in my den drinking a mug of hot coffee on a cold December afternoon, reflecting on the past hunting season, my mind goes back to all the grand adventures I've had in the woods and fields with my longbow swinging by my side. Venturing afield with the American Semi-Longbow and a simple method of shooting it has a unique way of bringing people together from different backgrounds in both archery and life. The desire to simplify life and enjoy that simplicity is important in this complicated world. This search for simplicity drives many in the sport of archery to the lure of the longbow and sometimes to the Hill style of shooting.

There is not much in the way of explanation concerning the Hill style of shooting. However, Hill wrote a little about it, taught the style to a few individuals, and showed how it's supposed to look on film. One of his students, John Schulz, took what Hill had taught him and competently put those step-by-step lessons into words and video. If the steps Schulz outlined are followed verbatim, an archer can have great success—provided the archer doesn't get in their own way as they try to learn.

That said, an archer struggling with target panic or a recent convert from the compound bow may require a more in-depth approach to learning what Hill and Schulz taught—not more complicated but more informative. There sometimes needs to be more to it than the simple "that's how you do it" approach they employed. What one person may deem a simple act requiring no further thought may prove awkward for someone else. An extra nudge in the form of a more detailed explanation may help. Knowing why and how something is working doesn't complicate the process; sometimes, I believe it can simplify it.

Steve Graf's insights forced me to dig deep into the nuances of the teaching style of Hill and Schulz to grasp what they were trying to say. I count it a great opportunity to spend time with John Schulz to understand how he taught face to face. Years later, those conversations with Schulz were followed by great conversations with Steve. Those results, combined with Steve's insatiable desire to know how things work, led to this great book. In these writings, Steve has shown the process, techniques, tools, and thinking that helped him on his journey to shoot the American Semi-Longbow using the Hill style of the swing draw. In this book, Steve gives us that deeper understanding, a nudge, if you will, that can help us overcome problems or stave off frustration as we learn the swing draw.

The entire approach that Steve outlines here will benefit both those who like to keep it simple and those who want to know more. We can all benefit from a deeper understanding of the Hill shooting style. A deeper understanding may be especially helpful for those who struggle to find their way. Steve's book will certainly help the student, whether they are completely new to this shooting style or an old hand wanting to refine their form.

I remember the day, about a year after he embraced the swing draw, when Steve told me about his first hunting success. He said there was no doubt in his mind about the outcome, and only 10 seconds after the game was in sight, the result was food ready to process for the table. That's what is so great about this style—its practical application to hunting and making good food and good memories. I'm glad Steve has written this book describing the methods and exercises that have worked for him. Not only did I learn from reading it, but it was also a joy to read. I know that you, the reader, will enjoy this book and learn from it as well. My sincerest thanks go to Steve for writing this book, and I wish him and each of you straight shooting!

Nate Steen
Bowyer, Sunset Hill Longbows

HANDEDNESS

I am a right-handed archer, and therefore, my descriptions of bows, arrows, form, shooting, and everything else archery are made from the perspective of a right-handed archer.

It would be tedious for the reader if (every time I mentioned something related to my shooting) I were to say, "For a left-handed archer, the arrow will go the other way." So I will say it once, here at the beginning, and leave it at that.

The left-handed reader will have to reflect about an imaginary plane (the sagittal plane) nearly everything I describe concerning how the archer-bow-arrow machine works. If I were to say (for example) that an overly stiff arrow flies to the left, you would have to translate that statement in your mind to understand that, in your case, an overly stiff arrow flies to the right.

I most sincerely and respectfully tip my hat to left-handed archers as they are routinely ignored not just by scribblers like me but by almost everyone, from makers of archery gear to those that set out the tournament stakes. We ignore them at our own peril, as I have found my left-handed friends to persistently outshoot me more often than not.

To my left-handed friends, please excuse and forgive my omissions to your perspective that force you to think harder than the rest of us in order to figure it out.

SWING-DRAW

I struggled mightily with the conundrum of what word or phrase to use to describe the shooting style I have outlined in this book. I struggled not because I had a hard time finding words to describe it but because of the connotations these words can invoke in those of us who have built our world and our sense of identity around archery.

The idea of a trademark recognizes the value that the connotation of a word can have. Owning the connotation of a word can literally mean the difference between success and failure for a business. Indeed, there are those who have made their living in the sport of archery by associating with this or that style of shooting and may claim authority or ownership over certain words or phrases.

Over time, certain words enter the lexicon of the common language. Take the ubiquitous Kleenex, for example. We use that word to describe a facial tissue without a thought to the fact that it is a trademarked word for a specific brand of facial tissue. The trademark suffered from its success and now connotes any tissue, not specifically the Kleenex brand of tissue.

I think there are several words that adequately describe the style of shooting outlined in this book. They are natural, automatic, and swing-draw.

I chose not to use the phrase swing-draw on the cover to avoid confusion with the specific teachings and style of those better archers that came before me, namely Howard Hill and John Schulz.

That said, I like to think that what I lay out in this book is indeed the swing-draw style as pioneered by Hill, Schulz, and many others, including the Wilhelm brothers. Hopefully, the book explains the method in more detail for those among us who are less talented, more hardheaded, and may be prone to the yips, like me.

On the cover, I used the word natural to describe the style because its connotations include innate abilities, simple approaches, and gentle attitudes while avoiding the mental conflicts or confusion that may arise from using a phrase like swing-draw.

In the body of the book, I do use (almost exclusively) the phrase swing-draw to describe the style as I think that, like the word Kleenex, it has evolved in our archery lexicon, and its meaning now includes most any dynamic method of shooting the bow wherein the bow is held low, moved up to target while the string is drawn to anchor, and then released. All in a smooth and fluid way.

There are those who may feel that what I have described in this book has nothing to do with the swing-draw as they know and understand it. I hope there are at least a few who will agree with me that the method I describe in this book meets the definition of the swing-draw.

As you read this book, you will have to decide for yourself what to call it. You will have to decide if it really matters.

Hopefully, in the end, what we call the method is not as important to us as what it has to teach us about ourselves, achieving balance with the bow, and maybe even finding our joy in archery.

DISCLAIMER

I do not speak for those whom I quote. I quote a lot of people in this book: people ranging from great archers to medical researchers, ornithologists, Zen masters, physicists, and statisticians.

The words of the people I quote affected my experience of learning to shoot more naturally. I present these quotes to help explain how I stitched my experiences and my thinking together into what is my understanding of shooting the swing-draw.

I do not have a special understanding of the people I quote. I use their words to illustrate a point I am trying to make. It may or may not have been the point that they were trying to make. This being the case, any mistakes and misunderstandings are mine.

Whenever we share our words (particularly in such a permanent way as writing a book), we hope that they will be understood as we intended them to be. But we must understand that our words will be viewed and understood through the prism of the readers' experiences. Such is life.

I share my understanding of the swing-draw in the hopes that it will speed struggling archers along their paths to finding joy in archery. The understanding I present in this book is my own and in no way claims to reflect the understanding or teachings of those better swing-draw archers who came before me, like Howard Hill or John Schulz.

FOREWORD

What is the value of following a path that was laid out by others? This is a question I have had some time to consider.

My son and I recently hiked the Appalachian Trail in its entirety. Starting from its southern terminus at Springer Mountain in Georgia, the trail meanders about 2,200 miles to its northern terminus at Mt. Katahdin in Maine. Through its course, the trail climbs nearly 550,000 vertical feet of mountain, and it took us almost six months of steady hiking to complete the journey.

Spending all our days hiking and most of our nights (occasionally, we stayed in a motel when we resupplied in town) sleeping on the ground gave me plenty of time to consider the merit of following a path laid out by someone else.

Doesn't following another's path show a lack of imagination? What is left to discover on a path already trod by so many others? Wouldn't I experience more by setting off on my own path? I bet I could find a better path than this mucky old trail.

The truth is that there are many answers to these questions, but none of them can really be known or understood until the path is actually followed from one end to the other.

Every single day spent on the trail is important. Every single day is unique. On some especially hard days, we may have walked only five miles. On our "easiest" day, we made twenty-eight miles. And even though my son and I walked every mile of the trail together, the experience was different for each of us.

The first truth about following a trail is that it will get you where you want to go. There is no way a person could walk from Georgia to Maine without help. At the very least, a hiker would need to resupply their food and have a compass and a map to navigate. In the end, it would no doubt take longer and be way more complicated to complete the hike off the beaten path.

Another truth is that the adventure—the *real* adventure—has little to do with the novelty of the path. The real adventure cannot be imagined beforehand. Exercising one's imagination requires that we have some memory or experience to build on. We cannot imagine something from nothing. Unless we have taken a long walk (defined as 2,000 or more miles), we cannot imagine what adventure awaits us.

I have spent many weeks at a time in backcountry camps roughing it. Even these experiences could not prepare my mind to accurately imagine the adventure of a six-month hike along the spine of an entire continental mountain range.

Perhaps the most important truth of all is the discovery that the path is where it is for a reason. We grumbled and griped our way through wind, cold, rain, snow, hunger, hard ground, mud, more rain, and perpetually sore feet as we shared our adventure. When we got to the end of the hike, we found that we were changed people. Even as the anniversary of the end of our hike nears, I find that it is still changing me. I will likely dwell on this adventure for the rest of my life, and it will probably continue to change me and bring me even more joy as the years pass. Having the trail laid out by those who came before me allowed me to focus on what was really important: Nothing worthwhile is ever easy.

All of these same thoughts apply to following the path of the swing-draw. Just as there are many trails to hike, there are many paths to learning archery. The point is to pick one and stick with it until you have reached your goal.

And what exactly does stick with it mean? How motivated we are to stick with a thing until we see it through helps define our personal adventure. That said, there have been a number of empirical studies that touch on the magnitude of commitment needed to master archery. Malcolm Gladwell tells us in his book *Outliers*:

> In study after study, of composers, basketball players, fiction writers, ice skaters, concert pianists, chess players, and others ... [10,000 hours] comes up again and again... No one has yet found a case in which true world-class expertise was accomplished in less time. It seems that it takes the brain this long to assimilate all that it needs to know to achieve true mastery.

One of the points that Gladwell drives home in his book is that the level of excellence we achieve is more dependent on how hard we work than it is on our natural ability. We don't all have natural talents for the things we love, but we can choose to work hard at it until we develop some decent skills.

Gladwell was able to put a number on what it takes to get good. It highlights the fact that if you want to get good at something, really good, then you have to be willing to work hard, really hard. There are no shortcuts, gimmicks, or quick fixes that will get you where you want to go.

This reminds me of another long-walker truth. It is the truth we have to remind ourselves of most often: The key to success is to keep putting one foot in front of the other. To be a long-walker, you must take the long view. It takes at least five million steps to walk the Appalachian Trail, and every step is needed. None can be skipped.

In the same sense, the title of this book, *The Long Fix*, illustrates the same truth. Following the path of the swing-draw is no afternoon stroll. The key to success is found in an almost infinite series of small improvements made possible by constant practice.

That said, there is such a thing as natural ability. No matter how hard and how well we practice basketball, most of us will never be as good as Michael Jordan. And by the same token, no matter how hard or how well we practice archery, most of us will never be as good as Howard Hill.

That doesn't mean there is no purpose in following the path.

While it took my son and me nearly six months to hike the Appalachian Trail, there were others who did it in much less time. Hardly a day went by that we were not passed by someone who had started a week or a month after we did. But in the end, we all arrived at the same place.

Now that we have completed the hike, does it matter that it took us longer?

And I wonder if, in the end, we didn't get more from the experience because it did take us longer to get there.

And I remember we never doubted that the trail would get us to Mt. Katahdin. Can you imagine if we doubted the path? If we doubted it would take us to our destination, why would we continue to follow it?

This book tells the story of my adventure to follow the path of the swing-draw. The path I followed was laid out by those better archers who came before me and were willing and able to blaze the trail so that I could follow in their footsteps.

Before I started this swing-draw adventure, I could not imagine the effect that following the path would have on me. It has most definitely improved my life, my archery, and my sense of joy.

Just as it shows good hiker etiquette to clear the trail and add stones to cairns that mark the way, it is my hope that this book will, to some small degree, improve the path for others who take up the way of the swing-draw.

There is one more truth to know about the path of the swing-draw that every long walker eventually learns about the path they hike. We come to realize that while there is a beginning to the path, as long as we are willing to walk, there really is no end to our trail.

Once we learn this truth, we free ourselves from the anticipation of getting to the end and open ourselves to the joy of being on the path.

The peak of Mt. Katahdin is the northern terminus of
the 2,200-mile Appalachian Trail.

PART I

A METHODICAL WAY

There are at least two approaches one can take to learn archery. The most common approach is to jump right in and start shooting at the mark. For some folks, this works out just fine, and they never look back.

For others, we head down this path, and everything looks fine. But then we begin to stumble, we begin to shoot poorly, and we lose sight of the joy of archery.

Lucky for us, there is another approach, another way. In this less common approach, this path less traveled, lies the opportunity to improve our shooting and to find the joy of archery again.

This less common path is what forms the core subject of this book and is outlined in Part 1.

In Part 1, the reader will find chapters that outline basic points of form, as well as exercises designed to ingrain that form into a reliable habit. The archer who reads these chapters and steadfastly practices the exercises described needs no further information or understanding to succeed.

The information in this first part is an expansion of the exercises outlined in the "Shooting Tips" chapter of my first book. If the reader has read that book, they will notice many of the same words, ideas, and pictures used.

One of the greatest hazards a writer faces in writing something down is that it doesn't always hold up to scrutiny over time. I am pleased and relieved that the words recorded in that first book do hold up as I read them again so many years later.

Therefore, I felt justified in using many of those same words again in Part 1. I hope the reader will not feel cheated, having paid twice for the same words. The value of reading those words again in this second book is that they are surrounded by more context, experience, and additional exercises designed to help the archer be more successful.

Finding this different approach to archery was a great relief to me. It allowed me to quit thinking about my form and just shoot. It gave me structure without the need for understanding.

The structure of this book mirrors, in a sense, the structure of the practice and philosophy that make up the "long fix" approach to learning archery.

As an enthusiastic archer, I wanted to get on with it. I am sure all enthusiastic archers feel the same way. Thus, Part 1 of this book allows the archer to get on with it. It allows them to begin finding their form, learning to balance themselves with the bow, and finding their joy in archery.

Understanding how the method works isn't important at this stage. Neither is understanding how your thinking may change as you commit to your practice. But if you do commit to practicing these exercises, then over time, you may find that you become curious to know more.

As a curious reader, you may read this whole book before you begin your exercises. That is a good thing. As you gain experience with the exercises in this book, you may read these chapters again and find that their meaning shifts. That is also a good thing.

But for now, the only thing you need to remember as you begin the exercises outlined in Part 1 is that there is no right or wrong. There is no good or bad. There is only practice.

There is no timeline. You are under no obligation to improve at any rate. The only obligation you need to set for yourself is a regular time and place to practice.

If there should be anything rattling around in your mind as you exercise your daily practice, let it be the words of the American dancer Martha Graham:

Practice is a means of inviting perfection.

Chapter 1

BASIC POINTS OF FORM

I n this chapter, I will go into detail about each of the basic points of the shooting form. After you have read about each of these points, you may want to scratch some simple notes that you can use to remind yourself of each point while standing in front of the blank bale (Chapter 2 will explain the blank bale) as you begin your practice.

As you read this chapter and see all the parts and pieces that must be put together to achieve good form, it might seem overwhelming. The good news is that most of these things will come naturally to you, and you will likely have trouble with only one or two.

In fact, an argument can be made that the information in this chapter is unnecessary—that all a person really needs to do is simply practice shooting into a blank bale, and if they practice long enough, they will develop good form. The argument continues with the observation that the morphology of our bodies is different enough so that what works for one person is not guaranteed to work for another, so why cloud the process with information that may not be helpful? Why not just let each person's natural ability develop as they practice?

I think this argument is 100 percent valid, and it is true that, given enough time, a person can learn all they need from shooting into a blank bale. Even so, I think there are a couple of reasons why reading this chapter may have value to a student of the swing-draw.

First, I believe that the points of form that I outline in this chapter are fundamental and applicable to most people. Therefore, reading this chapter will save the swing-draw student time by outlining the points of form upfront so that the student doesn't have to spend time discovering them.

Second, I believe that even if the points of form as outlined in this chapter don't work for the swing-draw student directly, they may inspire the student to try new things until they find what works for them.

There are two purposes in striving for good form. The obvious purpose is to develop consistency in our method and, thus, accuracy in our shot. This purpose is what this chapter is about.

AIMING AND FORM

There are only two reasons that account for why we miss our intended mark. Either our form is off, or our aim is off. That's it.

Contrary to popular opinion, I think aiming is actually the easiest part of archery. As we learn good form and apply it to our swing-draw method of shooting, we learn that we really don't *aim* the arrow in the commonly understood sense of the word. Instead, we point the arrow at the target just as we would point our finger at something.

Understanding this difference is key to success with the swing-draw. It is worth dwelling on this idea for a while.

We can easily point our finger at something without looking along its length with one eye to verify it is going in the right direction. We have a kinesthetic awareness of our body in space and time and can align our finger on a path that intersects with what our eyes are looking at.

Learning good form allows us to do the same thing with our bow and arrow. By developing good form, we learn to point our arrow at the mark. The things that make learning good form tricky are those pesky forces and torques we induce into the bow and arrow that are unseen by our eye. As we learn good form, we will begin to feel these forces and torques and learn to minimize or eliminate them.

As we learn to shoot, we will learn to draw the bow and to be aware of the arrow's position below our eye. We will point the arrow where we want it to go, and yet still (to our unending frustration), upon release, the arrow will often go somewhere else.

We are usually quick to blame our gear: bad arrow, low brace height, worn-out glove, whatever. Whether it is truly the fault of equipment—or more likely caused by ourselves—the real culprits are the unresolved and unnecessary forces and torques we apply to the bow as we draw it.

We can draw the bow (and unknowingly induce all sorts of torques and forces), and we can come to full draw and hold motionless for a perfect moment before release. And yet when we let go of the string, all sorts of unexpected things can happen to the arrow. How can this be?

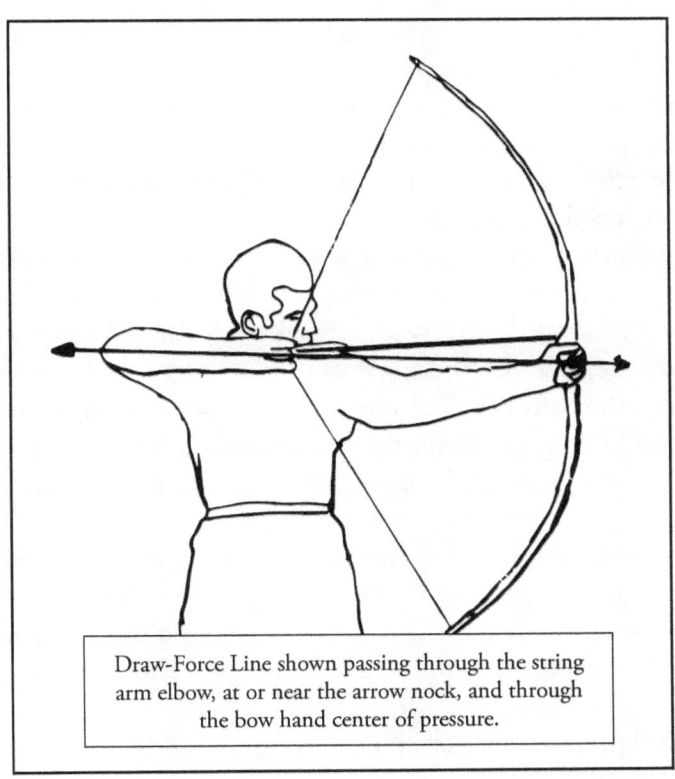

Draw-Force Line shown passing through the string arm elbow, at or near the arrow nock, and through the bow hand center of pressure.

When we draw the bow, our body applies forces against it. The bow, in turn, applies forces (equal and opposite) against us. It is a thing of beauty.

When we draw the bow and come to anchor and hold motionless, all forces are in static equilibrium. This is a fact proven true by observing that nothing moves. Static equilibrium. All forces add up to zero. But then we let go of the string, and half of the forces are removed. What happens?

Ideally, our draw-force line is in exact alignment with the arrow (in the direction of the target), and there are no torques. The draw-force line is the line that can be drawn from the pressure point under our bow hand to the center of our drawing arm elbow. This is the line along which the archer and the bow push against each other.

If we have perfect form, then there are no torques (twisting forces) between the bow and the archer. If this is so, then the bow will relax as its internal stress is relieved, and the arrow will be cast along the line we predicted.

On the other hand, if we have induced unnecessary forces (and thus unnecessary reactionary torque) into the bow, as it relaxes, it will twist off the line we set it to as we pointed the arrow at the bale, and the arrow flight goes awry.

Any unnecessary forces or torques in the bow are parasitic, and by definition, they take away from the perfection of the shot. Not only do they send the arrow on a trajectory different from what we want, but they also rob the arrow of speed (energy) and momentum.

A well-shot arrow will always be faster than a poorly shot arrow.

As we learn good form, we will develop a kinesthetic sense of these parasitic forces and torques. But it takes time, patience, and practice.

As our kinesthetic sense matures, we will be able to naturally and automatically point our bow at a target with the same ease and accuracy we are accustomed to as we casually point our finger. The idea of aiming our bow will seem as silly as the idea of aiming our finger when we point it.

As you practice the basic points of form outlined in this chapter, you will start to feel when you are doing something wrong. You won't necessarily be able to correct the flaw right away, and so you may become frustrated by it.

However, this is progress. First, we must learn to feel the shot. As beginners, we are likely doing something wrong, and thus the first thing we will feel is our faults. Don't worry about getting it right. Just concentrate on learning what the shot feels like.

There is no timeline. There is only commitment and practice.

NOCKING THE ARROW

Many years ago, I heard John Schulz say to nock the arrow above the nockset. I tried it off and on repeatedly. Sometimes it would work for a while, and sometimes not.

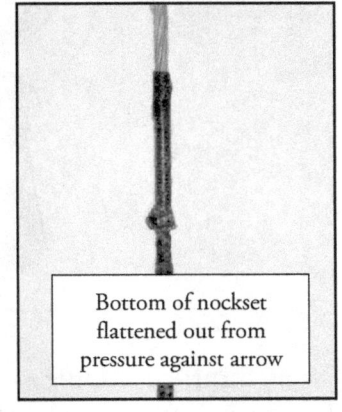

When it worked, the arrow would stay against the nockset during the draw, and then I could complete the shot. When it didn't work, the arrow would slide up the string, and my effort to draw the bow would fall apart.

Bottom of nockset flattened out from pressure against arrow

I would go back to nocking the arrow under the nockset, even though I knew my tied-on nockset would flatten out from the pressure of the arrow against it.

I was aware of this clue. The clue that there were unresolved forces at play in my bow as I drew it. Those forces, while unresolved, did show themselves in the flattened nockset of my string and erratic flight of my arrow. The nockset was acting like a pair of training wheels on my bike, keeping me upright but preventing me from learning how to ride.

I knew this, but what to do?

Then I read some of Jean-Marie Coche's words (translated into English by Google) from his book *The Discipline of Instinctive Shooting*. Coche said to hold the bow at about a 20-degree forward angle (70 degrees from horizontal) as you begin the draw. This surprised me.

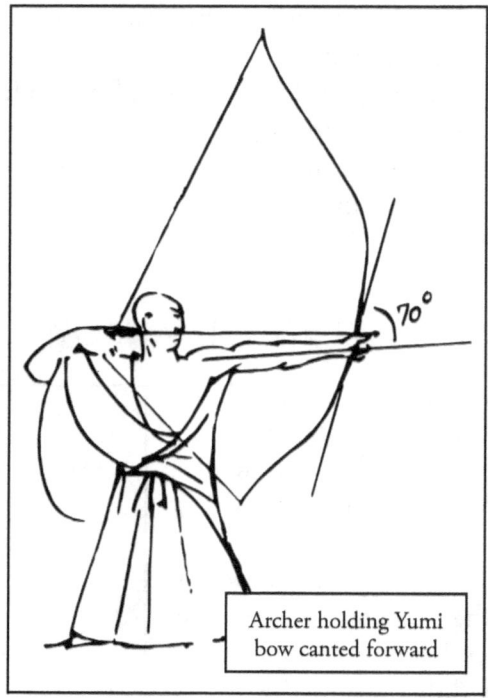

Archer holding Yumi
bow canted forward

It surprised me because I used to hold my bow this way. But I stopped because I thought it contributed to my problem of the upper limb lurching forward after the shot. As it turned out, holding the bow at a forward angle was the right thing to do.

There are other clues out there for the observant archer. Look how Japanese archers hold their Yumi bows, always tilted forward about the same 20 degrees from vertical (70 degrees from horizontal). Or watch old Howard Hill movies, and if you look closely, you will see the same thing.

Holding the bow at a forward angle keeps the arrow against the nockset.

Shooting a bow well requires that the bow-arrow-archer machine is in balance. Nocking the arrow below the nockset allows you to shoot the bow without achieving balance. Nocking above requires that everything be balanced and will improve your form and consistency.

Howard Hill keeps the angle by lowering his bow shoulder and bending his elbow.

Then something that Hill said in his book *Hunting the Hard Way* came to my mind. He said to hold the bow handle mostly with the bottom two fingers. By doing this, the bow is naturally canted forward.

In addition to holding the bow handle with the bottom two fingers, what I eventually ended up doing was leaving the thumb of my bow hand against the upper fade during the first few moments of the draw, then lowering it to its resting position. This allowed me to get a more consistent forward cant and didn't require wrist or finger action to achieve it. Less muscle tension gave me better consistency (see the "Gripping the Bow" section for more detail).

Aside from keeping the arrow against the top of the nockset, canting the bow forward has another benefit. It allows the hand to accept the bow in a more natural, ergonomic grip.

Lay your forearm and fist on the table. Rest your thumb on top of your fist. Notice the angle between the top of your forearm and the base of your thumb. It is not 90 degrees. It is closer to 70 degrees. If you take a bow in your hands, you will notice that the angle between your forearm and the back of your bow is closer to 70 degrees than 90 degrees.

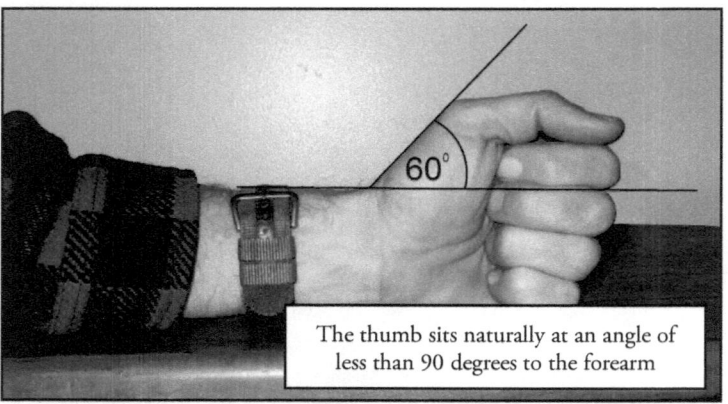

The thumb sits naturally at an angle of less than 90 degrees to the forearm

Recurves and compound bows take this morphology of our hands into consideration when they are built with locator grips that allow the hand to relax. Grips that are too deep go too far the other way, but that is not a discussion for this book.

Since longbows have no room for such grips, to shoot well, they must be sublimely designed to allow them to be drawn with this forward cant.

So as you take the bow in your hand, nock the arrow above the nockset. Cant the bow forward as you begin your draw just enough to keep the arrow against the top of the nockset. In my experience, 20 degrees can be hard to achieve. But when we start out, it's a good goal. Once we practice this for a while, the forward cant will become more subtle. Only the informed observer will notice it.

Study the pictures of Howard Hill and Justin Ma. They maintain the 70-degree angle by lowering their bow shoulders, raising their drawing shoulders, and bending their bow-arm elbows (at least a little). The result is that the bow arm angle is correct, and yet the bow appears relatively vertical to the eye.

Remember to relax your bow-arm wrist as the bow is drawn so that the bow can do what it needs to and so that you don't induce unwanted and parasitic forces or torques.

Justin Ma shows his
form as learned from the
writings of Gao Ying

SHOULDERS AND BACK

The shoulders and back provide the foundation upon which a good shot is made.

I don't think this fact is intuitively obvious to the average archer. Not many of us have to "put our back into it" much anymore. Most of the work we do involves just our hands and arms and is done right in front of our faces. But shooting a bow is a unique effort unto itself and does require a lot of work from the shoulders and back.

Having started my archery adventure with a compound, I never really had to learn how to use my back in a sustained way. I could easily pull my 80- and 100-pound bows, engaging my back muscles just long enough to pull the cams over their hump, and then relaxing into the low-holding weight compounds are famous for.

In my case, I think my shooting troubles stemmed from not using my shoulders and back correctly. Over time this form fault caused me to develop target panic.

Luckily, I picked up a book written by an ancient Chinese army general who spent the latter years of his life training new army recruits in archery. From his writings, I realized how fundamental the correct use of the shoulder and back is to good form, and I finally learned how to develop that form.

In Jie Tian and Justin Ma's translation of Gao Ying's 11th-century archery manual titled *The Way of Archery*, Ying's description of not being able to come to full anchor (target panic) because of incorrect form was spot-on in my case:

> Suppose you take the wrong path. When you are starting archery, your joints are free of problems, your muscles are strong, your concentration is sharp, and you can reach full draw. You become settled with your technique and have no problems hitting the target. But when you have practiced this way for a while, your joints will develop deep-seated problems... You suddenly lose the ability to reach full draw. The more you shoot, the more your arrows veer away from the target.

Gao Ying had my attention at this point. He then went on to provide a description of what one needs to do with one's shoulders and how to learn to position them correctly. I followed his advice. I found that with my shoulders correctly positioned, I could use my back muscles more efficiently and bring my string hand to my anchor.

Gao Ying provides an exercise to help the aspiring archer learn to position his shoulder correctly and recommends that the archer practice this exercise for at least a month before even attempting to shoot a bow. That's how fundamental it is to good form that we get the bow shoulder positioned just right.

Before I explain the exercise, I will explain the goal. The goal is to get the shoulder seated down and back so that it forms a solid foundation that is not prone to moving around and so that it will not shift unpredictably when the string is dropped. It is also the goal to get the shoulder blades correctly positioned so that the back muscles can be used efficiently.

The humerus (upper arm bone) has a ball on the end, which engages a socket in the scapula (shoulder blade). The key to understanding correct shoulder position is observing that the ball joint is not stuck right on the end of the humerus but is offset on the side of the bone.

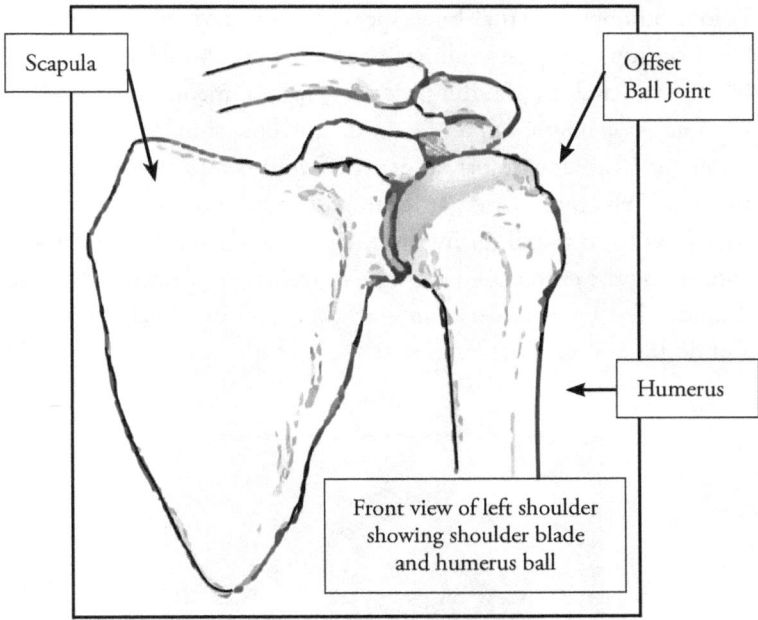

Scapula

Offset
Ball Joint

Humerus

Front view of left shoulder
showing shoulder blade
and humerus ball

If the ball joint were on the end of the bone, then rotating the bone would make no difference to how the arm reacts. However, since the joint is on the side, as we rotate our humerus, how it and the scapula sit on our shoulder changes.

If we can get our shoulders to sit down low and square (not up and floating forward), and we can pull both shoulder blades towards the spine, then we can have the most stable and strong form we are capable of.

When we are trying to learn a new motion of the body, it is often helpful to visualize some other motion that we may be familiar with that can help us find the muscles to use.

In learning to get my scapula pulled down and towards the spine and my humerus bone rotated correctly, it was helpful to imagine making my shoulder blade stick out like a wing. Looking in a mirror, I worked at making my shoulder blade stick out like Howard Hill's.

Then I would keep the image of getting the blade to stick out in mind as I practiced the exercise that Gao Ying explained:

> Before pulling an actual bow, spend several days with your bow hand on top of a post and... rotate your bow shoulder clockwise [right-hand archer]...[and if necessary] have someone assist you by rotating your bow shoulder forward. The bow shoulder should be lower than the drawing shoulder. If the arms and shoulders start to hurt, then stop... After a month, you can hold your bow while your bow hand is still resting on the post, and pull the bow while continuing the exercise... When the movement of rotating the bow shoulder has become very familiar, then you can nock an arrow and do the pulling without a post.

Howard Hill's bow shoulder blade sticking out

I found this exercise helpful in learning to rotate my upper arm bone and shoulder blade. We use the phrase manual dexterity to describe the ability to move our hands in precise ways. To become good at archery, I think we need to develop shoulder dexterity. We need to be good at moving our shoulder as required to balance the forces applied to it and to move the bow as we desire.

This exercise helped me develop my shoulder dexterity in the same way that using fat crayons helps young children develop their manual dexterity. It did take me about a month of daily practice to get it right.

After getting the hang of rotating my bow shoulder and learning what it felt like, I found that I could then rotate my string shoulder as well. I learned that if I rotated my string shoulder in the opposite direction (counterclockwise), it helped orient my string hand correctly and bring my arm more naturally to anchor.

The back of the string hand needs to be parallel to the bow. If it is not, then the bow hand must twist the bow to keep it canted. This is a common fault that can sometimes be traced back to the string arm shoulder and should be suspected when, upon release, the bow twists clockwise.

String hand twisting string, elbow higher than necessary

String hand parallel with bow, elbow in better alignment with arrow

Another way to get a feel for what the string shoulder should do is to stand with your arms out. Look down your bow arm as you would normally do and cant the bow hand clockwise like normal. Then, with the string arm still straight out to the side, rotate the string arm shoulder until the string arm hand is at the same cant as the bow arm hand (after it is brought around). Then bring the string

17

hand around to your normal anchor position. Notice that when the string arm is straight out to the side (as in the first figure), it is at an angle of about 90 degrees to the bow hand.

Rotate string hand CCW by rotating shoulder

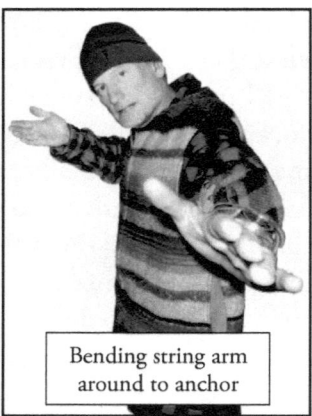

Bending string arm around to anchor

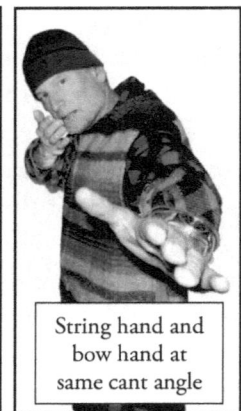

String hand and bow hand at same cant angle

Finally, here is another way to visualize the shoulder motion. Imagine drawing a line over your shoulder with an arrow point on the end indicating the direction of rotation. With the bow arm, the line would start on your back, come over your shoulder, and go down your chest with the arrow pointing down at your toes. With

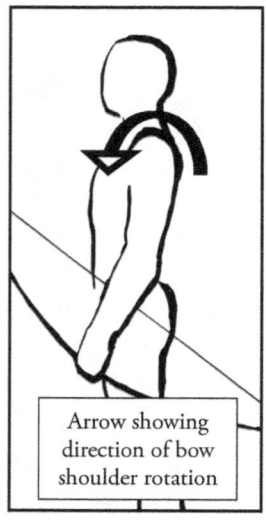

Arrow showing direction of bow shoulder rotation

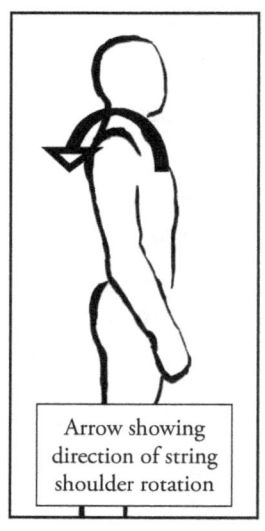

Arrow showing direction of string shoulder rotation

the string arm, the line would start on your chest, go over your shoulder, and go down your back with the arrow pointing at your heels. You are rotating your shoulders in opposite directions.

I found that if I position my shoulders correctly and pull my shoulder blades toward the spine before drawing the bow, it is easier to avoid the flaw of engaging the bicep muscle to pull the string back. If you find that you punch yourself in the face after letting the string go or that your string arm elbow is sticking way out to the side at full draw, then you are likely engaging your bicep to pull the string back.

If you wait to position your shoulders correctly and pull your shoulder blades toward the spine until after the motion of the draw has begun, it is harder to get it right.

STANCE

I think sometimes we archers forget that the only thing in archery we have no control over is the mark. We often stand rigidly in front of the target and shoot, wondering why it feels so awkward.

When we do bend, it is usually at the waist, which burdens our spine and forces antagonism on the latissimus dorsi muscles as they try to hold our draw while at the same time bending our spine. Our arrows generally fly high of the mark when we do this, since the forces we apply to the bow change, as does our sight picture.

There are two reasons we need to be able to bend. The first and most obvious is to adjust the trajectory of our arrow so that it falls into the target, whether it is high or low, close, or far. The second is to orient the shoulders so that the string-arm shoulder is higher than the bow-arm shoulder.

When we need to adjust the trajectory of our arrow, most of us are inclined to simply move our bow arm up or down. Doing so guarantees a poor shot.

We need to learn to bend (up or down) correctly so that our bow arm can keep its optimal position and our bow shoulder can stay seated down and back. This also allows our head to maintain its accustomed orientation to the string arm and bow so that our sight picture does not change, and our shot will prove accurate.

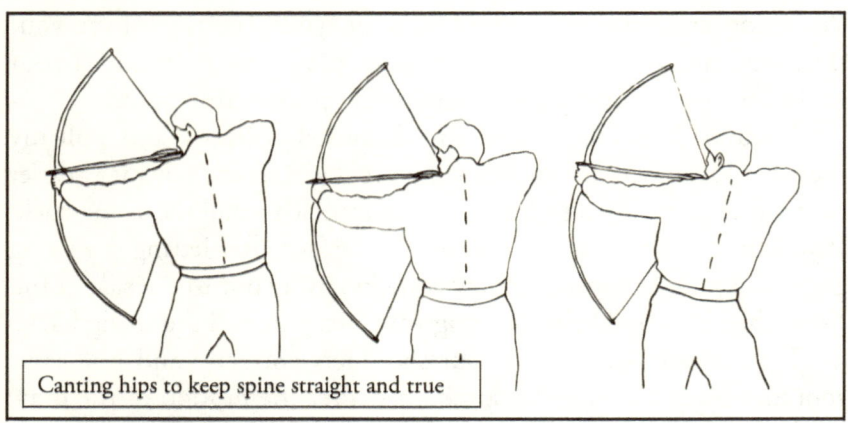

Canting hips to keep spine straight and true

What we must learn to do is to move our spine in the direction we want, not by bending it, but instead by balancing it straight and true upon our hips, which we angle, or cant, as required to put ourselves in position.

Learning to maintain a straight spine while canting the hips to allow us to bend down (most commonly) or up is a challenge. We must also add to this the need to lean slightly out over the feet, which does involve bending the spine.

The best way to bend down is to (by whatever combination feels comfortable to you) move the leading foot forward (toward the target) and bend the forward knee while shifting more weight onto the forward foot. The farther forward you move the leading foot, the less you must bend the knee to cant the hips.

While we don't want to bend our spine side to side because it is inefficient and unstable, we do want to bend our spine over our stomach so we can lean slightly over the feet so that when we draw the bow, our head is more easily positioned over the arrow for alignment down the shaft. It helps to crunch your stomach muscles tightly to make this posture solid.

Leaning slightly over the feet means that the hips will probably move subtly over the heels. This allows us to keep our balance and keep a solid foundation for our stance.

Howard Hill leaning over arrow

To make this happen, our feet must be well apart, and our stance must be (at a minimum) closed. I find for myself that if I take an extra closed stance, I do better.

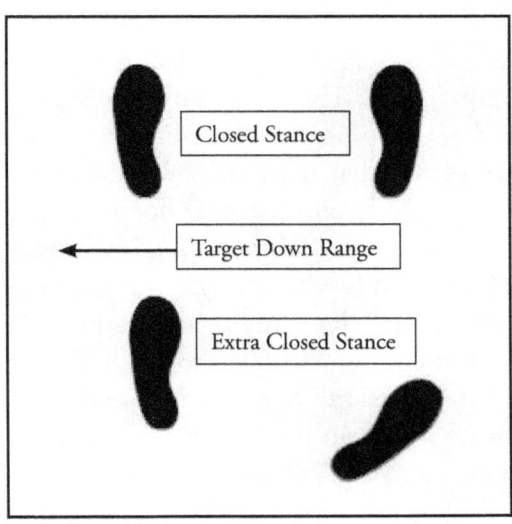

Closed Stance

Target Down Range

Extra Closed Stance

Practicing our stance is something we can do without shooting. We can benefit from taking our stance and feeling our balance steady as we settle. If we do this without shooting the bow, we can hold our stance as long as we want, learning the feel. We can experiment with moving our hips this way and that to steady our balance. We can lean our head out over our toes while moving our hips out over our heels and ingrain the feel into our form, ever mindful of keeping our bow shoulder lower than our string shoulder and our hips canted so that our spine can remain straight.

As we do this, we can draw an imaginary bow, going through all the motions required to come to full draw and release an arrow. As I take my morning walk, I make it a point to spy a leaf or a spot of lichens on a tree and draw my imaginary bow and send my imaginary arrow to hit it. After my imaginary shot, I hold my form until the arrow hits the mark, feeling the balance, feeling the power of a shot well made.

GRIPPING THE BOW

Some bow grips tell you what to do. There are only so many ways to hold a recurve-bow grip. That's why they are called locator grips. The bowyer shapes the grip so that you must grasp it in a certain way.

How we take the straight grip (and dished grip) of a longbow is open for interpretation. There are as many ways to hold that grip as there are archers holding them. Is one way more correct than another? I can't answer that question, but I can observe that if we hold the bow consistently and the bow doesn't fidget in our hands upon release, then we are probably holding it well enough.

I have tried several different strategies for grasping the bow, and I struggled to understand the many interpretations of Howard Hill's famous and often-invoked instruction to "grab it like a suitcase."

I just couldn't understand the "suitcase" reference for the simple fact that a suitcase hangs on the fingers when held, whereas a bow presses against the palm and wrist when drawn.

What did work for me was the method offered by Ray Axford in his book *Archery Anatomy*:

> With the traditional bow... The bow grip is either cigar-shaped of round section or a flattened barrel shape of oval section, and the bow hand can be positioned consistently by holding it with the thumb placed up the top limb before lowering it to the normal position with the thumb encircling the grip.

To take the bow into my hand consistently, I place my hand on the bow as Axford describes, with my thumb resting on the upper fade, and make sure I leave my fingers dangling and loose. Then I place some tension on the bowstring until my bow hand settles nicely into the grip. Once it feels right, I wrap my fingers around the grip, with the bottom two fingers doing most of the work. Then I lower my thumb and prepare to draw the bow. From this moment onward, it is important to keep tension on the string. Do not move your hand around on the grip. It should be glued in place at this point.

Feeling the relationship between the bottom two fingers closed around the grip and the thumb pressed lightly on the upper fade gives confidence. Feeling how they work together to position the bow hand upon the forward canted bow and to balance the arrow upon the top of the nockset helps to establish a smooth draw.

Before I started my swing-draw adventure, I would move my hand around several times as I drew the bow. I would start out holding it one way before the draw, let it slide around during the draw, and shift it again after reaching full draw. All this motion was in response to not having a consistent form and trying to balance things out as I went. Obviously, all this fidgeting only hurt my form and, thus, my shot.

Part of developing consistent form is learning to take the bow correctly in your hand and committing to that grip through the shot. When you have finished your shot, and you are holding your position after the arrow gets to the bale, take note of your bow hand position. Is it the same as it was when you began the shot? If not, why not?

Taking the bow in your hand, as Axford describes, will put the bow grip against the inside of your thumb and along the lifeline so that your hand will naturally and consistently fold around the grip. You will be able to take the bow in your hand exactly the same way every time, no question about it.

STRING HOOK

There are as many ways to take the string as there are archers. How we take the string depends on our body morphology as well as our chosen form of hand protection: Hill-style glove, Damascus-style glove, tab, etc.

However it works for us, there is one main quality to our hook that we should all strive for: We should try to keep all muscles in the arm and hand relaxed except for those muscles in the forearm responsible for bending the fingers around the string.

If we can learn to do this, then we will avoid faults, such as crabbing the string or cranking the wrist up or down and in or out.

Holding a bowstring in our hand this way is not intuitive. In fact, I think it is hard. In my experience, release faults seem to be the most common and persistently difficult faults to overcome. I don't know any archers who wouldn't like to improve how their string hand works.

I think part of the problem is that it is hard for us to isolate just those muscles needed to curl the ends of our fingers over. This is not a motion we use in our daily lives, and so we have little experience with it.

In our normal daily use of tools, computers, doorknobs, etc., when we grasp an item, we use all the muscles that close the hand (even if we hold something delicate with just the fingertips). When we open our hands, we pull every part of our fingers open.

Making a good hook on the string incorporates aspects of both gripping (closing our hand) and releasing (opening our hand) an object at the same time.

We need to keep the proximal phalanges (the first bone of the fingers after the palm) in line with the palm. This is the open-our-hand aspect.

We need to curl the middle and distal phalanges (the outer two bones of the finger) across the string. This is the close-our-hand aspect.

To make a good hook, we need to keep the proximal phalanges aligned with the wrist and forearm by engaging the extensor tendons (tendons that run across the back of the hand to open the finger) and relaxing the flexor tendons (tendons that run across the palm of the hand to close the finger). Ideally, we should relax all the muscles and tendons related to this first finger bone. But if we can't do that, the next best thing is to make sure we tense up the extensor tendon so that we don't crab the string.

Additionally, we need to engage the flexor tendons of the outer two phalanges while relaxing the extensor tendons.

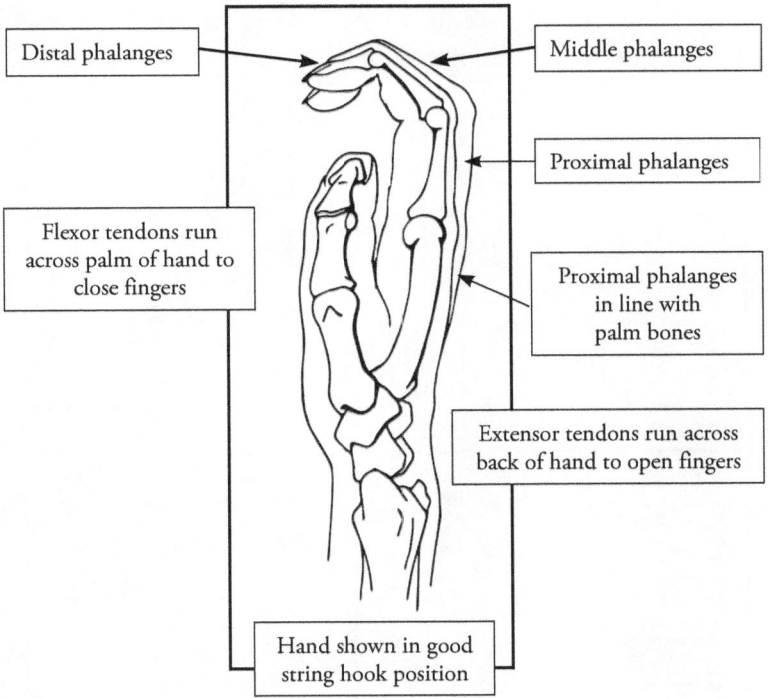

I used to find it easier to make an acceptable string hook using a tab or a Damascus-style glove. With these soft and pliable protective devices, the string can seat deep in the last joint of the hand, and our release faults don't usually get the better of us. But by the same token, because the string sits so deeply in the joint, we don't get as clean a release as we might be able to get with a stiffer glove like the Hill style.

Learning to shoot a Hill-style glove can be daunting because of the problem of the string not seating deeply in the joint. When we start using it, it feels like our grasp of the string is tenuous, and we are out of control. This can cause us to crab the string.

Learning to make a good string hook is a bit like learning to pat our head while rubbing our stomach. I found it was easier to learn to make a good string hook (that allowed me to use a Hill glove) by practicing an exercise outside my normal archery practice.

The following exercise can help the archer no matter what form of protective device they use. It will be especially helpful to the archer who chooses to use a Hill-style glove.

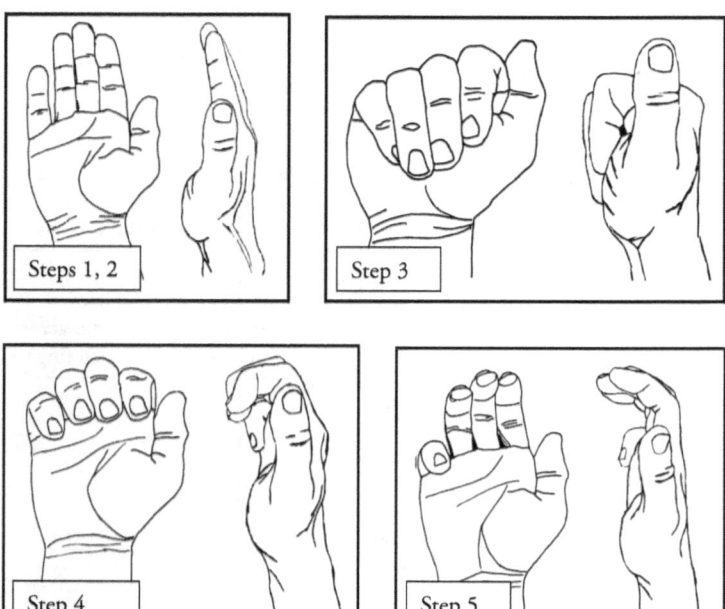

The purpose of this exercise is to help us learn to separate the open and close muscles and tendons and motions of the different phalange bones, and recombine them in a way that lets us grasp the string in an efficient and repeatable hook:

1. Hold your hand so that the back of your hand and your fingers are aligned with your forearm.
2. Rest your thumb on top of your hand.
3. Keeping your fingers as straight as possible, bend them at their base, the first joint at the edge of the palm. Bend them as far as you can before beginning to curl your fingers around to touch the base of your palm.
4. Keeping your fingertips in contact with your palm as long as you can and your fingers curled, bring the proximal phalanges bone back to the aligned position with the forearm (like in step 1).
5. Slowly uncurl the three string fingers into their hook position while leaving the pinky curled up against the palm.
   If you prefer to keep the thumb down and across the palm, this motion can be added after the fingers are in their final position.
   Hold the position for several seconds. Relax. Repeat.

When you first try this exercise, it may indeed feel as clumsy as rubbing your head and patting your stomach. With practice, it will become automatic.

It can be practiced while watching TV, riding in a car, reading, or any other time your string hand is free.

It is important to understand that the figures presented to help illustrate this exercise depict the hand as it would appear while practicing the exercise, not what it would look like under tension at full draw. In particular, the figure for step 5 shows the fingers extending past 90 degrees, which would make holding the string with a Hill-style glove hard to do. When drawing a bow, the fingers should establish an angle of about 90 degrees.

Another aspect of the hook that needs to be considered is the question of how much pressure we apply to the string with each finger. This is another example for which there are as many answers as there are archers. I will answer this question based on my understanding of balancing the bow-arrow-archer machine and placing the arrow nock above the string nockset.

When we place the arrow nock above the string nockset, we free the arrow from the bow. If the arrow is nocked below the nockset, it is trapped between the arrow shelf and the nockset. I think this is what accounts for (at least in part) the flattening out, or mushrooming, seen in the nockset of bows so configured (see the picture of the nockset at the beginning of this chapter).

When we draw the bow with the arrow above the nockset, we are forced to balance the bow as we draw. As mentioned in the section about nocking the arrow, if we don't balance the bow, the arrow will skate up the string as we draw.

In order to draw the bow in balance so that the arrow stays against the nockset (or nearly so), I have found that it is best to apply most of the force to the string with the bottom two fingers that are below the string nockset. Depending on the archer's morphology, this balance can extend to even pressure on all three fingers. However, the index finger should never see more pressure than either of the other two fingers.

There are a *lot* of conflicting opinions on this point. For example, Will Thompson makes reference to his release woes by describing his index finger as the "shirking first" in an article published in the April 1913 edition of *Forest and Stream* magazine. Thompson felt that because Roger Ascham (in his famous book *Toxophilus*) called for even pressure on all fingers, Thompson's natural tendency to leave the index finger under burdened meant that he was doing it wrong. I fell into this way of thinking as well.

Another opinion on the role of the index finger was expressed by Robert Elmer in his book *Target Archery*. I think Elmer finds the truth and exactly describes my experience:

> My own experience and that of many others is that shooting is steadier if very little pressure is made of the forefinger. If it be in the least overbearing, there is a tendency to pinch the nock and tilt the arrow up from the bow hand—a fatal blunder—and even

when the error is not of that magnitude, there still seems to be a residue of infirmity that will often make the arrow fly too high.

By nocking the arrow above the nockset and taking most of the draw force with the bottom two fingers, I find I can balance the bow and shoot the arrow more directly toward the mark.

THE STRING ARM

The way we should use our string arm to draw and shoot our bow is so very different from how we are accustomed to using our arms.

The muscles in our arms are there for a reason. We use them constantly in our day-to-day activities. But in the case of shooting a bow, most of these muscles that we normally depend on do nothing but cause problems for our good form.

To balance ourselves with the bow and to reliably place our arrow near the mark, there are only a few muscles in our string arm that should be engaged in the process.

Those muscles are the ones in our forearm that curl our fingers into the hook and those in our shoulder that connect to the spine of the shoulder blade and pull our arm back.

There is often controversy over how we should draw our arms back. Some will say that we should use our shoulder muscles, specifically our deltoids. Others will say we should use our back muscles, specifically our trapezius and rhomboids. Happily, the resolution to this disagreement comes in the realization that all these muscles must be used to pull our arm back. In the words of Russ Paine in a 2013 paper about the role of the scapula in the motion of the arm published in the *Journal of Sports Medicine*: "These muscle groups function through synergistic co-contraction to anchor [the shoulder blade] and guide movement."

It can be no other way after one observes the fact that there are no mechanical bone-to-bone connections between the arm and the rest of the body. The arm and shoulder essentially float freely and are connected to the rest of the body only by muscle and tendon.

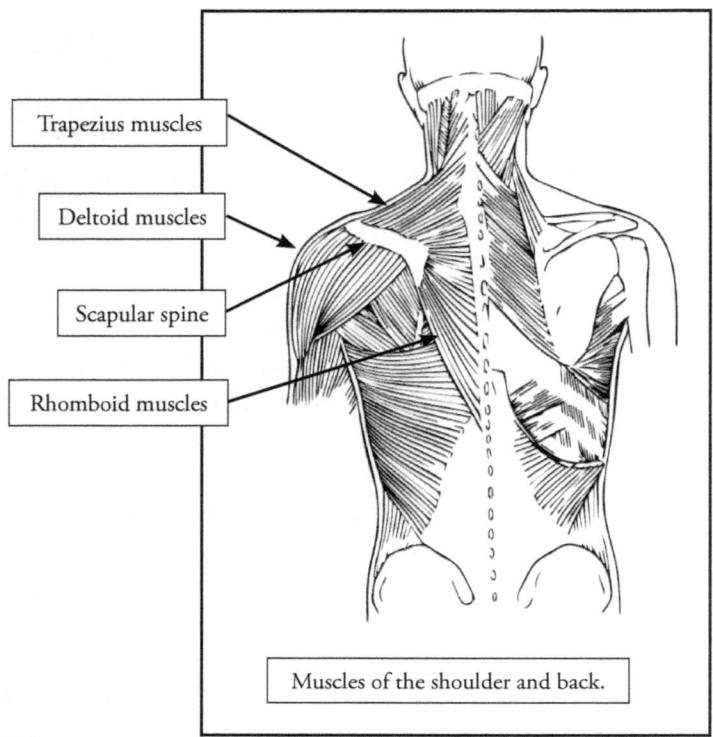

Trapezius muscles

Deltoid muscles

Scapular spine

Rhomboid muscles

Muscles of the shoulder and back.

This is what allows the amazing freedom of motion that our arms enjoy. But it comes at the cost of instability and complex muscle structure.

The shoulder muscles pull against one side of the scapular spine, and the back muscles pull against the other. All these muscles must work together at the same time to pull our string arm back.

Learning to pull the string arm back is part of developing our shoulder dexterity. We must learn to pull the arm back with these muscles while also learning to do it accurately. The goodness of our aim is dependent on fine muscle control in our shoulders and back.

While it has been established that no arm muscles should be used except those in the shoulder and those that make the finger hook, I have found that if I engage the muscles needed to keep my string-arm wrist straight, I can more easily and reliably pull my string arm back.

Keeping my string-arm wrist straight is my pragmatic fix to counter a common string-arm fault, which is to engage the bicep muscle to bring the string hand back to full draw.

THE BOW ARM

I have found that eliminating faults with the bow arm depends on eliminating faults with my stance and shoulders. The bow arm tries to compensate for faults in the stance and shoulders and ends up being blamed for them.

That said, there are a few faults that can be blamed directly on the bow arm, like the dropped bow arm that results from an archer's habit of peeking, which involves lowering the bow at the release to watch the arrow's flight. Inevitably, the archer lowers their bow arm before the arrow has left the bow, resulting in a low shot.

Most other bow-arm faults might be more correctly thought of as symptoms of a fault.

If a person moves their arm to the left at the shot, they are told to hold their arm steady and follow through. Instead, maybe they should be advised to close their stance. If they drop their arm at the shot, they are again told to follow through after the release. Instead, the fault may lay in poor posture (bow shoulder even or above the string shoulder) or a bow shoulder not set down and back so that it provides a solid foundation.

The bow arm, being extended as it is, is subjected to, and reacts more obviously to, parasitic forces and torques than does the rest of the body. Instead of trying to force it to do our bidding, we would be better served by sussing out the underlying cause of its erratic behavior.

If the rest of my form is good (and I am not *peeking*), my bow arm will behave.

About the only form fault that is directly related to the bow arm is the angle of the elbow. The elbow should be broken in that it is not held so that the arm is straight out; it should be bent.

If the bow shoulder is set correctly (down and back) and is lower than the string shoulder, then it is very comfortable to hold the bow arm with a bent elbow.

What angle the elbow takes is a function of the archer's physical morphology more than anything else. As long as the bow arm is held in a comfortable, relaxed manner (with a bend in the elbow), then that is just fine.

Some archers' elbows bend more than others. That's just how it is. No need to worry about it.

The bend in the elbow will help soften the impact of the shot on the bones, ligaments, and tendons of the bow arm. It will also help reduce some of the form errors that cause the arm to drop or move to the left at the shot.

Pay attention to your bow arm. It will tell you a lot about how the bow and arrow are reacting to your form. But don't be too quick to blame it for a missed shot. It can be your canary in the coal mine.

Is your bow-arm elbow or wrist sore? Maybe your elbow is not bent enough. This may be caused by the bow shoulder not being below the string shoulder. This, in turn, likely results from not setting your stance correctly before the shot.

Does the bow lurch to the left at the shot? Maybe your stance is too open.

Does the bow rotate clockwise at the shot? Maybe your string hand is out of alignment with the bow (twisting the string counterclockwise is a common fault), and the bow arm is trying to compensate.

Learning how your bow arm reacts to your shooting faults is a big step in learning to correct them.

DRAWING THE BOW AND RELEASING THE ARROW

In order to make a good shot with a bow, I think we must feel settled when we get to anchor and before we drop the string. This moment of feeling settled is very much shorter for the swing-draw archer than it is for the tournament archer. No matter how short it is for the swing-draw archer, I think it must still be part of the shot. We can learn to be settled, even though we may not stop our motion.

I think some of this sense of being settled in the shot gets transferred to the beginning of the shot for a swing-draw archer.

When we take our bow and establish our pre-shot stance, we learn to settle into it. Then we focus hard on what we want to hit and begin the draw. As we begin the shot, we go into automatic mode.

The success or failure of a shot is largely determined before the shot ever happens. I see this in myself, but I also see it in others. I can tell with almost complete certainty whether a fellow archer's arrow will fly true or not just by how they take their stance.

It's not about looking for a certain tell, like whether they hold the string exactly like Howard Hill or whether they position their feet just like John Schulz says to. No, it's simply an overall impression of the archer being comfortable and in control.

Feeling that sense of familiar comfort, control, and, ultimately, commitment is what we strive for in our practice. When we achieve this, it will be no surprise when the arrow hits the mark.

When we begin to draw the bow, we have settled ourselves into our pre-draw form and are committing to the shot. The deeper our commitment, the less we stumble. That said, there are times when it would be prudent to let down the bow instead of shooting. The better we get, the less we will be faced with the need to let down the bow.

So now that we have committed to the draw, how to start?

Our bow hand leads the way. In order to establish our bow hand's place in space, we should begin the draw by lowering the hand a few inches and then begin the upward motion. The value of this smooth drop before beginning the rise to orient our bow hand in space should not be underestimated.

As we continue to raise our bow hand, we can then begin to bring our string hand up and toward our face.

Our bow hand should arrive at the correct elevation just as our string hand gets to about the right level, but about six inches in front of our face.

While holding the bow hand on target, we bring the string hand straight back to our anchor, keeping our eye over the arrow. We can take these last six inches slowly and even pause as we get things right. Then we bring the string—finally—to our anchor.

As we pull through these last six inches, we will learn to feel everything come into balance. If there is inadvertent built-up tension somewhere, now is the time to relieve it.

As we become skilled in the swing-draw, our fingers will find that familiar place on our face that we call our anchor. We will hold deep into it as our string arm is pulled around that last bit by our back and shoulder muscles, and we narrow our focus onto the mark.

As I draw the bow, I inhale so that by the time I have my string arm in front of my face, my lungs are full (but not overly so), and I begin to hold my breath. I tighten up my stomach muscles, and I hold my breath until I have reached anchor. This helps to expand my chest and my draw, as well as to make my posture more solid.

There is something special about inhaling and holding my breath as I come to anchor. It helps to focus the mind. It also helps to separate the act of drawing the bow upon the target from the act of dropping the string. For those of us who suffer from target panic, this is no small help.

As I release the string, I release my breath. Not only does this release help me to be present in the moment, but it also helps the mechanics of the shot.

If I continued to hold my breath through the release, my chest (tight with air) would transmit the vibrations of the shot and the parasitic forces and torques to the bow and the arrow. By releasing my breath at the shot, my chest can collapse (some), and the escaping air can cushion the shot.

This effect is not unlike the action of an automotive airbag. If during an accident, the airbag simply inflated and stayed that way, the passenger would suffer almost the same injuries had the airbag not been deployed. Having the airbag deflate as the person presses into it takes the energy and momentum out of the impending impact with the dashboard.

By releasing the air from my lungs at the moment of the shot, I am giving the energy and forces pent up in my body somewhere to go.

The shot is not over when the string is dropped.

When we let go of the string, our string hand should remain at our anchor. As the string pushes its way past our fingers, it will push our hand away from our anchor momentarily. The string hand should gently settle back into position after the string is gone.

Our bow hand should remain up and on target until the arrow arrives at the mark. Assuming an arrow speed of 165 fps and a draw length of 28 inches, the arrow will be on the bow for something like 0.03 seconds after the string is released. That is plenty of time to send the arrow off course by dropping our bow hand.

Besides keeping the arrow on course as it passes the bow, by holding our posture until the arrow arrives at the mark, we give ourselves time to feel what went right and what went wrong with the shot. This helps us improve the next shot.

Something else that can help us learn the swing-draw is to watch an expert archer demonstrate the style. Watching John Schulz and his son execute the swing-draw flawlessly and listening to Mr. Schulz's advice in his video "Hitting them like Howard Hill" can be invaluable to the student of the swing-draw.

I struggled with the question of whether to include a picture of myself drawing the bow, since I am an average archer with imperfect form.

I grew up shooting compound bows, so my form will likely always have echoes of my old ways. In a sense, it is like an accent. Few people who learn a new language later in life can shed their accent. In the end, I decided to include a draw sequence figure for the sake of completeness and to illustrate the stages of the draw.

If the reader is wary of the trap of trying to exactly duplicate the shooting form of another, they can build confidence in their style by noting that the author has found joy and success in the swing-draw even while displaying some obvious faults (which shall remain unmentioned so as not to harm the author's tender ego). Despite these faults, the draw sequence shows the required stages an archer should endeavor to include in their swing-draw sequence.

The last stage of the draw, follow through, was not shown in the picture since to include it would have made the other stages of the draw too small to allow a clear view of what is happening.

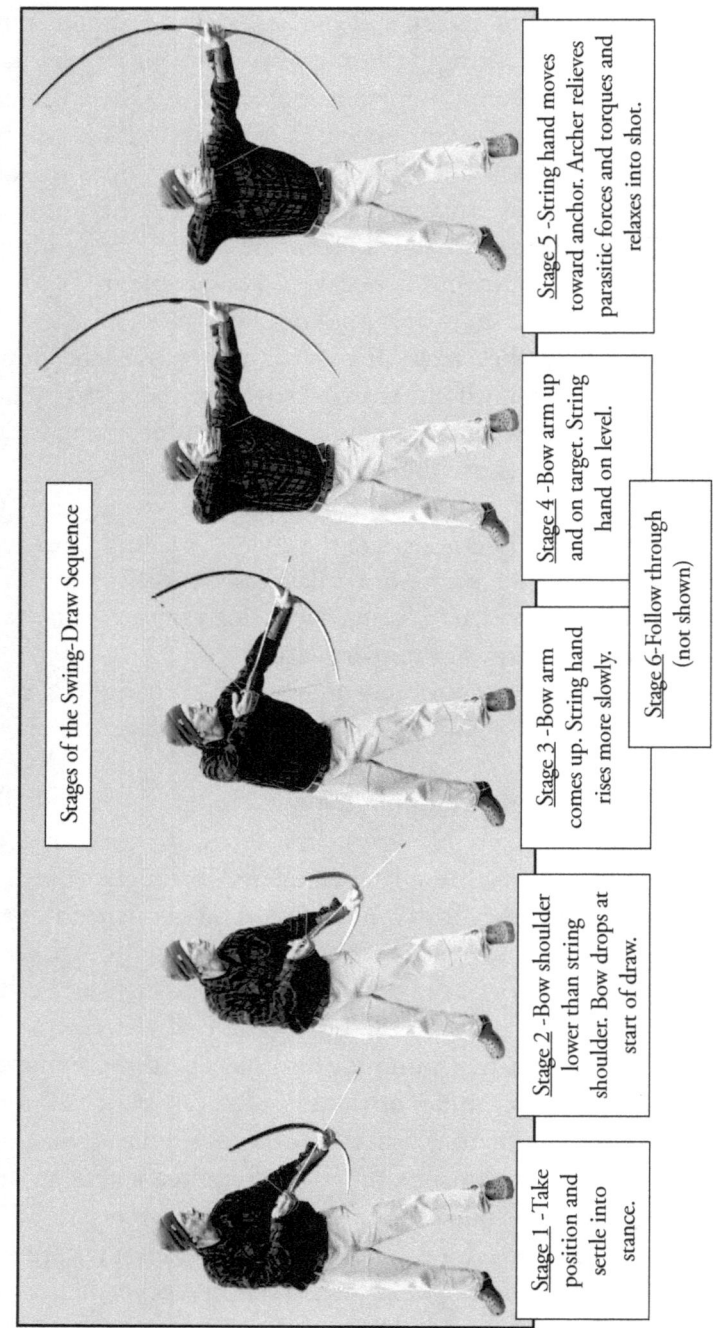

Stages of the Swing-Draw Sequence

Stage 1 - Take position and settle into stance.

Stage 2 - Bow shoulder lower than string shoulder. Bow drops at start of draw.

Stage 3 - Bow arm comes up. String hand rises more slowly.

Stage 4 - Bow arm up and on target. String hand on level.

Stage 5 - String hand moves toward anchor. Archer relieves parasitic forces and torques and relaxes into shot.

Stage 6-Follow through (not shown)

The follow-through stage will look very much like the last stage shown, except that the bow will be relaxed, the arrow will be gone, and the string arm elbow will be a bit lower.

At this point, the careful reader will notice that the end of the chapter is near and recall that I never addressed the second purpose in striving for good form that was mentioned on the second page of this chapter.

The beauty of archery is that it is, at the same time, both a simple act and one that can be practiced for a lifetime without danger of perfection. It is a contest we willingly enter with ourselves. What we learn while we patiently practice our form is personal. Calm and steady practice, without expectation, can be for the archer what meditation is for others.

I think the words of Master Awa that Eugene Harrigel recalls in his book *Zen in the Art of Archery* sum up this experience:

> You have become a different person in the course of these years. For this is what the art of archery means: a profound and far-reaching contest of the archer with himself. Perhaps you have hardly noticed it yet, but you will feel it very strongly when you meet your friends and acquaintances again... Things will no longer harmonize as before. You will see with other eyes and measure with other measures... It happens to all who are touched by the spirit of this art.

At the very least, if we are to be successful at improving our form, we must learn to be patient with ourselves and trust in ourselves that we can do this. What better purpose could there be?

Chapter 2

BLANK BALE PRACTICE

Ah, the dreaded blank bale. Often talked about, always (at least secretly) despised. I'm sure thoughts of detestable blank bale practice went through my mind as I began my adventure with the blank bale.

The blank bale is what we call a flat, uniform, amorphous surface into which we can shoot arrows while standing close by. It gets this name because a bale of straw or hay has historically been used for this purpose. A modern foam backstop will also suffice, though I feel that a hay bale is still the best, most economical choice.

The phrase blank bale practice is what we use to describe the act of standing in front of said bale while shooting arrows into it. Having learned so much about the value of shooting blank bale, I have come to wonder if the phrase is used too loosely.

Just as the question of what exactly constitutes art can stir heated debate, the question of what exactly constitutes blank bale practice can make for a good argument. My experience has shown me that blank bale practice goes much deeper than simply going through the motions. I have noticed that those who disparage blank bale practice are usually those unwilling to commit to it. That used to be me.

Taking four or five shots here and there when we feel like our form is suffering is not what blank bale practice is about. Four or five shots will improve nothing. Improving your form by blank bale practice will involve many thousands of shots. If you are of average ability (and perhaps burdened by target panic) like myself, then blank bale practice will likely be a lifelong commitment.

It is not possible to judge the value of blank bale shooting after just a few shots or a few practice sessions. The value of blank bale practice will only be revealed through committed long-term practice.

Standing in front of the blank bale is where we will learn most of the important lessons our bows and arrows have to teach us. If we pay attention, we will see that the lessons we learn are not just about archery.

TESTING COMMITMENT

The blank bale is where our commitment to the swing-draw will be most strenuously tested. As it has been observed that a journey of a thousand miles begins with a single step, so it is that our swing-draw adventure begins with that first shot into the blank bale.

As I write these words, I have in my mind's eye the image of my blank bale. I know where all its soft spots are: the large pieces of weed stem, the knots of wire grass, the shades of grey, brown, and green that blend together to make that bale. We spend a lot of time together.

In order to benefit from blank bale practice (in your effort to master the swing-draw), you have to flip a switch in your head. You have to commit, come hell or high water, to the method. You have to remove all doubt from your mind that embracing the swing-draw (and the blank bale practice that goes with it) is right for you.

This is not a judgment call or a moral call. Committing to the swing-draw does not require you to evaluate all methods of shooting to determine that one or the other is empirically better. This commitment is not that. This commitment is simply about knowing yourself and being honest about what you want from your archery adventure.

Some people like sports cars, while others like sport utility vehicles. One is not better than the other. When you watch people shoot bows and arrows, you will probably find yourself attracted to one person's style or another. Be mindful of that. What is it you like? Is what you like consistent with your archery goals?

Blank bale practice is not the sole domain of the swing-draw. Most all archery disciplines take advantage of what the blank bale offers to those who want to improve their skills.

The blank bale is a tool we use to improve our archery skills, just as a hammer is a tool we use to improve (hopefully) our world. We can hammer sixteen penny nails into wall studs or fine finishing nails into furniture, or we can hammer a chisel into marble to reveal a sculpture. How we use the hammer depends on what we want to accomplish. So it is with the blank bale.

In the case of the swing-draw, we want to use the blank bale to learn to shoot the bow and arrow with a dynamic style. If we are young and unencumbered with a lifetime of experience, the process can be fairly straightforward. If we are older, we will probably have to work through some bad habits before we can make "progress." I put progress in quotations because I think it is important to realize that by committing to the swing-draw and shooting in good faith, every arrow shot into the blank bale moves us toward our goal. Even if it doesn't feel that way at the time.

ATTENUATE EXPECTATIONS

This is where patience comes in. We must learn to be patient with ourselves. A poor shot means nothing. In fact, the whole idea of a poor shot means nothing when shooting the blank bale. Shooting arrows into the blank bale is not about good shots and bad shots. Shooting into a blank bale is about learning to balance the archer-bow-arrow machine.

This is where we must learn to focus on nothing and to unlearn expectations. Expectations are such an integral part of our lives that they come automatically to us, whether we want them to or not.

We expect to go to work every day, and we are expected to make a living. In many ways, expectations are good things. They keep us on track. But they can get in our way, too, if they are based on false assumptions. I wonder how many friendships and romances have gone awry because of expectations that went unmet—expectations that may have been based on assumptions that went unknown by one or both parties.

The same goes for our archery practice. How can we expect to shoot perfect shots every time when we haven't yet learned to balance the bow? How can we decide that today is the day we will shoot well? What is enough practice?

It is best to consider all expectations irrelevant and endeavor to put them out of your mind. We are only human, though. I know that when I have a bad day of bale practice, I can get impatient with myself. It is best to breathe deeply and let the feeling pass before taking the next shot.

Learning to be patient with ourselves and to attenuate our expectations can be a benefit to more than just our archery hobby. Working to improve these skills alone made blank bale practice worthwhile for me.

THE SETUP

Your success with blank bale practice is dependent not only on your commitment to practice but also on your commitment to the right setup.

In order to maintain a neutral posture, meaning that your bow arm is straight and level (elbow bent) and not pointing up or down, the middle of the blank bale needs to be placed at shoulder height so that you can shoot at it with your bow hand at shoulder level.

It needs to be located so that you can stand somewhere between twenty and twenty-five feet from the bale. This is an important distance because it allows you to learn an average trajectory. Once you can place your arrows in the bale consistently at this distance, it requires only a small correction (up or down) to hit targets closer or farther away.

Blank bale target with shooting platform about 25 feet apart. Pea gravel on path to improve walking surface.

Your setup needs to be made from something durable but not too hard on your arrows. In my case, I used a bale of hay backed up by a piece of stable mat (rubber mat placed on the floor of horse stables, available at farm stores). Hay is better than straw as it lasts longer and has greater stopping power. It must, of course, be protected from the weather. I have included plans for the blank bale enclosure I use in Appendix C of this book.

I have found that the correct elevation of the blank bale, the correct distance between the archer and the bale, and the durability of the bale are the critical elements of a successful blank bale setup.

In addition to these critical elements, I think it is important not to use your regular target for blank bale practice for several more reasons.

The first is mindset. When you are shooting a mark, your mind must be focused on hitting that mark. To be successful, there can be no thought about form. When you are shooting blank bale, your mind must be focused on your form. To be successful, there can be no thought about hitting a mark.

Blank bale target with rain flap folded up for practice

I think it is very hard to overcome the mental fault of thinking about our form when shooting marks and thinking about marks when shooting blank bale. These purposes are at odds with each other. For me, having different targets for each purpose helps to keep them from overlapping in my mind.

The second is position. Your regular target is probably not positioned ideally for blank bale practice. For the first few sessions, you may be willing to move the target to a better spot for blank bale practice, but after a while, the effort of doing so will likely interfere with your motivation to practice. Why handicap the process?

The third is durability. In a normal session, you will be shooting many more arrows into your blank bale than you would into your target. Due to the close nature of this work, your arrows will likely be focused on a small area of the bale. Foam targets, bag targets, and layered targets won't hold up long to that sort of abuse.

View of the blank bale target from the shooting platform

Finally, there is location. When we set up our regular targets, many of us like to put them in places that will allow for a variety of different shots. Shots from uphill, or downhill, from behind a tree, or around a bush. Hopefully, having a number of shot scenarios allows us to improve our skills and keep practice fun. Practicing shots on our blank bale while focused on our form requires a different setup. Hopefully, the ground is flat, and the view is clear. We don't want our environment to interfere with our focus.

I think this last point really has a big effect on our success with blank bale practice. At least, it has for me. Over the years, I have tried to improve my blank bale setup so that I can spend as little time as possible thinking about where I am and as much time as possible on the feel of the shot.

Repeating the shot over and over in exactly the same way is key to developing a feel for the balance of the bow. When our blank bale setup gets in the way of this repetition, it hinders the process.

It didn't take long for me to wear a deep path between my blank bale and my standing position when I started my practice. On dry days, this wasn't too much of a bother. But after a rainy day, well, it could be a mess. I did a lot of practice in my rubber farm boots. This problem was resolved by dumping some pea gravel onto the path. It took about four bags from the local home improvement store to make the path right. And after that, a bag every year or so keeps it in good shape.

Even with the gravel, eventually, I wore an uneven depression into the ground where I would take my stance to shoot. It got me thinking about the Japanese archery dojos I have seen in pictures and movies. They have a wooden floor in the shooting area, an open green space between the archer and the target, and a covered target area. So I took a lesson from them and built a platform upon which to take my stance.

This platform offers several advantages. It offers a level place upon which to take my stance. It allows me to stand in the same place for every shot. It keeps me out of the water when the ground is wet. And for some reason, it seems to help my focus.

These last suggestions of pea gravel in the path and a platform to stand on will not make or break your blank bale setup, but I found them a nice addition that makes an outdoor blank bale practice setup inviting and friendly to use, and they help to maintain a productive mindset.

MINDSET

Having the right mindset is even more important than having the perfect blank bale setup to meet the challenge of learning the swing-draw.

That said, I have found that committing to making my blank bale setup work well has helped me improve my mindset.

And that said, I have found that my mindset is as much a work in progress as is my swing-draw.

In truth, I believe that the physical aspects of learning the swing-draw are the easy part. The real nut to crack is the mindset. Already in this chapter, I have emphasized being patient with ourselves while we learn. I have also mentioned that every shot taken in good faith is progress. What I mean by taking a shot in good faith is that we need to honestly try to shoot without expectation or ego.

Where our arrow lands is no measure of our self-worth. This is doubly true when shooting at the blank bale. And yet I find it most difficult to avoid evaluating where my arrow lands. It is a constant challenge to keep my mind focused on my form.

I find my focus will ebb and flow, as does my form. Occasionally, I will have a stretch of four or five shots that land exactly where I am looking, and my form will feel good. Then my mind will invariably start to expect the arrow to land on the spot. The next shot doesn't. Then I'm back to square one again, and I have to remind myself why I am here and what I am doing, and then I start again. Enduring this ebb and flow of my form tests my resolve and is why being patient with myself is so important.

It is also important to evaluate your mindset before you begin to practice. If I am irritated by the day's events or feel particularly clumsy, I put off my blank bale practice. Because I am prone to such irritabilities, I like to get my practice done early in the day before I have had a chance to get too out-of-sorts.

Working on my mindset helps me work on my target panic as well. Developing a cool, collected, joyful mindset (together with the knowledge that practicing these time-tested drills is a solid strategy for improving my archery skills) has helped immensely in my effort to attenuate my target panic.

If I am successful with my blank bale practice, then I have managed to shoot most of the arrows without judging the results of their flight. I held my stance for a long moment after the arrow lands, and I felt my body adapt just a little more to the motions of the swing-draw. If this is the case, then I usually find that the rest of my day goes better as well. It is amazing how much brighter the day can be when we are happy with our practice.

It is important that when we start our practice, we take a deep breath, remind ourselves why we are here, and remember what we want from our practice. If we remind ourselves that what is important is not where our arrow lands but instead how the shot feels, how our body moves, and the joy that comes from a well-made shot, then we have set the foundation for a productive practice session.

As a final note on mindset, I recall that John Schulz advised me to smile when I shoot. There is plenty of scientific evidence that links the act of smiling with a happy attitude and a relaxed body. While we often smile when we feel good, it is also true that we often feel good when we smile. So as you stand there in front of the blank bale mulling over the results of your last shot and thinking about your next, take a moment to crack a smile. It may help you to shoot better, and it will make your friends wonder what you are thinking about.

TO THE BALE

Before starting your bale practice, it may be helpful to review the points of form outlined in Chapter 1.

Stand close to the target and find a place on the bale that is at the same height as your bow shoulder, and then remember that place. Don't put anything there; just know where that area is because that is the area you will look at while you are learning your form. Now, from your appointed position twenty to twenty-five feet from the bale, stand with your body at a right angle to the face of the bale. Your shoulder should be at a right angle to the face of the bale and to your side. This is what is commonly referred to as a closed stance. If you were to turn more to face the target, this would be more of an open stance. The better you can maintain this closed stance, the better you will shoot. Now, swing the bow up as you draw the string, find an anchor deep in your face, and release.

Make absolutely no effort to hold the bow at full draw. Period.

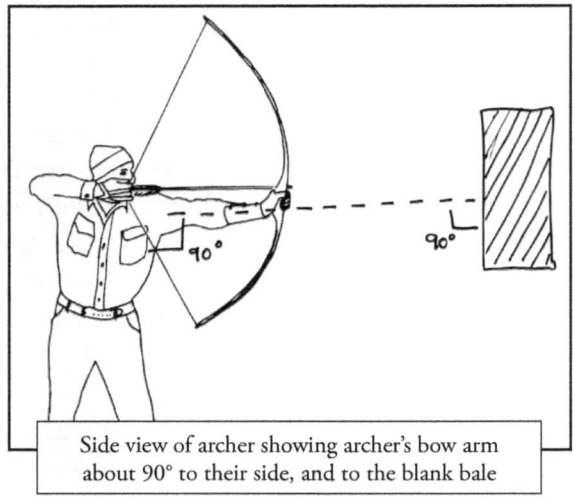

Side view of archer showing archer's bow arm
about 90° to their side, and to the blank bale

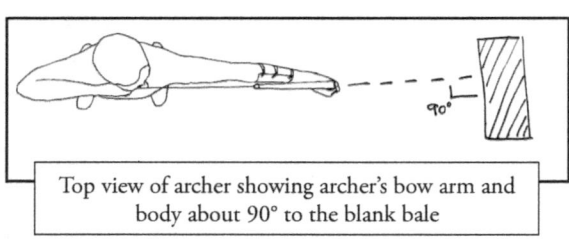

Top view of archer showing archer's bow arm and
body about 90° to the blank bale

When your string-hand finger settles well into your anchor, stop holding the string. You may find this disconcerting at first. Over time, it will begin to feel like the natural thing to do. It may help to have a place for your hand to come to rest after releasing the string. When I started my practice, I found it comfortable to have my hand come to rest on my ear. However you do it, your hand should stop shortly after letting the string go.

As you become more familiar with the swing-draw and more coordinated, you will find that your hand won't need a place to come to rest. It will just stay at your anchor.

Look at the area you identified earlier to be at shoulder height during the entire time you spend drawing the bow and releasing the arrow. **DO NOT FOLLOW THE ARROW IN FLIGHT WITH YOUR EYES, PERIOD. DO NOT SHIFT YOUR GAZE TO**

WHERE THE ARROW LANDS, PERIOD. Keep looking at the area where you want the arrow to go, and let your peripheral vision see where the arrow lands. Make no conscious adjustment to your aim or form while you shoot. Just swing up, anchor, and release. Do this all in one motion. Do it as fluidly and as casually as you can. Take one or two seconds for the entire sequence.

It helps to start the swing if you drop your bow hand just a little (two or three inches) at the beginning of the draw and then raise the arm through the swing. Why would dropping your bow hand be helpful?

Dropping the bow hand helps our body orient itself in time and space. Think about how swinging a hammer backwards helps us hit the nail on the head. When we swing a hammer to hit a nail, we don't start with the hammer statically suspended at its highest point; we start by swinging the hammer backwards, and then we smoothly swing the hammer forward to the head of the nail.

While this may appear at first as a simple time saver, which indeed it is, the real purpose is to ensure that we actually strike the nail on the head.

If you would like to prove to yourself that what I'm saying is true, give this a try: Hold the hammer steady for a moment above the nail head, then swing it toward the nail. See how successful you are at driving the nail straight and true. Then repeat the exercise by the more traditional method of swinging the hammer backward before swinging it forward to the nail. Which method do you find most successful in driving a good nail?

Don't worry about your release or any other aspect of your shot; just remember to keep your bow hand up and aimed at the target for two or three seconds after the arrow lands. A fluid motion and a relaxed feeling are your goals. Just feel the anchor as your fingers dig deep into your face. Don't just barely touch your anchor. Dig deep. Try to bury your fingers into your face. Remember that feeling when you get it right.

As you hold your stance after the shot, observe the mosaic of your bow hand and bow against the background of the blank bale and arrow. Do not worry about where your arrow is landing. Just keep looking at the area you intended to hit.

As I began to get familiar with this blank bale exercise, I realized that it incorporates two very powerful tools. I have come to think that (while they may have been used by others over time) these tools haven't really been identified, qualified, separated out of the midst of human thought, or named. By naming a thing, it helps us understand it. It helps us recognize the thing, qualify and quantify it, and see it. Sometimes the first attempt to name a thing doesn't go well, and the name changes over time. In an effort to help me explain these two important tools, I will attempt to name them as well. Maybe someone else will eventually give them better names.

The first and most powerful tool is what I call **trajectory awareness**. We learn trajectory awareness by forcing ourselves to focus entirely on one spot on the bale while seeing the arrow flight only in our peripheral vision. Learning this trajectory awareness will benefit you even if you never take up the swing-draw. Its value cannot be overstated. If your eyes focus on and follow the arrow in flight, how can your brain ever learn the arrow's trajectory?

If your eyes focus on and follow the arrow, your brain's point of reference is, by definition, the arrow. Your brain cannot trace and remember the parabolic path of the arrow if it never sees it. By watching the arrow in flight or moving your eyes to the impact point, you are effectively reducing the parabolic flight path of the arrow to a single point: (0,0).

This idea of making use of things you see in your peripheral vision can be the stuff of heated debate. Usually, the debate circles around whether we see the arrow in our peripheral vision when we draw the bow and whether this helps us to adjust the arrow's trajectory so that it hits the mark upon release.

I have heard no other discussion of this idea of seeing the entire trajectory of the arrow in our peripheral vision, this trajectory awareness, in all my decades of archery study. This is a new idea for me, and it was one of the most important things I learned from my blank bale practice.

Trajectory awareness—watching the arrow in your peripheral vision for its entire flight while being focused on the spot you want the arrow to land—is a skill that takes some time to develop.

The second powerful tool is what I call **form conditioning**. It is the understanding that if we keep our body in motion and allow it to do what it naturally wants to do, it will eventually figure out what is right.

Don't get into a knot about your form, your anchor point, or your release. Just keep focusing on the spot on the bale and attempting to shoot smoothly and without pause. Your body will figure out how to do it correctly if you give it the time and practice.

Form conditioning—learning to control your form by repeating (over and over) your shot without pause from start to finish—is the fundamental skill taught by all those who embrace the swing-draw.

As I alluded to at the beginning of this chapter, when I began my blank bale practice, I was dreading it. I had shot blank bale before in an attempt to improve my skill, but I was never able to stick with it long, and I was bored to death by it.

That is because I was not learning anything from it.

When you practice blank bale shooting, as described above, you will be learning something with every shot. You will be learning because you are focused on the desired point of impact, not upon the arrow. It makes all the difference in the world, and it brings joy to the practice.

I shoot just one arrow into the bale at a time. I walk up to the bale, remove it, and shoot it again. In the beginning, I would wear my back quiver and drop the arrow into it after pulling it free from the bale. I would then return to my shooting station, withdraw the arrow from the quiver, and shoot it again. As time passed, I found it easier and more convenient to leave my back quiver in the house and simply carry the arrow back to my shooting station. I get plenty of quiver practice while roving and hunting.

The one thing I do try to do is handle the arrow only by the nock, as John Schulz advises. Schulz advises this because it is the fastest and most efficient way to address the arrow for an archer who uses a back quiver. I find that even in my quiver-less bale practice, handling the arrow only by the nock makes sense. It is easier and faster to pull the arrow from the bale and affix it to the string if my fingers stay on the nock. It may seem clumsy at first. Just as a beginner shuns the long end of a hammer handle in favor of choking their grip up tight under the cheek of the hammerhead, the archer unaccustomed to withdrawing an arrow from a back quiver will grab the middle of the arrow. It won't take long to learn the benefits of taking the arrow by its nock.

That said, I cannot always remove the arrow from the bale simply by pulling at the nock. If the arrow is stuck, my fingers will likely slip from the nock before the arrow comes free. Therefore, I make it a habit to pull the arrow from the bale by its shaft until it is mostly free. Then I let go of the shaft and take the arrow by its nock to pull it free from the bale and nock it to the string as I return to my shooting station.

By shooting just one arrow and removing it from the bale with each shot, I maintain the blank nature of the blank bale and avoid the clutter that additional arrows in the bale would bring. This practice ensures that my arrows will not be broken by impact as they crowd into the same spot on the bale, which is an additional advantage.

Watching an expert execute this swing-draw is invaluable as we learn the skill. I would (again) recommend watching John Schulz's video "Hitting 'em Like Howard Hill," as well as any Howard Hill video you can find and those by the Wilhelm Brothers. All of these can be purchased on DVD or watched on YouTube.

BLANK OR BLIND BALE?

Blank bale and blind bale are two different exercises. Blank bale is the exercise of shooting with your eyes open into a bale. Blind bale is the exercise of shooting with your eyes closed into a bale.

There are different schools of thought on the merits of developing form with eyes open or eyes closed. I have practiced both ways and, in my experience, find that shooting with eyes open yields the best results.

Debating which, or if, one method is better than the other is a pointless exercise as there can be no definitive proof.

That said, there are several points that can be made in support of the notion that shooting blank bale is more appropriate than shooting blind bale for the student who wants to learn the swing-draw.

The strategy behind shooting with both eyes open into a blank bale while learning the swing-draw is based on the goal of developing a whole-body shooting system. Taking the eyes out of bale practice while learning to pull the bow removes important information that the brain uses to develop our kinesthetic sense.

If we don't see the bow being drawn against the background of the target, our balance is affected, as are our sensory feedback loops that our brain uses to position our bow hand and string hand. Our eyes are part of our body, and we should not exclude them from our form-conditioning exercises.

Shooting blind bale requires that the student stand directly in front of the bale so that the arrow is guaranteed to hit it. The additional (and really important) advantage of learning the arrow's trajectory while perfecting our form (trajectory awareness) is lost.

Shooting blind bale means you cannot see your arrow fly. If you can't see the effect of your form on the flight of the arrow, how can you tell if your form is correct? In my experience, the lack of visual feedback during the shot means I cannot know if I have balanced the bow.

I find shooting blind bale very boring simply because standing for any length of time with my eyes closed is boring.

Learning to focus your eyes on a featureless surface, and keeping them focused there through the entire shot and until the arrow lands on that spot, is an important skill. It is especially important to a hunter.

Chapter 3

LONG-RANGE PRACTICE

Context is everything. If I sit on a certain chair by the fireplace, our crazy cat will jump in my lap, purring and affectionate. But if I sit in any other chair, well, then that ends any hope of good rapport. While I laugh at the cat's limited capacity to deal with change, I must admit that I, too, have my issues with it.

The more we practice coping with new situations, the better we get at it. In fact, there is a part of the brain, the hippocampus, that is larger in individuals who demonstrate adaptive thinking. Does this mean that practicing adaptive skills will make your brain bigger? I don't know. What I do know is that the only thing that remains constant is change. Living life means adapting to change.

What is true for cats is also true for archers working to improve their fluid swing-draw shot. The more we shoot in different situations, the easier it will be to adapt to the next shot, no matter its context.

This chapter will describe two exercises that build upon the context developed in the blank bale exercise. The first one, blank range exercise, will (just like the blank bale exercise) involve no target. The second exercise, target practice, finally adds the target to our practice.

While the purpose of the long-range practice described in this chapter is to expand the context in which we can shoot, I found it helpful in my effort to overcome my target panic as well. For me, even the blank surface of the blank bale would (in the early days) present enough of a target to inflame my target panic.

The absolute lack of a target in the blank range exercise served the additional purpose of helping me calm my target panic. For those who do not suffer from target panic, spending many months on the blank bale before beginning to add blank range practice to your routine is good. For those who suffer from target panic, it might be helpful to begin this next exercise sooner.

A person with target panic can almost always close their eyes, draw their bow to anchor, and release under control. Unfortunately, in my experience, the context of shooting with my eyes closed doesn't help my form or my target panic.

Shooting into empty space with my eyes open did help. The context of the blank range exercise, while it doesn't involve a target, does involve seeing the bow, arrow, and background. And upon release, seeing the results of my form on arrow flight.

It will be up to you to decide when you want to add this next exercise to your routine. However you arrive at it, there will come a time to add some long-range practice to your training.

BLANK RANGE EXERCISE

The fluid motion you developed in front of the blank bale will be built upon with this exercise. Here is where you will begin to see the beauty of this system. It is at this point that I began to see how well this method works to hone our innate eye-hand coordination so that we can learn to be relaxed when we shoot.

When I think of a system, I think of a rigid method that must be followed exactly to result in the desired outcome. This system is different. It is true that you must follow the system exactly for the best results. But once you have learned what the system has to teach you, you will be free to shoot without the mental clutter so often associated with tournament form. You won't need a mental checklist to get through your shot. Instead, your shot will be dependent on the ingrained memories of your fluid and automatic practice that have been added to your neural network.

By learning to shoot in front of the blank bale and then at long range with no bale, we add context to our learning. The more context we add to our experience, the more adaptable we will be as archers.

Blank bale practice and the long-range practice described in this chapter shouldn't be thought of as discrete exercises through which you proceed in series but rather layers of exercises upon which you build. You don't *move on* to the next step. You simply *add* to your routine.

This next lesson is harder, and you may have to return to the blank bale and form shooting often to reinforce the swing-draw form. Shooting blank bale at close range allows you to concentrate on the feel of your form without having to worry about where the arrows are going.

While practicing on your blank bale, you may have noticed that your arrow began to hit the bale where you were looking without trying. The arrows began to go where you looked even though you weren't thinking about aiming the arrow because you became familiar with the context of your shot. This next lesson will challenge your progress because the context will change. Be patient with yourself. Renew your commitment.

We have used the word ingrained in the past to describe what happens when we repeat a motion over and over. We say the motion becomes ingrained, and we can repeat it without thought. I like the word and will use it to describe our motions that have become habits through repetition. But I do it with the understanding that we are building the strength of our muscles and the neural pathways and memories in our brain and spinal cord, not training some ill-defined subconscious self.

To get loosened up, you can start each session with blank bale shooting, maybe 20 or 30 shots. Then go out to an area where you can shoot long-range—at least 50 yards. If you have been adamant about looking at an area on the blank bale that was about shoulder height, you have ingrained the full swing-draw level form. (Without realizing it, you have ingrained the proper form for shooting at a target around 30 inches off the ground and about 40 to 50 yards away.)

This range is defined by the parabolic shape of the arrow's trajectory, the speed of your bow, and your physical height. In most cases, it is in the 40- to 50-yard range. What it is exactly doesn't really matter.

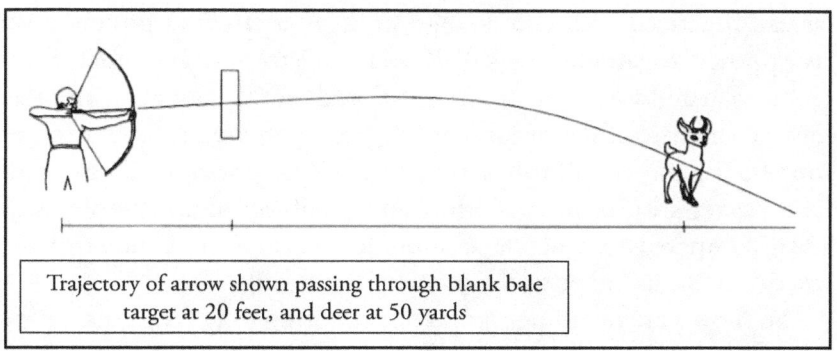

Trajectory of arrow shown passing through blank bale
target at 20 feet, and deer at 50 yards

With the arm extended so that the bow hand is about level with the shoulder, and because of the work you did to ingrain your form on the blank bale, you will be shooting arrows through an area shoulder-height off the ground at 20 to 30 feet. Because of the parabolic shape of arrow flight, when you shoot, the arrow will continue to rise above shoulder height and then drop down to shoulder height again at somewhere around 40 yards. The arrow continues on a downward path, depending on how flat the arrow shoots. The arrow will go through an area 30 inches off the ground at around 50 yards—the perfect height to pass through the chest of a deer.

With the basic form you ingrained at 20 feet, you have now ingrained the form necessary to shoot deer-height targets at 50 yards with no adjustments. If you have paid attention to the feel of the shot, you could, in essence, with eyes closed and concentrating on form only, shoot all your arrows into the same area on the ground at 50 to 55 yards just by how the shot felt because you have ingrained that fluid motion.

Hill told Schulz, "If your form is right, you won't be too far off at 50 yards." Basically, if you have practiced the proper swing-draw form at the proper height backstop until it becomes an automatic fluid memory, you have ingrained a 50-yard form. You will have only small adjustments to make in the height of your bow hand in order to shoot an animal standing on the ground at 20 yards or 50 yards.

The advantage of these small adjustments can be understood by comparing them to what you would have to do if you had instead practiced your short-range work on a target at ground level (as opposed to shoulder level). If you were to have ingrained form shooting at a block target on the ground, then to shoot at an animal's chest 30 inches off the ground at 30 yards, you would have to move your bow hand up almost a foot (instead of down an inch). This action takes a lot of mental effort and is subject to a lot more error when compared to practice at shoulder height. The context of the practice helps us adapt to the context of hunting.

So, now you are going to practice shooting long range, using the same fluid memory that you built at 20 feet. You are going to look at an area on the ground at 50ish yards. **THIS IS IMPORTANT! DO NOT TRY TO AIM.** Just look at an area on the ground, take your stance, swing your bow up and shoot, just like you did at the blank bale.

View down nice, flat, straight alley
for long-range practice

Chances are, when you begin this practice, it will not go well. No worries, it will come. When I added this long-range form practice to my routine, it took several days to get it going well. Things tend to fall apart, but they will come back together again. Just remember the following goals as you practice:

1. Keep your bow arm up. Keep your bow arm up through the entire shot until the arrow hits the ground.
2. Watch the arrow in your peripheral vision. Do not watch the arrow directly. Just see it without watching it. This will allow your brain to learn your arrow's trajectory.
3. Maintain form. Make sure you keep the basics right. Weight on the front foot, bow arm humerus rotated and shoulder blade pulled toward the spine, bow arm elbow bent, string hand to anchor.

Your goal should be to shoot at least 100 arrows in a practice session. When I started this, my form did indeed fall apart. As my form went south, my frustration went north. So, in the beginning, I never achieved this goal of 100 arrows of long-range practice. What I failed to do at 50 yards, I made up for on the blank bale. Each day, I had less to make up for as my long-range form improved. As you improve, you will find it easy to shoot 100 arrows at 50 yards.

If you can find a place that will allow it, shoot your quiver of arrows at your spot on the ground, retrieve the arrows, and then shoot them again back toward your starting point. This will save much time and walking.

It is best to use some sort of blunt on your arrow for this practice so that you don't lose your arrows. You will also want to have a rag handy to wipe the dirt off your arrows before dropping them back into your quiver. I use old socks for this purpose, and I leave them where I do my practice, so I don't have to remember to bring them each session.

Eventually, I stopped counting arrows while doing my blank range practice and simply set the timer on my phone for forty-five minutes.

By doing this exercise, you are practicing form shooting with the added visual stimulus of the arrow arc for your brain to see. This is what makes this exercise so difficult. No matter how hard it is, do not start aiming the arrow. Don't. Just look at that area, swing, and shoot. Concentrate only on the feel of the shot, just like during bale practice. The ground will actually become blurry in your mind's eye. You will feel like you are daydreaming because, even though you see the area out there on the ground, your mind is focused on the feel of the shot. You are leaving the trajectory and fate of the arrow to those parts of your brain and spinal cord that you are not conscious of.

If you shoot this long range with the same feel of the shot as you did at 20 feet, you will be surprised by how your arrows start grouping out there on the ground at 50 yards. They will start falling into an area around a 3-foot circle on the ground without you hardly trying to make it happen. All you are doing is looking, swinging, and shooting. Your *concentration* is on the feel and form of the shot, absolutely imitating the form and feel you did at the 20-foot blank bale.

Bucket on post to store rags for cleaning arrows

Another reason for the structure of this long-range exercise is that, at this point in time, you don't want anything close enough out there so that you start picking a spot to shoot at. Right now, you are just shooting at an area, a kind of blurry area at that, because you are still ingraining proper form with some added visual stimuli.

This exercise will be challenging. But for me, as I got better at it, I began to feel a realistic sense that I could hit a pie plate at 50 yards reliably. Before I began to learn the swing-draw, this would never have been possible. I spent two months shooting daily on blank range shooting before adding the next exercise.

TARGET PRACTICE

It's funny how many times I think I understand what someone is telling me when I really don't. The misunderstanding does not result because I am not listening. It happens because I don't have the same experience as the speaker, and thus, the words don't create the same image in my mind as they do in the mind of the speaker.

The oft-spoken phrase "bore a hole in it" is a case in point.

Howard Hill spoke these words oh so long ago, and they have been repeated by many good shooters since. I thought what it meant was to concentrate so hard on the point I wanted to hit that my sheer focus on that point would melt it away. Superman X-ray vision, if you like.

As it turns out, this is not the meaning at all.

The intent of blank bale practice and blank range practice was to build fluid memory and form so that the archer could produce the same shot time and time again without thought.

As our form improves, another outcome of these exercises is that our brain begins to learn the trajectory of our arrow. If the archer sticks with the same bow and the same arrow throughout these exercises, the outcome of the well-executed shot will be the same.

The purpose of this target practice exercise is to learn to place the trajectory of the arrow in space so that it intersects with the point we want to hit.

This is where the philosophy upon which the swing-draw is built deviates most obviously from other learning systems, and wherein it becomes such a strong method.

Practicing this exercise is where I also learned that I totally misunderstood what Hill and others were trying to tell me.

This exercise introduces an intended target. But the intended target in this exercise is like no other target you have shot before. It is that way for a reason.

Most likely, every target you have ever shot represented the terminal point of the arrow's journey. When the arrow hits the target, it stops.

That is not the case for this exercise.

In this exercise, you will shoot at a target suspended in the air at shoulder height, the same height you have been shooting since you started practicing. But this target is not solid. It will not stop the arrow. Whether the arrow hits the target or not, the outcome will be the same: The arrow will continue on its path, mostly undisturbed.

Let me show you what I do, and then I will explain why. After much fooling around, I came to a target that serves this purpose well and is durable. I took an old bowstring and wrapped it around the end of a long stick. Through the loop at the end of the string, I tied a small piece of orange surveying tape. I could then suspend the target in the air at whatever height and distance I wanted by simply moving the stick to different holes in my fence.

Target

Small piece of survey tape tied to end of old bow string and suspended in midair

From time to time, I hit the string, which throws my arrow off. But mostly, my arrow flies harmlessly by at some point near the survey tape.

I keep the role of survey tape in my bucket along with my old socks so that I can replace the target as needed. As you improve, you will shoot the tape off the string more often than you might imagine.

So, what is the point?

The point is to learn to change the way you think about hitting the mark. The point is to learn that the mark doesn't have to represent the end of your mental picture. The point is to learn that the mark should not be, in and of itself, the focus of your focus.

As you practice this exercise, you will come to realize, as I did, what the meaning of "bore a hole in it" really is.

You will not come to understand right away. You must practice this exercise a lot. As with the first two exercises, you will likely feel awkward, and your shooting will fall off. Do not fret. You will get better. Do not force it; it will come.

As you practice this exercise, you will begin to get a feel for it. Your aiming will become more automatic and more three-dimensional in nature.

Other aiming methods, such as string walking, secondary vision, gap, etc., all reduce the aiming process to the analysis of a two-dimensional picture intended to model the three-dimensional world. They all require some conscious estimate of distance. As a person gets comfortable using these methods, they can begin to feel natural. But they are all, at their core, reductionist methods that depend on knowing the boundary conditions of distance, elevation, and shooting angle.

I do not mean to criticize these methods of aiming. I simply want to highlight the differences between them and the swing-draw. These methods have proven not only outstanding for tournament archery but superior to the method outlined here, as evidenced by the fact that not a single tournament archer employs the swing-draw.

For the purpose of hunting, though, I believe that the ability to know your arrow trajectory and to be able to make that trajectory intersect with the deer is a more reliable way to kill the game. The situation a hunter finds themself in as a deer approaches can never be as predictable as walking up to a static target.

So, what is the meaning of "bore a hole through it" then?

As you become skilled in the swing-draw, you will begin to see the target as simply a point on the trajectory of the arrow. You will visualize the arrow trajectory both before and *after* the target. You will begin to focus not on the mark but on the whole of everything in front of you.

The mark will be at the center of your vision, but it will not be the center of your attention. It is just part of the whole shot experience.

As you become skilled in the swing-draw, you will begin to see through the target and see where the arrow would go if it passed through the target, just as it does as it flies past your survey tape. You will bore a hole through it.

I think it's safe to say that you will never forget the first time you succeed at this. When your swing-draw happens naturally, when you are 100 percent committed, and when your vision is clear and wide, you will see through your target and be genuinely surprised when your arrow stops in the mark.

So how do you get to that point?

Add this exercise to your routine. Shoot thirty or more arrows at the blank bale, shoot twenty or more arrows for blank distance, then set up your hanging target and shoot as much as you can. Proportion your shots for each exercise based on what you can do and what you have time for.

Again, just like you did with the blank range practice, remember the following points of form as you take your stance to shoot and as you hold your posture after the shot until the arrow has come to rest:

1. Keep your bow arm up. Keep your bow arm up through the entire shot until the arrow hits the ground.
2. Watch the arrow in your peripheral vision. Do not watch the arrow directly. Just see it without watching it. This will allow your brain to learn your arrow's trajectory.
3. Maintain form. Make sure you keep the fundamentals right: weight on the front foot, bow arm humerus rotated and shoulder blade pulled toward the spine, bow-arm elbow bent, and string hand to anchor.

As you become more proficient with this new exercise, vary the distance at which you shoot and the height of the hanging target.

After a month, and if you have the opportunity, take to the woods for a rove. Do not shoot at targets on the ground that will stop your arrows. Instead, shoot at leaves, branches, and snags that are off the ground.

On good days, just go for a rove and don't bother with the hanging target.

Keep at it until everything feels natural. Only then, add in targets that stop the arrow.

AIMING IS THE EASY PART

I know I have fretted about aiming, and I think that most people spend more time worrying about aiming than any other aspect of the shot.

In my experience, my usual miss was on line but up to six inches high. It didn't matter if I was five yards or thirty-five yards from the mark; the arrow would most reliably hit above the mark. I kept waiting for my subconscious to adjust, but it never did. The frustration was torture.

As I have gained experience with the exercises involved in learning the swing-draw (and, among other things, found a better explanation than a subconscious mind for how our body performs a fluid motion), I have learned that my misses usually have more to do with a form problem than with an aiming problem.

I have found that aligning the arrow to follow a trajectory that intersects the mark is the easy part. The hard part is to avoid fouling up the shot by inducing a force (and torque) into my draw that only shows itself upon the release of the string.

Once I started to make progress with my blank bale practice and my blank range practice, I started to feel the parasitic forces and torques in my draw that were robbing accuracy and power from my shot. I couldn't fix the problem right away, but at least I began to sense it.

It was at this point that I realized that my high shots were not the result of poor aiming but instead poor shooting. This was when the focus of my frustration shifted from the aim to the draw.

One of the goals of learning to shoot the swing-draw is to eliminate frustration from the experience. Frustration doesn't help us succeed, and it takes away from our joy in the process.

Every shot, taken in good faith, brings us closer to perfect form—not that most of us will ever experience perfect form. The increments of improvement are generally infinitesimal, but over time, they do add up.

After about three years of practice, I was able to sense what I did wrong during a shot that caused the arrow to flirt away from the mark. And I gradually came to see that most of my misses were due to poor form, not poor aiming.

I think this understanding might be the motivation behind Master Awa Kenzo's sharp criticism of his student Eugene Herrigel when he worried about hitting the mark:

> What are you thinking of? You know that you should not grieve over bad shots; learn now not to rejoice over the good ones... Learn to rise above them in easy equanimity... You cannot conceive how important this is.

The first big step to improved accuracy is learning to feel the balance of the bow and what goes wrong with the shot. Once we are aware of what went wrong, it would seem a simple thing to fix.

This reasoning is a trap. It is no easy thing to fix. Recognizing the fault is just the start. Again, Master Awa's words apply: "He who has a hundred miles to walk should reckon ninety as half the journey."

As of the writing of these words, I have been practicing the swing-draw for over seven years. The more I practice, the more I concentrate on my blank bale. There are times when my concentration moves to the blank range practice, and (truth be told) I probably should spend more time on it. Both of these form exercises help build our experience and broaden the context in which we can be comfortable and confident in our shooting.

The more I practice my form, the more it feels like hitting the mark becomes an afterthought. Instead of the goal to be pursued, it becomes the inevitable outcome of learning the balance of the archer-bow-arrow machine.

I guess these final words in this chapter are a caution. Don't rush through these exercises in your haste to hit the mark. The true joy of archery is not found in hitting the mark but in everything that happens before and leads up to that moment.

Chapter 4

MORE EXERCISES

To learn these advantages of form, the practitioner has to learn the pattern, which is initially unnatural, and practice it so well that eventually, it becomes natural to him. In the early stages, the student must learn and practice patterns exactly, paying careful attention to the correctness of form. This is the stage of "from formlessness to form"... At a later stage, when one is competent in the form, one may modify it to suit the situation... This approaches the stage of "from form to formlessness"... At an advanced stage, one may do away with form. It is [like] an adult fighting with a three-year-old child; the adult need not bother with any Kung Fu form; he or she is so comparatively powerful that the child simply has no chance.

This is how Wong Kiew Kit explained the progression of skill a person experiences as they learn the art of Kung Fu in his book *The Art of Shaolin Kung Fu.*

I know in my case that I will likely never achieve the transition of "from form to formlessness" Wong speaks of, but even so, I do get hints of it from time to time.

The real point of archery, of learning to shoot a bow and arrow as well as we possibly can, is not to hit the mark. Hitting the mark is the icing on the cake.

The cake is in the effort we expend to learn to move our bodies in harmony with our bows. The proximity of the mark to our arrow is simply a measure of our progress toward that harmony.

I don't think my experience is much different from others when I observe that my path toward this coveted harmony has been cluttered with quick fixes, misconceptions, excuses, frustration, and random changes in direction.

All of these distractions unsettle the mind and hinder our ability to make progress. They obscure our ability to focus on the one thing we can control: our willingness to repeat basic exercises relentlessly. Repetition of basic exercises is the clearest path toward finding this harmony we seek. It must be repetition without expectation, without strings attached.

That said, this chapter outlines some of the extra things I had to do to benefit from the basic exercises outlined in previous chapters. These exercises add layers to what has already been practiced. They are not substitutions.

If we learn to shoot a bare bow and arrow without the baggage of a lifetime of shooting bows adorned with big stabilizers, pulleys, or release aids, we can learn the skill more directly and won't need these extra exercises.

If we have a well-developed kinesthetic sense, we can learn to shoot well in a short time and will wonder what all the fuss is about. Again, these extra exercises won't be needed.

I think we learn more from our mistakes than from our successes. If we are successful right away with our shooting, then we have found our path to balancing the bow without the need for further effort. If we struggle with the effort to learn, then maybe we can benefit from additional exercises and can find new ways to clear our path toward achieving balance with our bow and arrow.

Learning to shoot a bow well requires that we not only find a balance with the bow but also that we learn to balance our desire to do it the right way with our need to learn what really works.

We are all different anatomically and neurologically. While we can all benefit from the same basic exercises, we may need to supplement those exercises with others that are tailored to our differences.

Sometimes, we need a little nudge to get on the right path. The exercises I outline here are things that I found nudged me in the right direction. I think others can benefit from these exercises as well, if only in as much as they give the reader the idea that they can think for themselves and come up with their own extra credit exercises.

As Wong says in the quote at the beginning of this chapter, the student must practice the patterns exactly. At a later stage, they may modify the pattern as the situation warrants.

With the exception of the first exercise (it's not really an exercise; it's more of an aspiration) described here, I did not add these exercises to my routine for a long time. I stuck with the basic exercises until the swing-draw motion became a part of me.

I used these exercises to become more effective with my shooting, not to learn the basic form.

KEEP YOUR EYE ON THE MARK

The need to keep your eye on the mark was addressed in the chapter on basic form. In that chapter, it was explained that we need to keep our eye on the mark so that our brain can learn the trajectory of the arrow relative to the point we want it to intersect.

If our eye tracks the arrow, then we never see the trajectory. If we can't see the trajectory, we can't learn the trajectory.

While the need to learn the trajectory of the arrow is critical to reliably causing the arrow to land where we want it to, there is another reason we need to keep our focus steady on the mark.

It has to do with the way the neurological system of our human organism works.

It's interesting to watch the state of human knowledge grow and change. We begin to explore different fields of study, and in the beginning, they seem unconnected. However, the more we learn, the more we find out that even things so far apart in scale and function as quantum mechanics (the study of structures at the smallest scale of matter) and cosmology (the study of structures at the largest scale of matter) are intimately interconnected. As it turns out, what happens inside quarks and gluons affects what happens inside stars and galaxies.

A similar thing is happening with psychology and neuroscience. Psychology is the science of learning about the mind, especially through studying behavior. Neuroscience is the science of learning about the brain and nervous system, especially through chemistry.

There was a time when we thought that the emergent property of consciousness and everything that goes with it could never be explained by the knowledge gained through neuroscience, and by the same token, psychology could never teach us about the functioning of the brain.

Even though these two fields of study were focused on the same thing, the human brain, they had little in common. As the tools of study have improved (the development of magnetic resonance imaging of a living brain, for example), scientists in both fields have started to find common ground.

One area where I think these two groups are starting to find common ground is the idea of agency.

If you ask a psychologist what agency means, they will tell you that a person's sense of agency is their ability to control their life and to make choices.

If you ask a neuroscientist the same question, they will tell you that a person's agency is their ability to control (and awareness of) their actions.

The difference in these definitions is subtle, but these definitions and what we are learning from studying the brain with magnetic resonance imaging while the test subjects are exercising agency give us our second reason for keeping our eye on the mark.

We have learned that agency takes time. This truth is counterintuitive to most of us. Our experience of agency (indeed even our experience of self) is instantaneous and timeless and leads us to believe that we must exist outside time. This belief is so strong that we expect that our sense of self, our agency that emerges from the biological and neurological activity of our brain, will exist even after that activity ceases in death. To learn that our agency emerges only after a complex cascade of neurological activity in the brain can be a hard pill to swallow. If we can breathe and relax our minds through this moment of existential panic, we can discover new reasons for joy in the simple act of shooting our bows.

There have been numerous studies on this topic. One of particular interest is titled "The Time Between Intention and Action Affects the Experience of Action" by Mikkel Vinding and others (this is a psychology experiment).

In this study, subjects were asked to press a button when they felt the desire to. They were also asked to record the exact time they pressed the button. Then the subjects were asked to delay pressing the button for a span of one to three seconds after feeling the desire to press the button. Again, they were asked to record the exact time they pressed the button.

The researchers found that:

Delayed intentions were followed by a stronger binding effect for the tone following the action compared to immediate intentions. The actions were reported to have occurred earlier for delayed intentions than for [immediate] intentions... This suggests that there is a general shift in the perceived time of action. The results imply that delayed intentions and [immediate] intentions have a different impact on the experience of action.

What they found was that the moment subjects reported pressing the button was a point in time before they actually pressed the button. In other words, the subject's recollection of events was faulty. They think they pressed the button before they actually did.

We have also learned that agency involves complex activity in our brains well before any action is taken. Again, there is a study of particular interest about this activity called "Decoding Action Intentions" from *Preparatory Brain Activity in Human Parieto-Frontal Networks* by Jason Gallivan and others (this is a neuroscience experiment).

In this study, subjects were asked to grasp and manipulate cubes and other geometric shapes in complex ways that required planning before the execution of the task. The subjects' brains were scanned during the performance of the task.

In this study, the researchers found that:

Although the motor cortex is predominantly engaged near the moment of movement and presumed... to be a relatively lower-level motor output structure... such descriptions likely only partially capture its complexity... The fact that we can decode each particular hand movement from preparatory responses in the motor cortex several moments before action execution might additionally speak to a more prominent role in movement planning processes.

What the researchers found is that (even for a specific simple planned task), there are brain processes occurring for a significant time before the task is executed. In other words, a lot happens in our brain between the time we decide to act and when we actually do act.

From these studies, we can see that our sense of agency is a complex process that takes time. And while we may be fully in control of our actions, our sense of time (relative to those actions) can be wrong.

So what exactly do these studies have to do with keeping our eyes on the mark when we shoot?

It is well known among archers that we must practice good follow-through, which means holding our form until the arrow reaches the target. And part of holding our form is keeping our eye on the target.

If we want to watch the arrow in flight, we must expend a substantial amount of brain power to move our eyes from the mark to the arrow as it is coursing toward the mark. Not only do we take our eye off the mark, but we must then search out the arrow in flight, lock on, and track it as it moves away from us. To be successful at this task, the planning associated with putting our desire into action must begin well before we let go of the string.

What we learn from these studies is that we are likely taking our focus off the mark even before we let go of the string. Is it any wonder that we miss?

In the psychology study, the researchers recorded an average of a quarter-second error in the subject's perception of when an event occurred. In the neuroscience study, the researchers were able to predict the movement of a subject's hands based on brain activity recorded the second before the action was taken.

Understanding that the agency we hold over our actions is dependent on some preplanning and is subject to chronological misperceptions as we plan helps explain why we must stay focused on the target.

Even if we shift focus from the target to the arrow a split second after the arrow has left the bow, the mental process involved in executing that shift must have started before we let go of the string. So (even though we don't realize it), we begin to lose focus on the target before shooting, and therefore, our accuracy will probably suffer.

I find it a hard habit to break. My desire to watch the arrow fly is a strong one. It is a constant battle to keep my eye focused on the mark and to see the arrow only in my peripheral vision. But if we can avoid watching the arrow in flight, the benefits are twofold:

- We will better learn the trajectory of our arrow.
- We will keep our mental and neurological focus on the mark, improving our follow-through and accuracy.

I think that other faults associated with not holding our form until the arrow hits the mark contribute to misses for the same reasons. If we drop our bow arm at the shot so that we can see the arrow fly, we have planned that action ahead of the shot. If we hold the bow grip lightly during the draw but then tighten our grasp on it as the string is dropped, we again plan that ahead of the shot.

We are aware of what we do when we do it and what we think when we think it. But by definition, we cannot be aware of everything our neurological system must do beforehand in order for us to sense our world and hold agency over our interaction with it.

But through these studies and others like them, we can be aware that our actions and thoughts take time to form before they can happen.

I think these studies formalize and find the root mechanisms of our delayed response to stimuli and the cautionary advice that our driver's education teachers drilled into us as teenagers—never follow a car too closely, or you won't be able to react to a problem in time to prevent a crash.

These studies illustrate the fact that even when we are simply acting on our own agency (instead of reacting to a driving problem), our senses and actions take time to form in our brains before they are executed and become part of our memories.

This understanding should give even more value to Howard Hill's advice of "with the hands at the shot, do nothing."

TEN-SECOND MODIFIED BLANK BALE PRACTICE

As I begin to describe this next exercise, the reader may conclude that it runs contrary to the fluid motion and relaxed style we try to develop when learning the swing-draw. In fact, when I first started experimenting with this exercise, I worried that it might hamper my efforts to improve my shooting.

Happily, after many months of adding this exercise to my routine, I found it had no negative effects on my form. Instead, my overall form improved. Therefore I feel comfortable sharing this exercise as I think for those (like me) that lack an excellent kinesthetic sense or the muscular physique of a mesomorph, this exercise can help develop both muscle and nerve.

Howard Hill and other strong archers speak of using extra heavy bows for exercise to build strength. While they promoted becoming as strong as possible, they also cautioned against using a heavy bow to attempt accurate shooting. Therefore, you would need both exercise bows and hunting bows.

This exercise has dual advantages in that it can be fit into a normal bale practice session, and it doesn't require a heavy exercise bow.

There are a few cautions I will make here that should be respected if you intend to incorporate this exercise into your routine:

- Perform this exercise only on the blank bale. Do not try this while shooting at a target.

- Build up slowly to the ten-second time. Begin with two-second hold times and no more than five repetitions.

To perform this exercise, I take my stance on my blank bale shooting platform. I make the decision to perform a repetition of this exercise before drawing the bow.

I draw my bow to anchor while focusing on the blank bale. As I reach anchor, I close my eyes and begin to count to ten. As I count, I am focusing on any one of the following form conditions: the feeling of my middle finger at the corner of my mouth, of my string arm alignment with the arrow, and of my back and shoulder muscles pulling hard. I focus on releasing parasitic tension from my string hand, wrist, and forearm. I focus on shoulders articulated to maximize stability. The list goes on.

Obviously, I don't focus on all these things at once. I focus on what I want to work on. If it feels right, I may shift my focus to something else.

As I reach the count of ten, I open my eyes, reacquire a spot on the blank bale, and drop the string.

If you are like me, you will find this exercise makes your deltoid muscles sore (and the trapezius and rhomboid muscles in your back). When I first started integrating this exercise into my routine, there were a few days when my deltoid muscles were so sore I could not pull the car door shut. Let that be a warning to the reader to proceed with caution when implementing this exercise.

The effect this exercise has on my archery shot is twofold.

The first and most obvious effect is upon my strength and the ease with which I can pull the string back. If I had opted to get a stronger exercise bow that had a higher draw force than my hunting bow, then I would be strengthening all the muscle fiber used to pull the string (through the entire length of the draw) beyond that required to pull my hunting bow. But I have observed that it requires very little strength to pull my bow through the first two-thirds of its draw. It is only the last third that taxes my ability.

I have further observed that in the performance of my normal swing-draw shooting, my muscles spend the least amount of time at full draw and under the full strain required to reach that point (if they even get there).

Different fiber groups within the muscle are responsible for different parts of the range of motion that the muscle (as a whole) creates. This is why weight-lifting coaches teach their students to lift those weights all the way up and, when doing squats, to bend all the way down.

And finally, I have observed that the strength of my muscles as I reach full draw, and my ability to control them at that point, has more effect on my accuracy than does my strength and control at any other part of the draw.

By drawing the bow to full draw, holding it for ten seconds, and then shooting, I am exercising those muscle fibers in my shoulder and back that are most responsible for getting me and my bow to full draw well beyond what is required of them during an actual shot.

Science has identified three factors that affect muscle growth:

- Frequency – how often an exercise is performed per week
- Intensity – how much resistance is applied to the muscle
- Volume – how long the muscle is exposed to the resistance (repetitions)

A study published in February 2007's edition of *Sports Medicine* called "The Influence of Frequency, Intensity, Volume, and Mode of Training on Whole Muscle Cross-Sectional Area in Humans" showed that:

Given sufficient frequency, intensity, and volume of work, all three types of muscle actions can induce significant hypertrophy [growth] at an impressive rate and that, at present, there is insufficient evidence for the superiority of any mode and/or type of muscle action over other modes and types of training.

Knowing that I can make my bow-pulling muscles stronger by increasing the volume of exercise (holding the bow at full draw) just as effectively as by exposing them to greater intensity (a stronger exercise bow) allows me to get stronger with less risk of injury, which is not to say that there is no risk.

Strengthening muscles through exercise is a controlled method of injuring them so they will heal stronger. But we need to minimize the risk of injury to bone, tendon, and cartilage as much as possible. Slowly building strength through the increasing volume of exercise, instead of the intensity of exercise, is one way of achieving this goal.

The second aspect of this exercise that helps to improve my shooting has to do with the effect of the hold time on my nerves and builds on what we will learn in Chapter 9 about how our neural network of the brain and spine and neurons works together.

There was an interesting article in the March 2020 issue of *Scientific American* called "The Brain Learns in Unexpected Ways." In this article, the author, Douglas Fields, outlines a new property he and his team found in the way that the grey and white matter of our brains work together to store memories and learn skills.

To begin his article, Douglas Fields notes the old adage among brain researchers that "nerves that fire together wire together." This mnemonic underscores the basic mechanism neurons use to store memories, which is to connect together at points called synapses. He then goes on to describe his research that builds on this basic understanding by outlining the role that the myelin sheath around axons (nerve fibers) plays in memory and repetitive tasks.

What he and his team discovered is that the more often neurons fire signals down axons, the thicker the myelin sheath around the axon becomes. The thicker the sheath is, the more efficiently the axon transmits the signal. Not only is the axon more efficient with a thicker layer of myelin, but it also transmits the signal faster.

In summary, Fields tells us:

Learning and performing complex tasks involves the coordinated operation of many neurons in diverse brain regions and requires that signals proceed through large neural networks at an optimal speed. The myelin sheath is crucial for optimal transmission... These novel concepts have begun to change the way we think about how the brain works as a system. Myelin, long considered inert insulation on axons, is now seen as making a contribution to learning by controlling the speed at which signals travel along neural wiring. In venturing beyond the synapse, we are beginning to fill out the stick-figure skeleton of synaptic plasticity to create a fuller picture of what happens when we learn.

While Fields's work was involved in studying how myelin sheaths formed in the brain, my studies (explained more in Chapter 9) tell me that this research will likely be extended to show that this mechanism is also at work in the spine and most other areas of our neural network that contain both white and grey matter.

By holding my bow at full draw, not only am I straining my muscles and stimulating them to grow stronger, I am stimulating my neural network to learn and build more efficient and faster pathways to help my swing-draw become more natural.

THREE-SECOND MODIFIED BLANK BALE PRACTICE

This three-second modified practice is simply a shortened version of the ten-second practice. The time to add this practice into your routine is after you have been doing the ten-second practice for many months.

Even after many months, the ten-second practice will wear you out as it requires a substantial amount of energy to perform.

Eventually, I settled into a routine where I would do ten or fifteen repetitions of the ten-second practice at the end of my daily routine two or three times a week. This volume of exercise gives my muscles time to heal and strengthen.

As I got better at settling into my draw and holding the full draw weight of my bow, I also got better at relaxing the tension out of muscles I shouldn't be using, like the biceps and wrist muscles of the string arm.

As I continued to practice the ten-second exercise, I found that when I opened my eyes, my arrow was still pointed near where it had been when I closed my eyes.

It was at about this time that I began adding the three-second version of this exercise into my routine.

This three-second version is different from the ten-second version in two ways. First, as mentioned, it is shorter. Second, the shooter leaves their eyes open during the count.

Again, the careful reader will note that this exercise runs contrary to the stated goal of building a smooth, fluid shot that does not require the archer to hold at anchor.

And again, I will note that this exercise is not for everyone. If you are progressing with your swing-draw satisfactorily by following the method and exercises of earlier chapters, then don't bother with this one. But if, after a year or more of practice, you are still struggling to get the feel of the bow (learning to balance yourself with the bow), then you may benefit from this exercise.

By confining this practice to the blank bale, you are free to work on your form and discover the feel of the shot without concern for hitting the mark.

By holding for three seconds instead of ten, it takes longer to get fatigued and so it is easier to incorporate many more repetitions of this exercise into a daily routine.

The purpose of this exercise is the same as the ten-second version. After performing the longer version for many months, the archer will be able to come to anchor using the correct muscles, relax away parasitic tension, release, and follow through in a shorter time.

I find it helpful in this exercise to count out loud as I come to anchor. "One... Two... Three..." Counting out loud keeps it real and keeps the time better. As I walk to retrieve my arrow from the bale, I often continue this counting mantra to keep my mind focused.

If it doesn't all come together in a count of three, then it is too early to add this exercise to your routine, and the archer should go back to the ten-second version for a while longer.

It is important to exercise agency over your practice. As I take my stance in front of my blank bale, I think about how I will take the next shot. I decide if I will take a fluid shot, dwell for a count of three at my anchor before release, or if I will just come to anchor, close my eyes, count to ten, open my eyes, and then drop the string.

Then I take the shot I intended to take, or at least I try.

After the arrow has landed in the bale, and while I am still holding my stance, I think about how the shot went—what went well and what didn't.

I let these thoughts and feelings inform how I'll take the next shot. I don't judge the shot just taken as good or bad. I don't admonish myself for some fault that may have crept into my form.

I keep quite a few of these three- and ten-second shots in my daily routine.

CHECKING FORM IN A MIRROR

We are lucky in this modern world to have all sorts of convenient technology handy to help us with our lives. One of these modern conveniences is the digital video camera.

This decidedly average archer displays a hunched-up bow shoulder and a string-arm elbow way out to the side as he watches his reflection in a mirror.

I use my video camera all the time to record my shooting from various angles. It is helpful to see where my form is lacking, and it is fun to review videos over time to see my form improve.

While video cameras are no doubt useful, I think an old-fashioned full-length mirror has been more helpful to me. I think it has been more helpful because I can use it in real time to see and correct form problems.

I have found it most helpful to place the mirror directly in front of me and to draw my bow at a target that I can see in the mirror.

By doing this, I can take note of faults with eye/arrow alignment, string-arm alignment, bow-shoulder alignment, and overall posture, and I can attempt to correct the fault in real time and see the results instantly.

The archer let his bow down and drew it again. He has now tightened up his form by rotating his humerus and pulling his string arm around with his back and shoulder muscles instead of his bicep. The mirror allows the archer to see the form changes he makes, while at the same time, feeling those changes.

I perform this exercise outside so that, in the unfortunate circumstance that I let go of the string, the destruction and ensuing mess are confined to my shooting area instead of the house.

The real-time feedback is surprisingly helpful in correcting faults.

It was impossible to find a camera angle that would show the exact view I had while drawing my bow in front of the mirror. As I drew the bow for these pictures, I focused on a leaf that was behind me about fifteen yards and drew the bow as if I would shoot the leaf. (I have found, through trial and error, that it is best not to shoot the leaf in the mirror.) I then looked at my form and attempted to correct faults.

Most faults in shooting are the result of incorrect muscle recruitment. This incorrect recruitment can happen in one of two ways. Either we recruit the wrong muscles, or (in addition to the correct muscles) we recruit additional muscles that antagonize the correct muscles. These faults reduce our strength and coordination.

Take, for example, the fault of recruiting the bicep muscles to pull the string hand back to anchor. For most non-archery activities we engage in during our day, if we want to move our hand closer to us, we fold our arm at the elbow by using our bicep muscles. We recruit the biceps for this common motion a thousand times a day, so it's natural that we would use it to pull the string hand back towards the face.

It's so natural that we don't realize we are doing it, even when we know it's not the right thing to do.

Without using a video camera or a mirror, we can know we are recruiting the biceps to pull our string hand back if we find we punch ourselves in the face upon release of the string. Or we glance over and see our string elbow way up in the air above our head (or way out to the side), or we see our wrist bent awkwardly.

In these extreme cases of getting the string hand to anchor by recruiting the biceps, it is easy to see where the fault lies. But as we get better and better at drawing the bow, the fault of using the biceps becomes more subtle and harder to see. We may engage it just a bit, for only part of the draw cycle, or just at the end. These more subtle faults will still ruin a shot and are the hardest to correct.

By drawing my bow in front of the mirror, I have been able to see the fault and find the muscles responsible for the fault more effectively than by watching a video.

I have found that it can be very difficult to isolate the correct muscles from the incorrect ones when trying to fix a fault. This is evidence that my kinesthetic sense is not perfect. When I have a newfound fault I am finding hard to correct, I will use a very light bow (kids' bows work well). A light bow eases the stress on muscles and nerves and makes it possible to find the right muscles.

Interestingly, I have found that time can also help fix a fault. I have found that if I spend a few minutes in front of the mirror every day concentrating on whatever fault I am having trouble with, one day, I will draw the bow in the mirror, and the fault will be gone. I will have found my neurological path to recruiting the correct muscles while avoiding the incorrect ones.

Once I find the correct neurological path, I repeat the exercise in front of the mirror until the correct paths become the dominant ones and the incorrect paths begin to atrophy. In my case, this can take a few weeks.

DRAW, BALANCE, LET-DOWN PRACTICE

Sometimes, it helps to mix things up.

If every time we draw our bow we drop the string, then we have only the experience of what happens next.

But if we mix up our practice by bringing in the exercise of drawing our bow to anchor, balancing ourselves with the bow, and then letting the bow down without shooting, then we give ourselves the additional opportunity to improve our mental focus, physical condition, and control over the shot.

For those of us who suffer from the yips, this exercise can be very helpful.

To perform this exercise, take your stance in front of your blank bale. Focus on the bale and draw your bow to anchor. Balance yourself with the bow and relax away all parasitic tension in your hands and arms to the point that you are confident that if you drop the string, your arrow will fly true. Then let down the bow.

Repeat the above exercise. Then rest for a few seconds.

After you have drawn the bow to anchor and balanced yourself with the bow twice, draw the bow again. Come to anchor and balance yourself with the bow, just as you did the last two times. Then drop the string.

Retrieve your arrow and do it again.

Repeat this sequence of two let-downs and two shots for fifteen minutes or for whatever time you have available to you.

When we shoot a lot, we tend to focus overly much on hitting the mark. We can forget what should be our true priority, which is to balance ourselves with the bow. By drawing our bow to anchor without any intention of dropping the string, we can practice the skill of balancing ourselves with the bow more efficiently.

It is a mistake to think that we should drop the string when we come to anchor. What we should do when we come to anchor is balance ourselves with the bow. If we are good, we will achieve this balance as we come to anchor. If we are not so good, it will take a moment longer to achieve this balance.

We should not drop the string when we come to anchor. We should drop the string after we have balanced ourselves with the bow.

The better we get at balancing ourselves with the bow, the easier it will be to reach this balance as we reach anchor. I found this exercise helped me improve my timing. It helped me reach my balance with the bow as I reached my anchor so that my shots came off more fluidly and naturally.

———✵———

There is comfort in letting others do the thinking for us, but there is also danger. One of the dangers is that we become so enamored, protective, and defensive of what we are being told that we forget that we ourselves might have something valuable to add to the process, and we forget that there might indeed be more than one way to peel a potato. This fault in thinking is as common in archery enthusiasts as is any fault in form.

There is also danger in thinking for ourselves. A prime danger in thinking for ourselves is the consequences of making a bad choice. If we are not accustomed to thinking for ourselves, we are likely not good at correlating cause and effect.

I think this is why Wong Kiew Kit emphasized that the beginning student must follow the form exercises of Kung Fu exactly as taught to them (if you have no experience, you cannot connect cause and effect). But then there does come a time when the student should be competent enough with the exercise that they can then stray from the fundamentals and explore the possibilities.

To be a successful student, you must have complete confidence in the method. To become a master, you must have complete confidence in your form.

We are all built differently and have different needs when it comes to learning. When we are starting out, we can all benefit from the same exercises performed in the same way. Then there will come a time when our form benefits from a more customized exercise routine. This is where the ability to think for ourselves comes in handy.

Just as it is hard to learn to balance ourselves with the bow, it is hard to balance our need to learn the basics with our desire to improve. It is up to each of us to decide when we will add to our basic routine the new exercises that we feel will help us.

Our success at improving our form will be dependent on our ability to be creative, reason clearly, and discern the real connections between cause and effect.

These extra exercises are just a starting point to help you think about how you can improve your shooting beyond the basics.

PART II

FRAME OF MIND

The instructor's business is not to show the way, but to enable the pupil to get the feel of the way by adapting it to his individual particularities.

—Eugene Herrigel, *Zen in the Art of Archery*

Presence of mind. Some say we need to develop our frame of mind; some say we need to get out of our own way. I like to think of it as developing presence of mind. Whatever you call it, almost everyone who works hard to get good at something will agree that practicing the right mental state is at least as important as practicing the right form.

Developing the right mental state is harder and more elusive than developing the right form simply because we don't have a path for it as clear cut as the one we have for practicing our form.

There is one thing that our physical practice has in common with our mental practice, though, and that is context.

The exercises in Part 1 are designed to build form through practice set within specific contexts (shooting into a blank bale to build form, shooting arrows into space to build trajectory awareness, etc.). The chapters of Part 2 don't outline exercises per se but instead outline ways of thinking about our practice that should help make the process of learning more effective.

As we strive to become the best archers we can be, we naturally look to those great archers that came before us. This is good. This is good if we seek inspiration from their style and success. But it would be a mistake to think that we should exactly imitate their form.

Because of our unique morphologies, both physical and neurological, we must each develop our unique style. There may be only small, subtle differences between how we shoot as compared to others, but in those subtleties lies the perfection we seek.

While our shooting forms may vary, our goal is the same: to shoot an arrow accurately to the mark and to find joy in the act. To achieve this goal, we all have the same task in common: to balance ourselves with the bow.

Just as some of us are lucky enough in that we have no need for physical exercises to help us develop our form, some of us will have no need to think much about it. We can develop our mental form, our frame of mind, without any help.

For those that may need a nudge in the right direction, the following chapters may prove useful.

The last chapter in this section is about troubleshooting problems you may be having with your shooting. It is not strictly about developing your shooting frame of mind. It is about developing a can-do attitude toward solving problems.

Building confidence in your problem-solving abilities helps you build confidence in your shooting, and in this way, it helps each archer adapt to their individual particularities.

Once we accept our individual particularities and learn to adapt our shooting to them, we truly free ourselves to find joy in archery.

Chapter 5

THE CHOICES WE MAKE

As I write these words, there are at least 367 known proofs for the Pythagorean theorem. The Pythagorean theorem, which we learned in grade school, is the theorem that tells us that the square of the hypotenuse of a right triangle is equal to the sum of the square of its sides. $C^2 = A^2 + B^2$.

Pythagoras, who lived around 500BC, is given credit for discovering this property of right triangles. But it was likely well-known as early as 1600BC since Babylonian stone tablets were found that contained a list of special integers, which we now call Pythagorean triples.

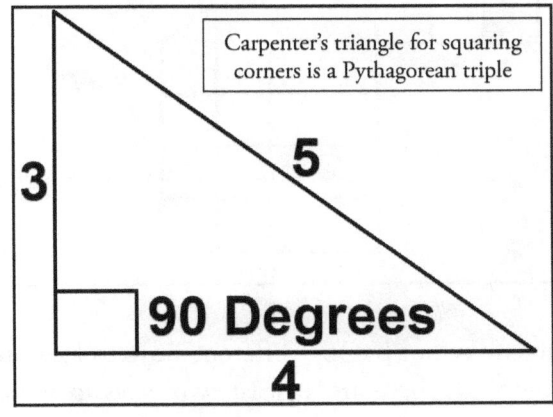

Carpenter's triangle for squaring corners is a Pythagorean triple

3

5

90 Degrees

4

One such triple is the set of three, four, and five. The carpenters among us will know these numbers as they are handy to use for establishing a square corner in a structure: If you measure three feet along one side from the corner and four feet along the other, and if those two measured and marked points are also five feet apart from each other, you have a square corner.

These 367 proofs include algebraic, geometric, and calculus methods. Some require many pages of calculations, while others require just a simple illustration to establish the theorem as true.

The point is that there can be many ways to arrive at the same truth. While only one proof is required to show that the Pythagorean theorem is true, the value of having so many proofs is that their different natures and approaches appeal more or less to different people. I, for one, can more readily understand (and appreciate) the geometric proofs that seem self-evident at a glance.

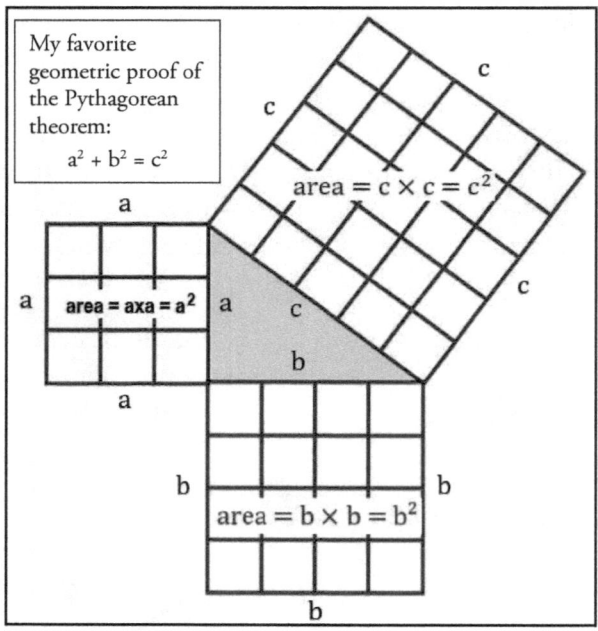

While there may not be 367 different ways to learn to shoot the bow and arrow well, there are at least two ways in which a person can end up becoming a good shot. The first is to simply be a natural athlete. The second is to work really hard in an efficient, confident, and thoughtful manner.

Sometimes, the merit of listening to a teacher is obvious. Consider those famous archers Howard Hill, John Schulz, and Byron Ferguson. These fellows shot well during their entire lives. They racked up many examples of their excellent shooting, like winning contests, giving demonstrations, or killing game. There is no doubt they knew what they were doing, and they did it well.

If we read Howard Hill's book *Hunting the Hard Way* or one of his many brochures on how he shoots, and then we watch John Schulz's video demonstration of his shooting and read his booklet *Hitting 'em Like Howard Hill*, and then we read Byron Ferguson's book *Become the Arrow*, then we must have everything we need to learn how to shoot well. Right?

I guess I would answer that question with a yes and a no. For some of us, that is indeed all the information we need to learn to shoot well. Others of us may still struggle. Why is it enough for one person and not enough for another? I think it boils down to different aptitudes, natural abilities, and life experiences.

Experience and time leave indelible marks in our brains and our bones that reflect the life we've lived. These changes and adaptations can sometimes hinder our efforts to learn a new skill. And yet our bodies are always willing to adapt themselves to our next adventure. But we must remember that as we age, the process of learning a new skill can take a little longer.

In the same way that it can be helpful to use different methods to prove the Pythagorean theorem for people with different mathematical aptitudes and life experiences, it can be helpful to illustrate different methods used to learn the swing-draw.

Some of us have a better-developed kinesthetic sense. When we start out with a better sense of our body in time and space, it makes it easier to learn a new physical skill. Our kinesthetic sense is supplied by an array of nerves in our joints and muscles that transmit information to our spine and brain. I will talk about this more in a later chapter, but for now, suffice it to say that we can all improve our kinesthetic sense with practice.

If our kinesthetic sense is good, this simplifies the exercise of learning to shoot the bow and arrow. If it's not so good, the need to improve it adds to what we must learn. From what I know of the aforementioned fellows, they were all good athletes who demonstrated above-average skills even before picking up the bow and arrow. For example, Howard Hill had the opportunity to pursue careers in both professional baseball and golf.

When we struggle to learn something and feel we are not making progress, we can get frustrated. Frustration with archery is likely the number one reason people give up on it.

When someone who is accomplished at archery shows us (or tells us) how to do something as "simple as that," and we try but just can't get it right, then that's a formula for frustration and failure.

Sometimes, all we need is just a little more, a small nudge in the right direction. If we can get pointed in the right direction, our ability to teach ourselves takes over, and we make progress.

Once we find ourselves on the right path, once we gain confidence in our strategy to learn, our frustrations will begin to ebb. Even if our improvement is not obvious in the short term, our confidence allows us to have fun.

I think this is really the point. What good is shooting a bow and arrow if it isn't fun? Fun is a word, the meaning of which I think changes as we get older. For me, having fun with archery means learning, feeling the progress towards perfection in my form, and becoming a better person through effort.

Notice that I didn't say having fun with archery means becoming the best archery trick shot the world ever knew.

No matter how efficient our training is, no matter how good our teachers are, we all don't rise to the same level. A variety of skills and abilities is what makes a species robust. It's what allows a species to survive a never-ending string of challenges to its very existence. In the case of humans, it can also make us frustrated as we try to achieve the same level of skill as those who became famous for theirs.

For many years, I found myself haphazardly trying this and that. I'd change something about my gear, brace height, arrow spine, gloves, draw length, stance—whatever—all in the hopes that it would improve my shooting. Each thing would offer promise, but eventually, it would not pan out.

I was shooting in the dark. I had no plan. I didn't see the big picture. Once I found the right path for me, the dominos began to fall, and it all made sense. The sensation I felt was similar to the feeling one gets when a good mystery novel wraps up. All the seemingly unrelated evidence suddenly transforms into pieces of the puzzle that neatly fit together.

As with most endeavors, I ended up with more than I bargained for. Not only did I end up more skillful in my hunting with the bow and arrow, but I also ended up having more fun. I also learned a lot about how our bodies and brains work together to do what we do. So what exactly does it mean to be more skillful?

WHAT'S THE DIFFERENCE?

How we measure the quality of our skill set depends on what we want to accomplish, our goals. The two main forms of archery evolved from the goals of target shooting and hunting. Those who pursue target shooting will do so with the ultimate goal of succeeding in tournament archery. Those who pursue hunting will do so with the ultimate goal of harvesting game.

Those who want to excel at tournament archery find success in a static form. Those who want to excel at hunting usually find success in a more dynamic form. We often call that which tournament archers do tournament form. By the same token, we call what hunters do instinctive form.

So what is the difference between tournament form and instinctive form?

The look of tournament form is static. Its stability and success are based on bone alignment, steady anchor, and minimal muscle antagonism. Its objective is pinpoint accuracy.

The look of instinctive form is dynamic. Its stability and success are based on bone alignment, momentary anchor, and muscle coordination. Its objective is general accuracy.

If you are going to win the tournament, you need the best score, but you can take all day to get that score.

If you are going to kill the deer, you just need to get the arrow in the chest cavity. You don't need to center-punch the heart, but you *can't* take all day to shoot.

This is why Howard Hill, in his book *Hunting the Hard Way*, advised his readers to decide what they wanted to shoot—target or game—and why he said that the two don't mix.

There are rules to good tournament form. There are rules to good instinctive form. These styles are equally valid, but they serve different purposes.

If someone says, "Come to the target range and prove instinctive archery is just as accurate," this challenge is based on the false assumption that the purpose of instinctive form is the same as tournament form. Generally, a tournament shooter will get better scores than an instinctive shooter on targets, as it should be.

But if the challenge is made to come to the woods and chase squirrels, well, the tide will turn. The instinctive shooter is more likely to kill the squirrel before the target shooter even takes his shot, as it should be.

The bottom line is that the style you employ should be determined by what you intend to shoot: targets or game. One is not better than the other. But your wise choice, based on understanding the merits of each style, will make you a happier archer.

THE ACCURACY TRIANGLE

The point remains that archers may employ either of these styles and shoot a reliably accurate arrow.

How can this be?

The answer is that all accurate styles of shooting hold three things in common. However you choose to shoot, you must do three things to ensure that your arrow arrives at its mark.

These three things may be thought of as sides of a triangle. The archer that makes a good shot must do all three things. In other words, the archer must close the triangle before letting go of the string.

- *The archer must balance themself with the bow.* This means that there can be no parasitic forces or torques that will throw the arrow off course when the string is released. An example of a parasitic torque would be twisting the bow handle. An example of a parasitic force would be applying pressure in the grip too low or too high.
- *The archer must come to anchor.* This means that the archer must fully draw the bow and pull the string to a known and repeatable position. For most of us, the anchor point is somewhere on our faces. This doesn't have to be the case, though, as demonstrated by Mongolian archers whose anchor appears to float in the air.
- *Finally, the archer must aim or point their arrow at the mark.* I used both words to describe this side of the triangle so that it most generally represents what has to be done. Some archers literally aim their arrows like a marksman would aim a rifle. They use the tip of the arrow or a site pin to positively align the arrow to a mark. Other archers simply point the arrow at a mark in the same way that we can point our finger at a bird sitting in a tree without actually looking down our finger like a gun barrel to do it. For the purpose of closing the triangle, it doesn't matter how the archer aligns their arrow with the mark.

These two methods of aligning the arrow with the mark work equally well. They serve as another example of the truth that there is almost always more than one way to arrive at a goal. How we align the arrow should be informed by our general style of shooting. If we tend more towards a tournament form, then a gun-barrel aiming technique is more appropriate. If we tend toward a more instinctive form, then learning to point the arrow is more appropriate.

However we shoot, we must close our accuracy triangle if we are to make the shot count.

To shoot with a tournament style, the archer will most often assemble their accuracy triangle in distinct steps. They will usually come to anchor first, as step one. Then they will settle into the shot, which is to say that they will attempt to relax away parasitic forces and torques so that the arrow is not pulled off course when the string is released. "Settling into the shot" is the more common way of saying "balance yourself with the bow." Finally, they aim their arrow at the mark.

The challenge of this style is in keeping the triangle together as we build it.

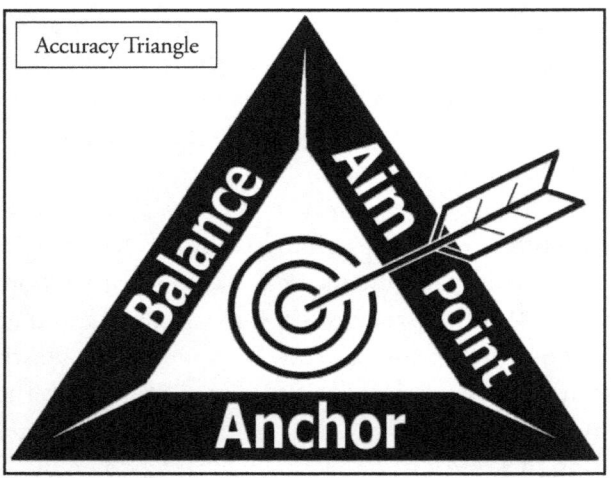

Say the archer comes to anchor perfectly. Step one is done. Then they begin to feel their balance with the bow. They settle into the shot. But this takes a few moments, and in that time, their string hand has drifted away from their anchor. Finally, they aim the arrow and release. The arrow will miss the mark.

Or say the archer comes to anchor perfectly. Then they settle into the shot and achieve perfect form. Finally, they begin to aim the arrow. The arrow is well off the mark, and as they bring it to the mark, some tension creeps into their string-arm bicep muscle to keep their string hand against their face. This causes a torque that throws the arrow to the side at release. The arrow will again miss its mark.

To shoot with an instinctive style, the archer will most often assemble their accuracy triangle in one simultaneous event. When someone like Howard Hill demonstrates a fluid shot, what they are doing is bringing all three sides of the accuracy triangle together at the same instant.

It's a thing of beauty to watch. It's even more beautiful when you experience the feeling of what it's like to shoot this way.

The challenge of this style is in the timing. The archer must bring all three sides of the accuracy triangle together at the same instant and then release the string. This is no small challenge.

If the archer manages to bring all three sides together, the arrow will hit the mark.

If any one side of the triangle is off-kilter, not connected to the other two, the arrow will miss the mark.

I think the biggest mistake people make when attempting to learn instinctive archery is that they focus on letting the string go without pause.

In the best case, they get into the habit of reaching anchor and then letting go of the string before achieving balance or pointing the arrow at the mark.

In the worst case (target panic), I think they may manage to point the arrow toward the mark but never achieve balance or anchor before letting the string go.

The purpose of this book (in the simplest terms), then, is to provide methods and mindset that will help the archer learn to bring all three sides of the accuracy triangle together at once.

WHICH STYLE TO CHOOSE?

This is the place, in reading this book, where you should stop and consider what you want to accomplish.

If you want to shoot well in tournaments, this book may not help you much. If you want to get better at hunting or roving through the woods with your friends, then you may benefit from further reading.

A defining characteristic that (in my opinion) makes the swing-draw a better method for hunting is that the archer never takes their eye off the target. The swing-draw employs an upward motion of the bow to the line of sight. This allows the archer to keep their eye on the squirrel from the moment tension is placed on the string until the arrow has arrived at its destination.

By contrast, tournament form requires that the archer employ the high draw (or the T draw), where the bow is drawn from a position above the shoulders and brought down onto the target. This style of draw has the bow, at least for a moment, blocking the archer's eye from the squirrel. Anyone who has hunted knows that if you take your eye off the squirrel, it's apt to disappear.

Everything in life is a balancing act. If we choose to act in a certain way, hopefully, we have done the math correctly and found that the addition of the pros and cons will result in a positive sum.

This principle applies to how we choose to shoot our bow and arrow. Is the swing-draw the perfect way to shoot? I don't suppose it is; there are a few drawbacks. But in total, for the purpose of hunting, roving, and shooting at distances of fifty yards or fewer, I think it's as good as it gets.

The major drawback to the swing-draw I have found is that it does rely on muscle coordination. Our aptitude for coordinated motion is individual. Some are more coordinated than others. We all stumble, but we can all improve our abilities with practice. That said, I believe this aspect of the swing-draw is what limits its ultimate accuracy for each person who practices it.

A person who is highly coordinated and athletic can become highly accurate with the swing-draw. Howard Hill and Ken Wilhelm are prime examples. Most of us will end up shooting less accurately since we are not so athletic.

Another example of this same point might be all the kids who go to the Michael Jordan basketball camps. We can all practice basketball like Michael Jordan, but only a scant few will ever be as good as he was at the sport. That doesn't mean we can't all have fun with it.

Another con of the swing-draw is that it does not take full advantage of skeletal alignment and can involve some muscle antagonism for most of us who are not highly coordinated.

If we acknowledge these limitations and keep our expectations real, then we can enjoy the advantages that the swing-draw gives us. The two advantages I mentioned earlier, namely being able to keep your eye on the target and attenuating target panic, are not the only advantages.

Another advantage is that we can shoot from just about any position with the expectation of achieving our normal level of accuracy. We can shoot from our knees, we can shoot downhill or uphill, or even from a treestand without the usual decline in accuracy that would be experienced by someone who shoots tournament style.

Yet another advantage is range estimation. The swing-draw is, for most people, effective at fifty yards or fewer. The method outlined in this book will allow the archer to develop an intuitive understanding of the trajectory of the arrow and be able to keep it on target without much concern for the distance.

And yet another advantage (subjective, I admit) is that we need less stuff to shoot. We don't need a range finder to know the distance. We don't need a score sheet to tell us how we did. We don't need a lot of time to take the shot. We shoot, and we move on.

While I have emphasized the point that we need to keep our expectations realistic, I don't want to give the impression that those of us who are athletically challenged have limited capacity to excel at shooting the bow and arrow.

If the only measure of excellence is hitting the bullseye every time we shoot, then some of us will be disappointed. But if we expand our idea of what excellence is, we can see more opportunities for it.

By adopting a method of shooting that is well-defined, has a specific approach to learning, and is supported by an understanding of why it works, we can be confident in our ability to continue improving. Fred Bear once said that archery is a competition with yourself. This simple observation encapsulates all the reasons why we average archers can nonetheless endeavor to excel at archery.

There is no better feeling than to look back at our shooting and see improvement. We can improve our score, but we can also improve our style.

We can become more relaxed in our shots by learning to use only the necessary muscles. By using the correct muscles, and no others, we reduce what is called muscle antagonism. Muscle antagonism is what we call muscles fighting for control of a motion. One muscle is pulling this way, and another is pulling that way. Our hand may go where we want it to, but the effort fatigues us and usually introduces torque (twisting) into our shot. The resulting arrow flight is never good.

We can stop chasing dead ends. When there is no plan, we are prone to constantly try new things, see if they work, and then abandon them shortly. This never-ending cycle of change inhibits our ability to learn. By committing to and adopting the swing-draw, we can stop this hunt for the quick fix.

By having a plan, we can stop looking for a plan. This alone is great progress. Learning the swing-draw is a step-by-step process. It will not be completed in two weeks, but rather takes a lifetime. We can spend each practice session improving our shot, becoming better than we were the day before, if by only the slightest amount. Yet this frees us up to think about other things. A better glove? White arrows instead of brown? The list is endless.

We can find joy in the process. As the old saying goes: "It's not the destination that matters; it's the journey." It used to be that when I hit the bullseye, I felt good. How the arrow got there didn't really matter. Now I feel good when my form feels right. When I smoothly bring the bow to full draw and release the arrow cleanly. When my bow hand stays put after the shot. When my string hand rests quietly at my anchor once the arrow is gone. When I hold my stance calmly, waiting for the arrow to complete its arc. These good feelings would not be possible if every shot did not build on the experience of the one that came before.

So, winning this archery game, this competition we have with ourselves, depends more on our commitment to getting it right than it does on getting it right, right now. If we commit to the process, to regular practice, to staying the course, we win. And if we stay the course, we will eventually get better at actually hitting the mark.

Enjoying the time spent hunting is very important to me. Enjoying my time in the woods is in no small way affected by my confidence in my shooting. If I am not confident that when the moment comes to shoot, I can hit the mark, then everything that leads up to that moment is tarnished. If I am confident that I can make good on the shot, then even if the opportunity never comes, I am still happy with the day.

We can follow a random path, or we can learn to choose our way. The more we practice making choices, the better we can get at making good choices, and the more we can discover about ourselves. Weighing the pros and cons in our mind and choosing a path lends confidence when we find trouble in our way. That confidence, in turn, helps us get by those bumps in our path.

None of us need to shoot the bow and arrow to survive in this modern age. It is purely an optional activity and, as such, should contribute to our happiness. If you find yourself frustrated with your shooting, randomly changing up what you do, feeling a lack of progress and flagging confidence, then maybe it's time to stop and consider your archery path. The choices we make can make all the difference.

Chapter 6

COMMITMENT

Kung fu means supreme skill from hard work. A great poet has reached kung fu. The painter, the calligrapher, they can be said to have kung fu. Even the cook, the one who sweeps the steps, can have kung fu. Practice, preparation, endless repetition until your mind is weary and your bones ache, too wasted to breathe. This is the way, the only way, one acquires kung fu.

—One Hundred Eyes, *Shaolin Monk*

Perhaps the hardest thing to master while learning the swing-draw is commitment. **The only thing that really endangers our ability to learn the swing-draw is giving up on it.**

If your intention is to learn to shoot the bow to the best of your abilities, then the swing-draw method offers a means to that end. But it does require commitment and hard work. There are no shortcuts, no quick fixes, and no tidy little secrets to success.

The quote at the beginning of this chapter comes from a character (based on a real monk by the same name) in the Netflix movie short *One Hundred Eyes*. I think it perfectly summarizes the understanding and commitment required to succeed at learning the swing-draw.

Learning the swing-draw is like learning to ride a bike. When we are children, our parents give us a few pointers about steering, braking, looking where we are going, and tucking our pants into our socks, so they don't get tangled in the chain. After that, it's up to us. You cannot teach a person to feel the balance of a bike; they must learn it for themselves.

There is really only one way to learn to ride a bike, and that is to do it. We can't really learn to ride until the training wheels come off. If we are lucky, our parents never put them on in the first place.

My memories of learning to ride are faded, but from my experience as a parent, I remember that it took about a week of diligent effort on the part of my children to learn to ride.

They would have a bike for a while and fool around with it, never really caring if they got it to work. It would lay discarded in the yard until put away by an adult.

Then one day, the child would look at that bike a little differently, with a look of commitment in their eye. I knew it wouldn't be long after that.

There would be a few days of short straight attempts, always ending in a tip over. Then one day, a long run would be made, again ending in a tip-over as steering hadn't yet come into the picture. And shortly after that, longer and longer runs with turns to avoid obstacles. Hours later, total control of the bike was had.

In learning to ride a bike, children benefit from the plasticity and architecture of a young brain. Their brains are wired to learn new skills. Skills don't require critical thinking, and the child's brain has a limited capacity to think critically. This ability to learn new skills without the worry of thinking it through allows young people to become naturals at the skills they learn.

With age, our ability to learn basic skills fades as our brains take on the higher tasks of reason and survival. Children learn languages easily and can become fluent in several, while as adults, we struggle to learn even one new language and may never lose our accent.

It's not that we can't learn a new language as adults; it's just that we need a strategy to do it (and commitment to the task). Additionally, we must accept the fact that we may never lose our accents.

THINKING WITHOUT WORDS

In Zen, there is a concept called the "unborn mind." Those who practice Zen understand that our rational mind can interfere with our ability to learn a new skill. They understand that for us to really master a skill, we must learn it as a child learns it, without reason or preconception. The mind most free from reason or preconception is an unborn mind.

The concept of an unborn mind is a description of the mind before it is exposed to language and rules. As we learn rules and language, we gain new abilities to imagine things that are or can be while we simultaneously confine our imaginations to the limits of words.

If we fail to recognize these limits of language, we can never move past them.

While the student wants to learn a skill, the teacher wants to teach it. The teacher who has truly mastered a skill likely recognizes the danger of using too many words in an attempt to fully explain their experience to the student. Every word conveys meaning, but each word can also limit the student.

This is why you may see such cryptic descriptions from masters to their students. What seems cryptic to the student may be crystal clear to the master and all that is needed to really understand the message without limiting one's thinking and actions.

There is a fine line between saying enough and saying too much. To teach children a new skill, little must be said. Teaching adults a new skill may require a more substantial strategy to overcome our current physical limitations and mental habits. This book sets out such a strategy in (hopefully) as few words as possible. All that is required to benefit from this strategy is commitment.

Every action we take is the result of a commitment to motion. There is a Zen concept called "mo chih ch'u," which means to "go ahead without stopping." It seems simple, but what it means is that to master an action, you cannot break it into parts. You must commit to the whole thing.

To illustrate this idea to his fencing students, 17th-century Zen Master Takuan Soho asked his students to observe a tree and notice that even though a tree has innumerable leaves, we can instantly see all of them without stopping to look at each one.

In the same sense, shooting a bow requires (depending on how finely we want to divide it up) innumerable actions that must be performed together. Alan Watts, in his book *The Way of Zen*, conveys the words of Master Takuan as he explains this idea that if we don't encumber our minds with rules and words, then:

> Our natural organism performs the most marvelously complex activities without the least hesitation or deliberation. Conscious thought is itself founded upon its whole system of spontaneous functioning, for which reason there is really no alternative to trusting oneself completely to its working. Oneself is its working.

As children, we trust ourselves completely. We jump into new skills and experiences with joy. The idea—the concept—of doubt is learned as we grow. One of the side benefits of learning the swing-draw as adults is having the opportunity to, at least in this one instance of shooting bows and arrows, unlearn this concept of doubt. **The strategy laid out in this book helps us unlearn doubt through repetition.**

FINDING JOY IN COMMITMENT

I found that the joy of archery returned to me as I committed myself to the process of learning the swing-draw. When we attach our sense of success to the measurable distance our arrow falls from the intended mark, we open the door to doubt.

I think we confuse confidence with commitment. I have heard many people give the advice that to hit the mark, we must be 100 percent confident that we will hit it. While this advice has the merits of being neat and tidy, it never rang true to me.

Early on, as I worked through the experience of learning the swing-draw, I thought that the only thing needed for success was my confidence in the method. I expected that as I practiced, my confidence in the method would transmute itself into my confidence in the shot.

In a sense, I still think this is true. As I understood it at the time, I had confidence in the swing-draw method. But as I look back at it through the prism of hindsight, I see that confidence is a complex idea based on words and carries with it judgment and values. When it all boiled down to the basic truth, I was committed to the swing-draw. That's all there was (and is) to it. There was no further need to doubt my progress or judge the distance between the mark and my arrow. There was only practice.

As adults, we carry a lifetime of experiences in our minds that affect everything we do. For the most part, this is a good thing and helps us to survive and thrive, but it can also make us impatient for success. We are used to doing things and getting results pretty fast. As we age, we get better at anticipating the outcome of events simply because we have been exposed to similar events in the past and have become good at extrapolating from our experience. We take action, and then we judge our progress.

With archery, this means that we may try a change in our form or a different shooting glove, or whatever, for a short time. Then we judge our progress and likely make another change.

The beauty of the swing-draw is that we don't have to go through this process. This beauty can become a pitfall if we don't recognize it for what it is and instead try (in vain) to change it.

I will say it again, the only thing we need to do mentally to succeed at the swing-draw is commit to it. In itself, the simple mental act of committing to a method brings relief and joy to an archer frustrated by years or decades of poor shooting.

While I thought I understood the process and anticipated that my confidence in the swing-draw would transfer to my shot, what really happened is that my commitment to the swing-draw became my commitment to hitting the mark.

What is the difference between commitment to hitting the mark and confidence in hitting the mark?

The difference is joy.

If I am 100 percent confident that I will hit the mark and I miss, then what? I was wrong.

If I am 100 percent committed to hitting the mark and I miss, then what? I missed.

Even though I may have missed, I still felt the joy one experiences in doing an activity while being totally committed to it and without the need to judge the rightness or wrongness of the outcome.

When a child runs screaming across a field, do they feel joy? Is it joy in some expectation of what they will find when they get to the other end of the field? Or is it simply joy in the act of running without hesitation and without expectation?

Many people have said it, and it is certainly true that archery is a contest we enter with ourselves. But what is that contest? Is it simply a contest to place the arrow closer and closer to the center of the mark?

We can put training wheels on our bikes and convince ourselves that we have learned to ride. We can put sites and stabilizers on our bows and pull the string to our anchor using a trigger release and convince ourselves that we have learned to shoot. We can even strip our bows of these aids and instead rely on other visual cues and form tricks to get our arrow to the mark.

By doing these things, have we made progress in our contest?

When you shoot, do you experience joy only after the arrow has hit the mark? If you shoot and miss, do you find joy in the process?

For me, one of the most unexpected outcomes of committing to the swing-draw was that almost immediately, I began to experience joy in my shooting. This joy came from the act of shooting itself, not from the outcome of the shot.

I felt joy in taking the shot. That joy was not enhanced or diminished by where the arrow went.

Feeling my body learn to shoot was an unexpected and joyful experience. I can only guess at the joy children feel from running hell-bent and screaming across a field. But if I did guess, I think it would be the joy of feeling their bodies working perfectly.

We live in a fast-paced (and getting faster all the time) world. We live in a world of deadlines, instant information, super-fast travel, and expectations of productivity. Accommodating ourselves to this world makes us unaccustomed to the experience of letting something happen in its own good time.

Learning the swing-draw cannot be rushed.

Archery is truly a contest we enter with ourselves. But it can be more than that. Committing to learning the swing-draw, however long that takes, can be a gift we give to ourselves.

By committing to a single way, we relieve ourselves of the need to second-guess. By eliminating this need to second-guess, we clear our path to success and free our minds to simply focus on doing the thing.

If we can approach learning the swing-draw this way, not only does it provide us the greatest chance for success, but it also gives us the opportunity to get to know ourselves a bit better, and that is the gift we give ourselves.

TESTING OUR COMMITMENT

Let's take a step back, though. What actually am I proposing? To commit to a thing so steadfastly that no experience or reasoned argument could dissuade me from my cause? Am I proposing that a person should commit to the swing-draw like a lost soul seeking purpose, any purpose?

No.

There is a world of evidence that stretches across time, culture, and even science in support of the thesis that the swing-draw is an effective way to shoot the bow and arrow. That said, as with all things, including the swing-draw, there are pros and cons. The basic swing-draw posture requires some muscle antagonism, and if the student tries to shortcut the learning process, it can result in new faults and bad habits, to name just a couple of the cons.

In a sense, the main purpose of this entire book is to provide enough evidence for the efficacy of the swing-draw and enough advice to the student on how to learn the swing-draw so that the student will be able to decide for themselves if this style is right for them and then commit to it.

Once this accounting of what is important to us has been made, and the business of finding the right way to learn is finished, and we commit ourselves to it, then we can get on with what is really important. In his book *The Way of Zen*, Allen Watts explains:

> A world which increasingly consists of destinations without journeys between them, a world which values only "getting somewhere" as fast as possible, becomes a world without substance. One can get anywhere and everywhere, and yet the more this is possible, the less is anywhere and everywhere worth getting to. For points of arrival are too abstract, too Euclidean to be enjoyed, and it is all too very much like eating the precise ends of a banana without getting what lies in between. The point, therefore, of these arts is the doing of them rather than the accomplishments. But, more than this, the real joy of them lies in what turns up unintentionally in the course of practice, just as the joy of travel is not nearly so much in getting where one wants to go as in the unsought surprises which occur on the journey.

The experience of learning the swing-draw really is like a journey. If we commit to our journey, then the inevitable rainy days become part of the trip. If we are committed to the journey, we don't wonder to ourselves if we should quit the trail simply because it's cold and wet today. The idea never crosses our minds. The rain is irrelevant to a committed journeyman. In fact, the rain adds to the adventure. If the rains don't come, then the flowers don't bloom along the trail, and the newts don't show themselves. What fun is that?

Master Awa Kenzo chastened Eugene Herrigel, "Where the arrow goes is no concern of yours!" when Herrigel lamented his poor accuracy. "What?" you may ask. Isn't hitting the mark the whole point of archery?

If hitting the mark is all that matters to you, then I respectfully suggest that you put this book away and get yourself a compound bow with sights, stabilizers, and a trigger release.

But if there is even an inkling in your mind that there may be more to shooting a bow and arrow than simply hitting the mark, then I suggest that you keep reading.

This book is a summary of my journey to learn the swing-draw, and none of this adventure would have been possible without taking that first step, the step of committing to the way of the swing-draw.

The most important thing I have learned about this adventure is that it is never-ending. As long as I am willing to practice, there is always room for improvement, and there are always things to be learned from it.

Each person's experience of learning the swing-draw will be unique, and therefore, it is impossible to put a timeline on how long a person can expect it to take before they learn to shoot "well." That said, each practice arrow shot in good faith brings us closer to our goal, whatever that may be.

Commitment is not a transactional guarantee of success. That's not the point. Commitment brings clarity of purpose and calms the storm of doubt that can plague our shooting.

If we are committed, we don't pick and choose those parts of the process that we think will help us find a shortcut to success. There are no shortcuts. There is only practice.

If you find yourself thinking that you might try this or that part of the form or shoot a little bale practice now and then, then you are wasting your time.

For most people, when they begin learning the way of the swing-draw, there is a long period without perceived progress. This time is when your commitment will be tested. This is when the student must learn to shoot without expectation. If there is no expectation, there is no need for success or the gratification of seeing the arrow hit the mark.

This is where most people give up. They can shoot a blank bale for a week or two, maybe even a month, but more than that? The excitement of hitting an arbitrary point in space (the mark) is too great a temptation.

But what is the thrill of occasionally hitting the mark compared to the joy of learning how to shoot? I mean, learning how to *really* shoot?

These words are not meant as a pep talk.

If we are young and no one gets in our way, we can pick up the bow and learn to shoot well with little effort. The older we get, the longer it will take to learn the way of the swing-draw, but happily, the more opportunity we will have to learn other things along the way.

Reading these words is no guarantee of success. At most, these words simply tell the story of another who took the journey to learn the swing-draw. Your adventure will be your own.

However your adventure goes, it cannot start without the conscious decision to commit to the swing-draw. The student must commit to it and then let it go. That's the end of it and the beginning of it.

These words may sound confusing, mystical, or just stupid. Perhaps so, but after a few years of daily blank bale practice, performed without expectation, they may begin to ring true.

When I am with my archery friends and we are shooting our bows, I can almost always tell how their shot will go simply by watching them take their stance and draw their bows. Any angle will do. I don't need to be behind them so that I can see the target or how they are lining up. I can be leaning against a tree ten feet away and tell. Their body language foretells the shot.

The same goes for starting to learn something new. How a person begins their journey of new experiences says a lot about how they will eventually end up.

Whether it's learning how to ride a bike, learning how to drive a car, learning about chemistry, or learning the swing-draw, how we choose to start matters.

If a person can mix equal parts enthusiasm and patience with a big dose of commitment, all the while curbing their expectations, then I think they will have given themselves the best chance to learn.

The method outlined in this book is not something that a person tries to see if it works. It won't. It is a method that the student makes work through their efforts and commitment.

Archery has waxed and waned through the ages, but it manages to hang on as a pastime that always seems to capture the imagination.

It has inspired some really good writers through the ages: The Thompson brothers, Aldo Leopold, Art Young, Walt Wilhelm, and

Erle Stanley Gardner, to name just a few of the dozens of writers who have seen the world through new eyes as a result of their experiences with the bow and arrow. Maurice Thompson summed it up best:

> I have yet to find a person so grave and dignified that archery could not coax him into a bending humor. Indeed, the bow is the natural weapon of man, and it affords him the most perfect physical and mental exercise that can be conceived of. It is to the mind and body what music and poetry are to the soul.

Through our hard work, patience, and commitment, we give ourselves the best chance to truly appreciate this most "perfect physical and mental exercise" Thompson speaks of. What could be better?

Chapter 7

BALANCE

What an essential property of both matter and mind, this idea of balance. As children, we were likely introduced to this property (as it relates to matter) at our local playground when we tried out our first seesaw. Little could we know then that our need to find balance would become a constant effort in our lives.

This idea of living in a sustainable way on our planet of finite resources is an effort in balance. Balancing the available resources against our needs and trying to find ways to keep those needs from getting out of hand is a constant challenge.

Closer to home, we work to balance our expenses against our checkbook. This can be an effort that takes most of our time and leaves little of it for spending on family and self.

In mathematics, no matter how simple or complex, the challenge is to make the expressions on each side of the equals symbol, well, *equal*. In chemistry, we balance reactants with products. In physics, we balance one set of forces against another.

And on the grandest scale of all, one of the biggest mysteries still left to solve is whether the universe is destined to expand forever or eventually implode upon itself. Again, this is a question of balance. Are the forces compelling the universe to expand greater than or less than the force of gravity that is pulling the universe together?

As we go through our daily lives, there are forces at work on us that we are so accustomed to feeling that we don't even notice them: economic, physical, social, psychological, gravity, etc. These forces affect us whether we notice them or not. I think the better part of wisdom is the ability to recognize these forces and see their effects on our lives. We may not be able to alter these forces, but being aware of them allows us to adjust our response to them and maybe avoid their worst effects.

Living with intention, and living mindfully, are expressions of this awareness that we live in a world of forces. If we are aware of these forces, we can learn ways to balance them and improve our lives.

So it is with archery.

When we drop the string and send the arrow on its way, the arrow's trajectory is the result of all those forces (physical and mental) and how they are balanced at the moment of the shot.

When we say, "Don't torque the grip," what we are really saying is, "Don't let the sum of all the forces and torques be greater than zero." As any archer who has shot much knows, this is not a trivial exercise. Even if the archer's bow hand is completely relaxed and applies no muscular force to the grip, there can still be a twist induced simply as a result of where the draw force is applied by the hand.

In fact, there are several ways that forces and torques can be induced into the bow-arrow-archer machine that are invisible to the eye yet will throw off the intended arrow trajectory.

As with all things, there are a number of ways to cope with these issues. At the most basic level, if you see your arrow impacting the target a foot to the left of the mark, simply aim a foot to the right. This solution does not address the problem; it merely addresses the symptom. We often confuse the problem with the symptom in our rush to improve. When we have a headache, we usually don't care what caused it; we simply want to relieve the pain with aspirin.

The same is true with the pain of a missed shot. In our rush to hit the mark, we often skip over any thought of the underlying problems in our effort to hit it again. Oftentimes, addressing the

114

symptom will allow us to hit the mark for a while, but eventually, the root cause (the problem) resurfaces to take away our accuracy.

My adventure with the swing-draw began because I had run out of quick fixes for my accuracy problems. The more fixes I put into place, the shorter the time that they worked. The more fixes I employed, the dimmer the feel of the shot became in my mind. Eventually, I reached a point where there was no feel for the shot at all. My shooting had become nothing more than a sequence of quick fixes that were strung together from the time I nocked the arrow until it left the string.

What is the difference between a consistently good shot and a quick-fix junky like myself? Boiled down to its essence, I think the difference is simply an awareness of the forces involved: basic forces like draw force and derivative forces like those that develop in the joints and muscles as a result of drawing the bow and the effort to balance them completely before letting go of the string.

Before we can learn to balance these forces, we must learn to recognize them. Some of us have a good kinesthetic sense and can recognize and nullify all parasitic forces and torques so that only the draw force remains. Most of us struggle to some degree just to sense these forces. But we can get better at it.

Aside from a less-than-perfect kinesthetic sense keeping an archer from finding balance, the misconception that the blame can be placed on the bow needs to be addressed.

Byron Ferguson named his book *Become the Arrow* in part to convey to his readers that the arrow was more important to a good shot than the bow. On page 2 of his book, he suggests an experiment to his readers to prove the point:

> Go into your backyard and cut a slender sapling. Make it into an arrow. Buy a $1,000 custom bow and see how well you can shoot that green stick arrow. [Now] spend $40 on a set of decent arrows, go out to your backyard and find a sapling big enough to make into a bow. Those arrows will shoot consistently. That is why I say the arrow is more important than the bow.

I know from my childhood experience that this is true. I remember the first time I shot aluminum arrows from my sapling bow. Oh, what a difference!

Ferguson identifies this truth in his book and leaves it there. But I think it can be taken further and, by doing so, can help us better relate to our bow and arrow and give us a complete understanding of the bow-arrow-archer machine so that we can shoot even better.

A bow cannot change itself. An arrow cannot change itself. They both react to the forces that are applied to them in a predictable and repeatable way. A bow and arrow shot from a stable shooting machine will shoot the same way every time. At reasonable distances and with no wind, an arrow can be expected to hit the same hole in the target shot after shot. Not so with a human shooting the bow and arrow. We are the changeable, sometimes unreliable, part of the machine.

We have the ability to adapt ourselves to our bows, proven by the fact that there is great variety in the form that bows take, yet all can be shot accurately. From the very short, highly reflexed Turkish bow to the straight and true English longbow to the really long Japanese Yumi bow, all can be shot well by the archers who embrace them.

In my bow-making adventures with the American Semi-Longbow, I have made bows that varied from a one-inch-longer bottom limb to a four-inch-longer top limb. I was able to adapt to each bow and shoot them all with about the same level of accuracy.

The bow simply reacts to the forces and torques applied to it. The same goes for the arrow. As long as we are shooting decent arrows, as Ferguson explained, the bow and arrow will react in a predictable manner. We, on the other hand, are responsible for making sure the bow-arrow-archer machine is well-balanced.

The bow-arrow-archer machine can be thought of as an onion.

The arrow is the center of the machine. It is the thing upon which the bow does work (the heart of the onion). The bow wraps around the arrow (like an onion layer) and supports it in all dimensions. It is the thing upon which the archer does work. The archer (like another onion layer) wraps around the bow and supports it in all dimensions.

Parasitic forces show up as torques in the bow at the moment of the loose. As we reach our anchor point and pause for a moment, there is no motion. All forces are in equilibrium. That which we did right and that which we did wrong are hidden at that moment. Once the string is dropped, the truth becomes evident.

If there were no parasitic forces in our draw, then the arrow would come away from the bow cleanly and fly true. The bow rests gently in the bow hand, and the string hand rests gently at anchor. The archer's body is poised but relaxed until the arrow reaches its mark.

If there were parasitic forces in our draw, then the arrow may clatter as it leaves the bow. It may fly erratically, nock porpoising (up and down), or fishtailing (side to side) toward the target. The bow hand may move left or right, and the bow may rotate clockwise like a propeller, or the string hand may flail out or back or into the face. The archer's body may shudder as the parasitic forces expend themselves.

In our rush to shoot the next arrow and try yet again to hit the mark, we may ignore these telltale signs. Every time we ignore them, they become more common to us. They become expected, part of our routine—ingrained.

No matter what kind of bow we are shooting, no matter how well or poorly made, it should be our purpose to shoot it well. To shoot it well, we need to find our balance with the bow.

An engineering term that is used to describe the relationship between elements of a device is the word *communicate*. This word has a common meaning with which we are all familiar, and the engineering meaning is similar. When we say that one element of a machine communicates with another, we mean that they are in contact with each other by means of a fastener or a bearing, for example, and so have the ability to transmit force or energy to each other.

The archer communicates with the bow.

The bow communicates with the arrow.

Defining the relationship between an archer and his tackle in terms of the device elements, machines, and communicating parts risks making the relationship seem inanimate. I don't mean to degrade the joy we feel from shooting our bows and arrows, but I think it is important to dispel at least some of the mystery that surrounds our shooting.

I think we imbue too much credit (or blame) into the bow we are shooting. By understanding that the bow simply reacts to the forces we apply to it, we can free ourselves to look at that part of the machine that is truly responsible for a good (or bad) shot: ourselves.

I initially referred to this machine by putting the bow first in the hyphenated phrase because that is how it has always been referred to historically. We always say, "Let's go shoot our bow and arrow." From now on, however, I will refer to it as the archer-bow-arrow machine in deference to the relationship between them, as defined by how they communicate.

Whatever forces we communicate to the bow, it, in turn, communicates to the arrow. In an ideal situation, the only force we would communicate to the bow would be the draw force. Because drawing the bow requires a high level of coordination and application of significant force, we generally communicate other forces (parasitic forces) that are the result of our physical morphology and level of skill.

Finding this balance cannot be rushed. It will take as long as it takes. Learning to shoot well means learning that we can't force the arrow to go here or there. **We shoot the bow; then, the bow shoots the arrow.**

Being mindful of this search for balance and the consequences to the shot of not finding it is crucial to success for the archer.

We may be inclined to try to solve our accuracy troubles by changing bows. One after another, we abandon bows in an attempt to find one that works for us. In truth, they will all likely work just fine if we just give ourselves enough time to find our balance with the bow.

The same goes for the rest of the gear that makes up the archer's tackle. When an arrow flies to the side, we blame it. When we pluck our release, we look to our glove for fault.

While I am a firm believer in keeping an excuse or two handy to explain away the fact that the deer is still alive and now on the other side of the woods or that the squirrel is unharmed and chattering at me from the top of the oak, there does come a time when we need to face the truth that a good shot is due more to execution than to equipment.

As you begin to practice the exercises described in this book, you will probably start to feel even worse about your form and shooting than you do right now. While no doubt frustrating, this feeling is totally normal.

When Thomas Grey penned his famous (and long) poem *Ode on a Distant Prospect of Eaton Collage* and ended it with the words,

> And happiness too swiftly flies.
> Thought would destroy their paradise.
> No more; where ignorance is bliss,
>   'Tis folly to be wise,

he had no idea that just three of those words would ring so true that they would live on as a proverb: Ignorance is bliss. Intellectually, it is easy to understand the idea that what we don't know can't hurt our happiness. And yet (ignorant though we may be), we can still be unhappy.

Here is yet another lesson my trusty longbow has taught me: Ignorance really isn't bliss.

I can shoot my bow, oblivious to my faults. I can be unhappy with the results of my shot, and yet I have no idea why. Why don't I know why I missed? Why am I concerned only with the miss and not with the cause of the miss? In the end, not understanding can lead to misery.

As our western civilization advances, life gets faster all the time. If we are caught up in it, we may not stop to think about cause and effect. We become ignorant of the cause and focus only on the effect.

When we discover our cholesterol is too high, we take a pill instead of looking at the junk food we eat. Instead of eliminating the cause of our poor health, we take the easy path to attenuate the problem.

When we hear on the news that more communities are suffering from blue sky flooding (floods on sunny days due simply to high tides) or that the earth is suffering from some new calamity, we turn the channel until we find one that tells us that it is not our fault.

Ignorance is bliss. And yet, in the end, we still suffer for it.

We have to learn to see past the outcome to the cause and the consequence. This is not an easy thing to do.

When we encounter trouble in our shooting, we usually blame our equipment. That said, we may sometimes go so far as to try to change something small about our form.

We may change how we take the string in our hand, how we hold the grip of the bow, or where we anchor before dropping the string. There are an infinite number of things we can change about how we shoot. But until we learn to feel the balance of the bow, none of those things will really matter much.

As you practice the exercises outlined in this book, you will start to notice things about yourself and how you shoot that just don't seem to work correctly. This dawning awareness is a step in the right direction for the student. Progress.

If you are committed to learning the swing-draw and are diligent with these exercises, you will gain a new awareness of your form—of how your body works with the bow to shoot the arrow.

This new awareness will be centered around feeling the balance of the draw. You will learn how to shoot the bow without imparting parasitic forces and torques.

But it starts with awareness.

You will become aware of the fault, but you won't be able to do anything about it right away. That's OK. It takes time for your body to figure out how to move more efficiently.

How much time it will take to learn to balance the bow is unique to the individual. At the very least, it depends on age, experience, aptitude, and morphology.

In John Schulz's booklet *Hitting 'em Like Howard Hill*, Schulz says that under Hill's tutelage, he practiced shooting at a blank bale for three weeks before being allowed by Hill to shoot at a target.

Eugene Herrigel, in his book *Zen in the Art of Archery*, says that it took at least a couple of years of shooting at the blank bale before his master would allow him to shoot at a target.

In my case, I spent a year on my form before shooting at a target. I probably should have spent even more time.

John Schulz took up the swing-draw as an athletic youth. This is the ideal situation. Young, strong, and free from bad habits. Herrigel and I began our archery lessons later in life, so it took us longer.

So now that you are aware that a good shot is based on a balanced archer-bow-arrow machine, what to do next? How do you set out to make this balance happen?

Balancing the bow is not something that you can make happen; it's something you can feel happen.

Stand on one foot. If you haven't fallen down yet, you will notice that the foot you have on the ground is wabbling this way and that and that your arms are likely swinging here and there, adjusting your balance to keep you vertical. Are you in charge of how your foot and arms are adjusting your balance? Or do you simply feel it?

If you stand on one foot every day, you will get better at balancing. Your foot will move less, as will your arms. You will become more comfortable with the task. Eventually, it will take little effort to stay standing. You can begin looking around as you stand on one foot. You will begin to look casual and relaxed, as if the exercise of standing on one foot is effortless. As usual, this task is easier for younger people, but it is a worthwhile exercise for any age.

Just as you can't force yourself to balance on one foot, you can't force yourself to balance the draw. You can be aware of the need for balance, and with practice, you can begin to feel it.

At first, what you will learn to feel is that you are out of balance. You may feel clumsy and that your form is not working efficiently to draw the bow. This period can last a long time. It doesn't matter. **Every shot taken in good faith brings you closer to a good shot.**

I will say again: You cannot force yourself to balance the draw. What you can do is give yourself the opportunity to develop this feel for the balance of the draw. This is the point of shooting an arrow into a bale without a target.

If you are well skilled at standing on one foot, then it will take no special effort to stand on one foot while riding in a boat rocking in the waves. But that is not how you start. You start on a flat, solid surface that does nothing to interfere with your balancing exercises. You cannot learn to balance on one foot if you are worried about falling overboard.

By the same token, you cannot learn to balance the archer-bow-arrow machine if your mind is focused on some mark and your ego is intent on hitting it with an arrow.

Stop and think about it for a minute. What a stroke of genius is the idea that we can get better at hitting the mark with an arrow if we commit ourselves to shoot at a bale with no mark.

That stroke of genius was only possible because the person who had it was able to separate cause from effect. They were able to step back, and instead of just hoping their arrow would hit the mark this time, they were able to think it through and realize that one must learn a skill before one can use the skill.

Eventually, you will make a balanced shot. You will likely recognize it and want to repeat it right away. In your bliss, you will try to parrot that shot again. That is a formula for failure. Instead, remember how the shot felt. Dwell on the joy it brought you. And remember that it will eventually happen again.

Every aspect of life is predicated on balance. Indeed, the very world we live in would not be here if not for the fact that the centripetal force of its orbit around the sun exactly balances the gravitational force pulling it into the sun. Nor even would the sun be here save for the fact that the forces of nuclear heating in its core exactly balance the crushing weight of its mass.

As we struggle to balance all the other needs and wants in our lives, should it come as a surprise that in order to shoot a good arrow, we should need to balance ourselves with the bow?

Chapter 8

TROUBLESHOOTING

C hances are that if you are not a natural, you will develop some form faults as you follow your path to learning to shoot. When boiled down to their bare essence, almost all form faults are the same. A fault induces parasitic forces and torques into your shot.

Parasitic forces and torques will send your arrow away from the mark and rob it of energy.

You cannot see a force or torque with your eye, but eventually, you will learn to feel them build and then dissipate as you draw your bow, come to anchor, and drop the string.

Before you learn to balance yourself with the bow, it can be frustrating to draw your bow to anchor and see the mark sitting there on the end of your arrow (fuzzy in your peripheral vision) and then watch the arrow leap this way or that as it veers off to land somewhere other than where you had intended.

The frustration can become maddening as the arrow goes off course, over and over. The harder you try to stop it from happening, the more likely it becomes. I am surprised more bows don't end up in the pond alongside all those golf clubs.

I think this frustration we feel with ourselves because we can't seem to stop making the same mistake over and over is one path that leads to target panic.

There are a few faults that are obvious and easy to fix. They are the low-hanging fruit. A stance that is too open, dropping the bow arm at the shot, and leaning away from the target instead of toward the target, to name a few. They are easy to identify and (relatively) easy to fix.

On the other end of the spectrum are the parasitic forces and torques that result from nothing more than extra tension in the hands and wrists. Invisible tension is able to move the arrow four or five inches off the mark. These faults are the hardest to fix (in my experience).

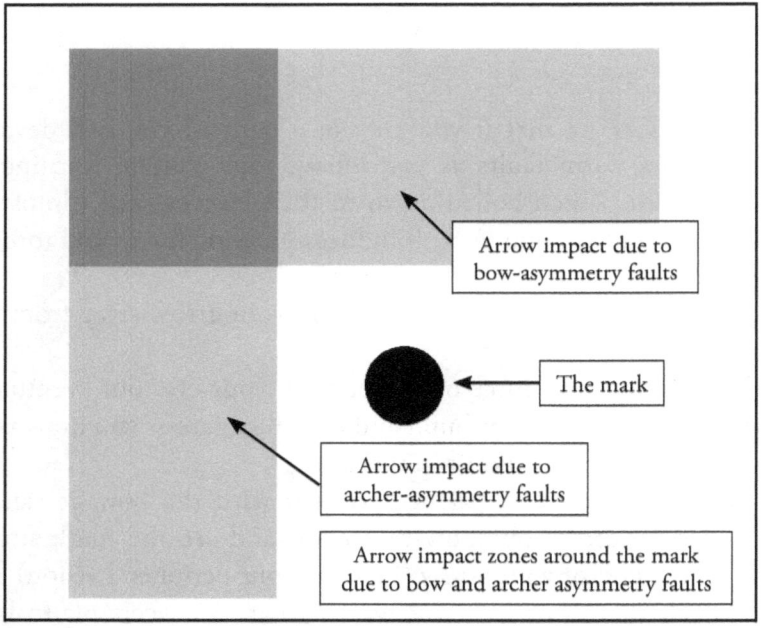

Arrow impact due to bow-asymmetry faults

The mark

Arrow impact due to archer-asymmetry faults

Arrow impact zones around the mark due to bow and archer asymmetry faults

Howard Hill boiled down the solution to all shooting faults with the bare bones basic truth: **"At the shot with the hands, do nothing."** This can only be accomplished if there are no parasitic torques and forces.

If we can understand why their effects are so disastrous to our shot, it may help us commit to eliminating them. The reason is simple. In a word, *asymmetry*.

Our bow is asymmetrical. No matter its design, we shoot our arrow above our hand. This makes our bow asymmetrical. If we shot the bow through its center (like a crossbow), then all forces would be symmetrical and self-correcting. But that would require us to shoot the arrow through our hand, an obvious disadvantage.

Our body is asymmetrical (in the sagittal or shooting plane). When we draw our bow, it's across our chest, not through the center of our body. Because the bow is drawn on one side of the body instead of through its center, our draw is asymmetrical. Again, if we drew the bow through the center of our body (obviously impossible), then all forces would be symmetrical and self-correcting.

Knowing that high-shots are usually the result of faults rooted in the asymmetry of our bow, and left-shots are usually the result of faults rooted in the asymmetry of our body, helps us troubleshoot the cause and work to fix it.

Knowing, too, that most poor shots are the result of a combination of faults helps to explain why most misses tend to land high left of the mark for a right-handed archer (as shown by the darkened zone in the figure) and high right for a left-handed archer.

Any seesaw can be balanced, even if the fulcrum is nowhere near the middle. That is our job when shooting the bow. We must balance our asymmetrical seesaw of an archer-bow-arrow machine.

So how do we eliminate parasitic forces and torques so that we can do with our hands as Hill advises? The answer is yet another simple bare-bones truth that applies to all faults and in all situations: **No matter what, keep practicing**.

If we practice with commitment and without expectation, then these two basic truths are all we need (along with simple shooting instructions) to get us started.

So how are we mere mortals—who suffer doubt, who strive to shoot without expectation, and are prone to shooting faults—supposed to bridge the frustration gap that forms in our minds as we practice (day in and day out) without visible improvement?

I think it helps to alleviate our frustration if we can at least understand what is causing our arrows to go astray, even if we can't fix it (yet).

I've said it before, and I'll say it again. I think aiming is the easy part. Drawing the bow and shooting it without inducing unwanted forces and torques is the hard part. The reason it's so hard to get rid of these parasitic effects is that their tells are so subtle.

If we can start to recognize some of the tells, then we can at least know why our arrow has gone off-mark, and we can be less frustrated by it. To recognize tells, we must first understand what forces and torques are.

A force is any interaction that, when unopposed, changes the motion of an object. In the simplest terms, it is a push or a pull.

A torque is a force that acts at a distance from the centroid of an object. In the simplest term, it is a twist.

I think most of the bad stuff we do to bows results in some unwanted twist to the bow or to the arrow.

The push-pull draw force that the archer generates between themselves and the bow exists on an imaginary line that can be drawn between the archer's elbow and the bow hand pressure point on the bow handle. We call this the draw-force line (DFL). Any torque (twisting) induced around this DFL as a result of recruiting extraneous muscles (like the bicep muscle of the drawing arm) is parasitic and diminishes both accuracy and arrow speed.

Eliminating shooting faults, then, is the process of eliminating pushes, pulls, and twists that can occur around the DFL as a result of recruiting extraneous muscles. The trick, the challenge, is to recognize when we are engaging the wrong muscles, what the effects on arrow flight are, and what we can do to fix the problem.

One of the best consequences of committing to a simple shooting system like the swing-draw is that it gives us a chance (through constant repetition) to become familiar with how our bow and arrow react to our shooting style. Having spent so much time shooting at a blank bale and struggling to balance myself with the bow, I have picked up on several cause-and-effect relationships between some of my worst faults and what they do to the flight of the arrow.

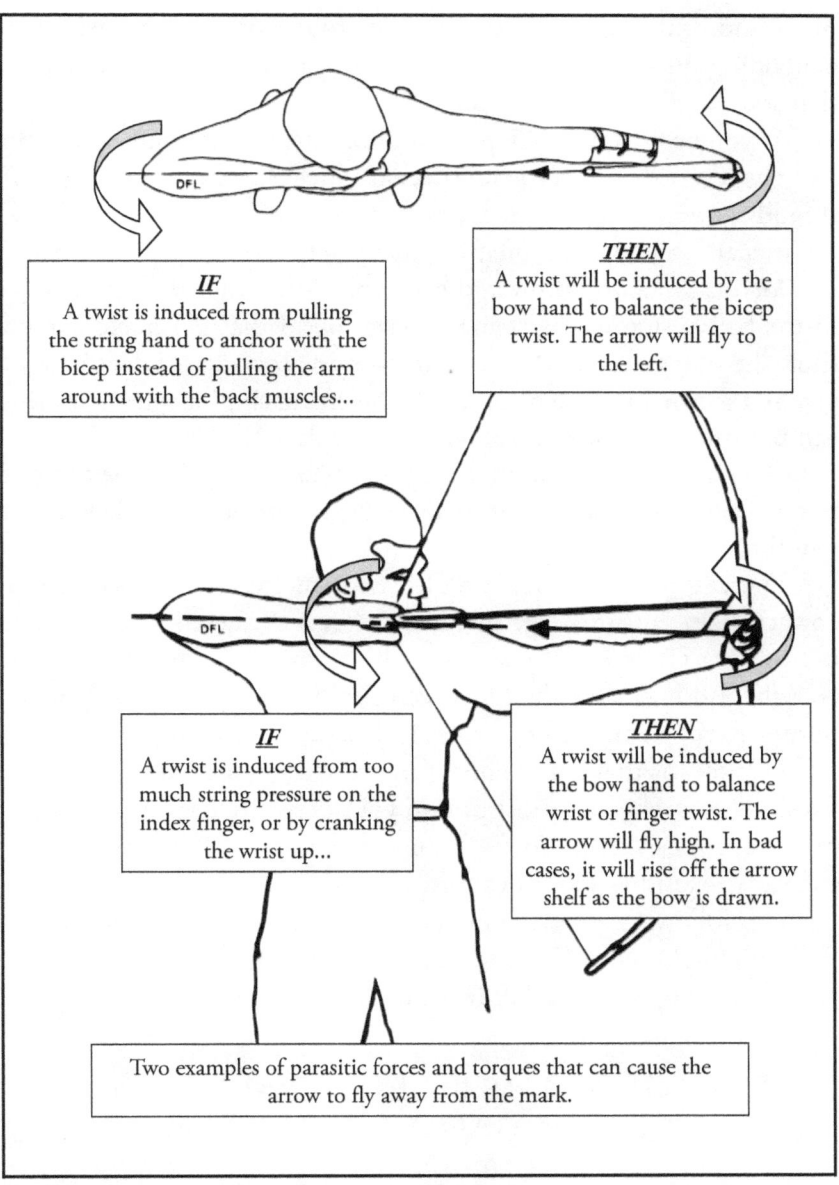

IF

A twist is induced from pulling the string hand to anchor with the bicep instead of pulling the arm around with the back muscles...

THEN

A twist will be induced by the bow hand to balance the bicep twist. The arrow will fly to the left.

IF

A twist is induced from too much string pressure on the index finger, or by cranking the wrist up...

THEN

A twist will be induced by the bow hand to balance wrist or finger twist. The arrow will fly high. In bad cases, it will rise off the arrow shelf as the bow is drawn.

Two examples of parasitic forces and torques that can cause the arrow to fly away from the mark.

As I go through a list of common faults, I will describe the consequences of arrow flight and how the bow reacts. That said, there is another tell that I like to keep track of as I shoot, and that is the sound of the string at the shot. The sound of the string will vary depending on the quality of the shot, but I cannot say exactly how that sound will change for you.

As you begin your daily practice, hold the bow in your bow hand and give the string a gentle but decent pluck. Listen to the sound. It should sound sweet in your ear and fade away before it gets tedious. Do it again so you can remember that sweet note.

As you shoot your bow and hold your form until the arrow stops in the bale, listen to the string. I have found that if I make a good shot, the string will produce about the same sound as it does when I give it a gentle but decent pluck. If the string sings a sour note, this can be your first clue that something is amiss.

Of course, if you employ string silencers on your bow, then your bow's song will be stifled, and you will miss out on all it has to tell you through its melody.

There are as many form faults as there are archers working to correct them, but there are just a few effects all these faults can have on arrows. These faults can cause the arrow to fly high, low, left, or right. Additionally, the arrow can fishtail (wiggle left to right) or porpoise (wiggle up and down) as it flies toward the mark.

This means that many faults can cause the same effects on arrow flight. This is why you must put on your detective hat and see if you can find more evidence for one cause than another. Test your theory, analyze the results, and move forward.

The following list of faults is in no way comprehensive. These faults highlight what I have found to be the most common causes of poor arrow flight and archer frustration.

ENGAGING THE BICEPS TO BRING THE STRING HAND TO ANCHOR

If your arrows are flying to the left, you may be engaging your bicep muscles to pull your bow hand to your anchor that last inch or two.

The most common tell that you have engaged your biceps is that after you drop the string, you punch your hand in your face.

If you are using your string-arm biceps to come to anchor, then you are pushing the string sideways into your face. This makes the bow want to rotate to the right (clockwise as viewed from above, looking down at the top of the bow). When you push the string sideways into your face, your bow hand must compensate by twisting the bow handle to the left (counterclockwise as viewed from above) in order to keep everything lined up. When you let go of the string, the bow twists to the left and sends the arrow to the left.

Using only the back and shoulder muscles, the string hand can be brought around to touch your anchor (wherever it is on your face). Ideally, the biceps should remain relaxed throughout the draw cycle.

If you find that your arrows are flying to the left and that your string hand ends up hitting your face after the shot, you may want to give the ten-second and three-second exercises described in Chapter 4 a try.

These exercises can help you to feel the balance of the bow, relax away the tension in your string-arm biceps, strengthen your back muscles, and improve your shoulder dexterity.

CRABBING THE STRING HAND

If your arrows fly to the right (or, for some people, to the left), or your arrow falls off the shelf as you draw the bow, you may be crabbing your string hand.

A person is said to crab their string hand when it takes a balled-up, crabby-looking shape. If the archer engages only those essential muscles and tendons necessary to hold the bowstring in the distal joints of the fingers, then the hand will appear stretched out, relaxed, and in line with the forearm. If the archer recruits additional muscles of the wrist, hand, or fingers, in addition to the essential muscles, then those extra muscles tend to antagonize the essential muscles and distort the appearance of the hand.

The consequences of crabbing the string can vary due to individual physical morphology, hook style (three-under or split-finger), and bow and arrow tuning. Though the things that cause us to crab our fingers are easy to identify, they are not necessarily easy to correct.

The first cause is simply a lack of skill or experience. Pulling a bowstring without crabbing can be difficult for those who have never before drawn a bow. In fact, it is almost universally true that new archers have the least intuition for, and are most clumsy with, addressing the bowstring.

When using tabs or soft gloves, most people learn to minimize the crabbing of their fingers without much trouble, at least enough so that the arrow doesn't fall off the arrow shelf. That said, any amount of crabbing will reduce the pressure of the arrow against the side plate and affect left-right accuracy.

The second cause of crabbing can be attributed to shooting with a thicker and stiffer Hill-style glove. When used with the split-finger style, the thicker glove tends to exert more pressure than a thinner glove would on the arrow. The thicker glove is then more prone to rotate the arrow off the shelf (away from the bow) if the hand crabs. Add this to our natural tendency to want to grab the string harder as we feel less control through the thicker glove, and the troubles can start.

Breaking in a new and stiff Hill-style glove can throw us into this bad habit of crabbing. As much as I love the Hill-style glove, it is nearly impossible to buy an off-the-shelf glove and have it be the right stiffness, size, and shape (even after breaking it in) to be useful.

The benefit of the Hill-style glove is that you can develop an excellent feel for and control over the balance of the bow. Additionally, when the string is dropped, it will come away from the glove without interference common to other styles. Unfortunately, all these benefits are negated if we start badly crabbing our string hand.

If you are shooting a Hill-style glove and are having problems with crabbing your string hand, I encourage you to think about making your own glove. It is easy and personally rewarding, and you may be pleasantly surprised at what a difference it can make to your accuracy and confidence. See Appendix A for instructions on making a glove.

No matter what style of string hand protection you choose, reviewing and practicing the string hand exercises in Chapter 1 will help if you are crabbing the string.

CRANKING THE STRING-ARM WRIST

If your arrow tends to fly high of the mark, no matter what you try or how near to or far from the target you are, you may be cranking your string-arm wrist.

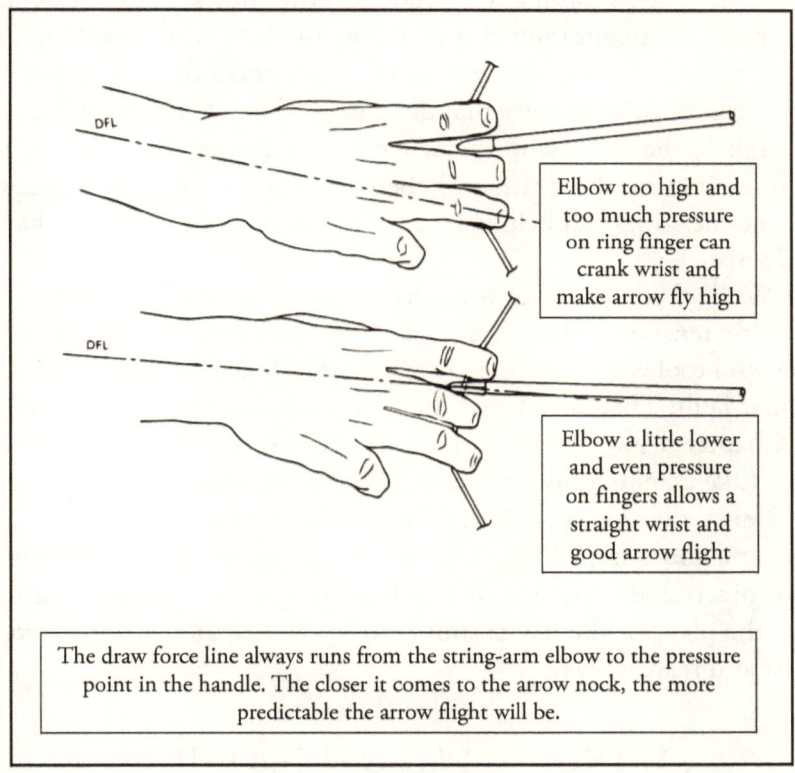

DFL

Elbow too high and too much pressure on ring finger can crank wrist and make arrow fly high

DFL

Elbow a little lower and even pressure on fingers allows a straight wrist and good arrow flight

The draw force line always runs from the string-arm elbow to the pressure point in the handle. The closer it comes to the arrow nock, the more predictable the arrow flight will be.

A related problem is applying too much tension to the string with the ring finger. Sometimes, it's hard to know what came first: the cranked wrist or the overly tensioned ring finger.

Yet another related fault is applying too much tension with the index finger. If you pull the bowstring perfectly in every way, and yet you apply just a little too much force with your index finger, the added tension can lift the arrow off the shelf and send the arrow flying high.

Whenever we exert a lot of force with our limbs, we tend to tense up more muscles than are strictly necessary for the job. I am sure there are many reasons for this, not the least of which is self-preservation. Muscle tension helps to protect bones, cartilage, joints, and tendons when we are exerting ourselves.

In my case, shooting a compound bow with a strap release aid for many years conditioned me to draw the bow while cranking my wrist upward. Each of us has had life experiences that compel us to tense arm muscles in ways that don't help when we are shooting.

Taking the string with the first and third fingers sharing an equal load, beginning the draw, and then allowing the middle finger to engage the string can help balance the DFL through the string hand and wrist.

While I don't have any specific exercises to help eliminate parasitic tension in the string-arm wrist, I can observe that the most powerful tool we have to help us eliminate a fault is simply awareness of that fault. That said, I find that the ten-second practice described in Chapter 4 gives me the time to isolate, feel, and relax whatever fault (like cranking my wrist) I may be working on.

Being aware of a fault while practicing on the blank bale is the first and most important step to eliminating it. When you begin your practice and are standing in front of the bale, remind yourself that the plan for the day is simply to try to feel the tension in your wrist and relax it away.

STRING-ARM ELBOW TOO HIGH

If your arrow tends to fly high of the mark, no matter what you try or how near to or far from the target you are, you may be holding your string-arm elbow too high.

It is important to remember that our faults don't exist in isolation and act alone. How we shoot is the result of the interactions between everything that we do well and everything that we do poorly. It all adds up.

Say, for example, we notice that we hold our string-arm elbow maybe a bit too high as we draw the bow. The question is: Do we have our elbow a bit too high simply because that's where we put it, or is it too high as a consequence of some other fault(s)?

Remembering that all forces in the bow revolve around the DFL gives us a tool that we can use to figure out what the root cause of our high elbow might be.

If our elbow is high, but our string-arm wrist is straight, then the problem could be that we are simply recruiting the wrong muscles to pull our string-arm back. Another cause in this scenario could be that our bow arm elbow is not broken, and the pressure point in our hand is too low. It could also all trickle back to not having the bow shoulder set down and back.

Remember that the back and shoulder muscles meet at the spine of the shoulder blade. Both sets of muscles must be used in equal measure to pull the string arm into alignment. Failure to recruit both sets of muscles in equal measure means that the biceps will likely take up the slack. This usually results in the string-arm elbow rising too high or too far out to the side.

Another cascade of faults that can lead to a high elbow is having the bow-arm wrist cocked up so that the top limb leans toward the archer as the draw is begun. I think this bad habit gets its start from shooting a bow with a stiff top limb and nocking the arrow under the string nockset.

Nocking the arrow under the string nockset allows us to draw the bow while displaying a number of faults that tend to unbalance the bow. If you use a string nockset and see that it has flattened out, or mushroomed, from pressure against the arrow, this is a clue that you are relying on the string nockset to keep things steady instead of learning to balance the bow.

If we nock the arrow above the string nockset, we may find that the arrow skids up the string as the bow is drawn. This is what happens when the bow is drawn without balance. If we commit to nocking the arrow above the string nockset, we will be forced to balance the bow.

As described in Chapter 1, the bow hand should take a forward angle of about 70 degrees as the bow is drawn. If the archer holds the bow at this angle, they will find that the arrow remains against the top of the string nockset, and the bow will more easily balance.

Regardless of how our bow is tillered, we can balance ourselves with it. If we draw a line from our elbow to a spot about 1 1/2 inches below the arrow shelf (or wherever we feel the bow pressure focus on our hand), and that line flows through our string forearm, wrist, and hand, and also passes somewhere near the nock of the arrow, then we can visually confirm that we have learned to balance ourselves with the bow.

DROP THE STRING, COME TO ANCHOR

If your arrow tends to fly all over the place no matter what you try or how close to or far from the target you are, you may be dropping the string and then coming to anchor.

This can be a difficult fault to recognize because it's so hard to learn to feel. As we draw the bow and come to the place where we pull the string straight back to our anchor point, we may develop the bad habit of letting the string go and then feeling our hand come to rest on our anchor point in one harmonious and satisfying motion.

What makes this fault so hard to detect and correct is that it feels so good, and we can hold our form so well after the shot.

The easiest tell to see for this fault is that the amount of arrow sticking out in front of our bow when we shoot is much greater than the amount that sticks out when we come to anchor and then let the bow down without any intention of shooting. As we get better and the fault gets harder to see, the arrow may only stick out an extra 1/4-inch, but our arrows still won't fly true as often as they will if we do things in the correct order. The correct order is to first come to anchor and then drop the string.

But, you might ask, what difference can 1/4-inch make? It can make a lot of difference when you consider what it means to come to anchor before letting go of the string. When we bring the string to anchor, it is not just checking off a box on our list of things to do. It is the high point of all the work we have done to perfect our form. When we reach anchor, we might need to pull our string arm around just a little more as we come to complete balance with the bow. Only after we have balanced ourselves with the bow should we let go of the string and hold our form until the arrow settles in the mark. When we drop the string, our string hand should relax and move just a bit farther back on our face, and our string arm elbow should settle down and back.

If your string hand is exactly on your anchor after you let go of the string, you may want to take a video of yourself shooting to see if you can find the tell. First, draw the bow to anchor as you stand in front of your blank bale, and let down. Then draw the bow and shoot. Look at the video and watch for a difference in the amount of arrow hanging out in front of your bow.

The three-second and ten-second exercises described in Chapter 4 can be helpful in learning what it feels like to come to anchor and balance the bow and to find that resting place for your hand to seek out after the shot.

In my case, when I feel I have made a good shot, the tip of the thumb of my string hand is usually resting in the hollow behind my jaw or touching the lobe of my ear. This represents a motion of about one inch past my anchor (my middle finger pressed into the corner of my mouth).

If I was a natural, I could come to anchor, pull my string arm around that last bit using my back and shoulder muscles, let go of the string and keep my hand settled on my face with my middle finger near the corner of my mouth. However, I am not a natural. And so, I err on the side of pulling a little too much instead of a little too little.

Pulling a little too little will result in creeping, shooting left, flinching, etc. Pulling a little too much has no ill effects on arrow flight or my form, as far as I can tell.

BOW SHOULDER, NOT SET

If (in addition to having your arrows fly all over the place no matter what you try or how near to or far from the target you are) you experience any of the following, then you may not be setting your bow-arm shoulder correctly before you begin your draw:

- You have a hard time bringing your string hand back the same way twice and have a hard time touching the same anchor consistently.
- Your chin touches or even rests upon your bow shoulder at full draw.
- You throw the bow this way and that after the shot.
- You lean away from the target as you draw.
- You cannot bend your bow-arm elbow as you would like.
- Your sight picture seems to change from shot to shot.
- You can't take a consistent grip on the handle.
- Your bow arm trembles when the bow is fully drawn.

Any one of our faults is as apt as any other to cause our arrows to fly astray. That said, we can have no hope of solving our form problems until we get our bow arm and shoulder working correctly. It all begins with setting our bow shoulder correctly.

Correctly setting the bow shoulder is foundational to shooting the bow and arrow well. Correctly setting the bow shoulder forms the bedrock against which our body can successfully oppose the compressive forces applied to our bow arm as we pull the bowstring to anchor.

If the bow shoulder is not anchored correctly, then it can shift about. As the shoulder shifts about, the forces that the bow arm must apply to the bow change rapidly, and as they do, our response to them can be unpredictable.

If the bow shoulder is anchored correctly, the amount of effort to keep our arm extended and stable is minimized. Additionally, when the shoulder is anchored correctly, we don't need to recruit extra muscles to keep it steady and under control.

Keeping the bow shoulder set correctly requires us to do just two things. First, we must rotate our humerus bone clockwise and pull the shoulder blade down and toward the spine before we draw. Second, we must keep the bow shoulder lower than the string shoulder as we draw (this is what happens when we lean into the shot).

If we can do these two things repeatedly, then we have established the foundation for good form.

There is a more comprehensive explanation in Chapter 1 on how to develop your ability to control the bow shoulder. If you are finding that you are feeling out of control in several aspects of your shot, there might be a root cause to all of them, and that root cause may be a bow shoulder that is not set correctly.

CREEPING AT THE SHOT

Creeping at the shot means that as you come to anchor but before you drop the string, your back and shoulder muscles relax, and the string drags your arm forward. When you eventually let go of the string, the energy left in the bow to drive the arrow is reduced, and you have collapsed from your ideal anchor position.

The effects on the arrow can vary, but it will surely not have the speed it would have had from a crisp release, and it will likely fly left, though it could go in just about any direction.

Working to master the swing-draw means developing a rhythm in which you complete the accuracy triangle described in Chapter 5 and then drop the string. Once we get good at this rhythm, creeping usually isn't a fault we need to worry much about.

As we work to develop our rhythm, it is very important to remember that **we don't drop the string because we have come to anchor; we drop the string because we have balanced ourselves with the bow.**

I used to shoot with a more static style. Holding longer at full draw was part of my routine, and creeping was a constant concern, especially with the higher draw weight of my hunting bow.

Since committing to the swing-draw, it has become much less problematic. I do notice that if something unexpected happens as I draw my bow to anchor that requires my attention and makes me pause (like the wind blowing a branch into my arrow's likely path), then I need to tighten up and make sure I pull hard to my anchor before dropping the string.

I think the better we get with our swing-draw, the less likely we are to creep at the shot. If you find yourself creeping, it might be a sign that you haven't fully developed your swing-draw rhythm. The more you practice, the better you will get.

STATIC HIPS

If your arrow tends to fly high when you shoot at something low or low when you shoot at something high, then you may not be positioning your hips correctly.

You've likely heard the advice that you should bend at the waist when shooting from a tree stand, or you will probably shoot high. Before we develop a natural shooting style, it is common to simply lower our arms and aim at whatever is below us. This changes the geometry between our arms, head, bow, and spine from what it was when we were standing on level ground. This almost always results in a high shot.

By rocking our hips, we can learn to keep our spine stacked nice and straight upon them. As we change our shooting angle by rocking our hips and keeping our spine straight, we can maintain the same geometry between our arms, head, bow, and spine, no matter how high or low our target appears.

Spreading your feet well apart provides a solid base upon which you can then rock your hips side to side. As you shoot arrows into your blank bale, stand for a moment and be aware of how you can rock your hips side to side (allowing you to establish the best shooting angle) so that you can keep your spine straight, lean into the shot, and keep your string shoulder above your bow shoulder.

To begin to get a feel for it, stand straight with hips even and spine 90 degrees to hips (normal posture). Set your feet wide apart. Glue your feet to the ground.

Then rotate your right hip up and your left hip down while at the same time keeping the spine 90 degrees to the hips. (You will be ready to shoot low.) Hold the position a moment.

Then go back to level hips. (You will be standing straight and ready to shoot a target at shoulder level.) Hold the position a moment.

Images of archers through the years pivoting
their hips to maintain consistent geometry
between bow, arms, back, and head as shown
in *Archery Anatomy* by Ray Axford

Then rotate your left hip up and your right hip down, remembering to keep the spine 90 degrees to the hips. (You will be ready to shoot high.) Hold the position a moment.

Repeat several times.

TOO MUCH HEEL PRESSURE

If your arrow tends to fly high and your top bow limb tends to rotate forward at the shot, you may be applying too much pressure to the heel of your hand.

There are two approaches to addressing the bow. Target bows with locator grips require that we address the bow with the upper part of our hand, including the web between the thumb and index finger. Straight-limbed bows with straight grips require that we address the bow with our whole palm, including the heel of our hand.

The straight grip gives us more flexibility in how we shoot. But with that flexibility comes the chance to make more mistakes. If we apply pressure too low in the grip, the bow becomes unbalanced, and the top limb rotates towards us an imperceptible amount. This rotation can cause the arrow to shoot upwards and thus land high of the mark.

Learn to feel where the bow bears against your hand. Intentionally move that point up into the base of your thumb and watch the effect on your arrow flight. Once you become aware of the relationship between where the bow bears on your hand and how high your arrow flies, steady bale practice will attenuate this fault.

KEEP ON KEEPING ON

The faults outlined in this chapter are by no means a complete list of all the possible ways we can find to add parasitic forces and torques to the draw force line. These faults are merely the ones that come to mind as I think about my experience and what I have seen in those around me as they strive to perfect their shooting.

I have found that as I continue to find my balance with the bow, learning to feel my faults is the first step on the path to eliminating them.

I have also found that my ability to resolve my shooting faults is not a function of how hard I work to avoid a fault, but rather how hard I try to find my balance with the bow.

It is also not a matter of working harder in a literal sense; it is a matter of learning to be relaxed. **Since every fault (except for creeping) is the result of adding parasitic forces and torques around the DFL, it follows that every fault is a matter of doing too much, not a matter of doing too little**.

Recruiting only those muscles necessary to bend the bow to full draw is the essence and the challenge of balancing ourselves with the bow. If we cannot find a way to practice that helps us improve our form, and a way to think that helps us understand our form, then we are liable to suffer much frustration.

There is no archery fault so subtle that we cannot find it with our mind and feel it with our body. Constant practice without expectation is the way.

The more we practice, the more we will become aware of the DFL, and the easier it will be to detect those parasitic forces and torques that are likely to collect around it.

It is important to practice not only our shooting but also our thinking. As we think about each shot, it's important to think about how each shot went, both how the bow reacted and how we reacted. It is important to gather up in our minds all the threads that lay between and tie together our thoughts and actions as we shoot our arrow at the mark.

When something goes wrong, it is nice to figure it out right away. With archery, the answers don't always come as fast as we would like, and thus, we get frustrated. In those moments, it is important to remember that the first step to solving the problem is simply to keep practicing. The rest will follow if we keep our mind open for the answer.

Keep on keeping on.

PART III
WEAVING IT ALL TOGETHER

We are always weaving what we see and learn together. The first time we look at a bow, what we see are a stick and a string. Then we almost instantly weave together our understanding of those two parts and how they relate to each other into a new thing, into a bow.

According to the Merriam-Webster dictionary, the English word *context* has its beginning in the 15th century and is defined as "the weaving together of words in language." Merriam-Webster goes on to say that this meaning is now obsolete.

I think this old and obsolete meaning of the word describes what we must do to really learn something like archery, to make it part of ourselves. As we weave together our experiences and understanding, we see larger patterns, and then we can weave those together as well. It never ends.

We build context.

We build understanding.

The third part of this book details some aspects of how the bow works and how the archer works. To paraphrase Aldo Leopold as he describes the third part of his book *A Sand County Almanac*, only the most sympathetic reader will wish to wrestle with the physio-mechanical machinations of Part 3.

If you think about it just a little, we humans are the universe made manifest. We are little bits of stardust that have, through the process of life and evolution, been assembled in such a way as to provide energy to this emergent property we call consciousness.

We are aware of our surroundings, and we are self-aware. The most powerful aspect of archery is that it helps us to hone these twin aspects of our consciousness.

As we drive down the road, we can glance at a hillside; we may only see the grass and trees as a tangled background. Once our eyes have moved away from this scene, we instantly forget it. But what if, in that instant of looking, we catch a pattern? What if our brain weaves that pattern into an object we recognize as a deer? If we see the deer, we can then look at this scene, and the once-meaningless tangle of trees now has meaning we won't soon forget.

We may even put together the context of why the deer is there. The tangle of trees now resolves into an oak glen with ample acorns to draw the deer. We may even notice the creek drainage the deer walked up, and that leads to public land we can hunt. How quickly this random tangle of trees has changed into something that has value and meaning to us.

A curious glance is all it took.

A quick glance through these chapters that describe how the body and bow work to cast an arrow to the mark might allow you to catch a pattern that has meaning to you and may spur you on to weave together an evermore complete picture of shooting the bow and arrow naturally.

Learning to hit the mark with our bow and arrow is but one thread in the tapestry of our lives. The more effort we put into understanding it, the tighter our shooting is woven into our sense of self and the more chance we have of finding joy in it.

What better way can there be for us little bits of stardust to celebrate our place in the universe than to find joy in archery?

Chapter 9

HOW THE METHOD WORKS

I like to know why things work the way they do. I think we all harbor curiosity about the world and how it works, at least to some degree. But here is where a pitfall can present itself.

If we are just curious enough to want an answer but not curious enough to want to know if that answer is true or false, then we can be satisfied with something less than true.

There was a time when we were happy with the answer that gods were responsible for the changing seasons. Or that the reason the stars, moon, and sun crossed the sky was that the earth was the center of the universe. It took centuries of debate, religious excommunication, and even death by execution for those who searched for better, truer answers (to these questions) to find them.

What makes a better answer? Is it one that completely fits the facts? One that can be used to predict future events more accurately? One that can be used to build new technologies that improve our lives?

Sometimes, it doesn't matter to our way of life if we have the right answer or not. Old wives' tales are a case in point. The notions that "chicken soup will cure a cold" and "carrots are good for the eyes" are both true. But the deeper truth to chicken soup is that there are compounds (now identified by scientific research) that help reduce inflammation and are antiviral. By studying these compounds, we have improved our understanding of various immune processes in the human body. And carrots contain beta-carotene that the body converts into vitamin A, which is necessary for good vision.

By studying chicken soup, we have learned about nutrition and antiviral compounds and can now come up with new, even more effective, ways to fight colds and flu. By learning what compounds in carrots help us to see better, we can expand our understanding of good nutrition and those foods that provide it.

If our curiosity about fighting our cold had stopped by simply eating chicken soup, then we might not have the new antiviral drugs that help so many people today. By the same token, preventable childhood blindness caused by vitamin A deficiency has been significantly reduced.

But what happens if we stop short in our pursuit of the question, why?

Even today, with a planetary network of weather satellites that show us a view of clouds over our globe, the network of communication satellites that allow us to talk and share information around the world instantly, and the fleet of probes we have sent to other planets in our solar system, and the international space station with the hundreds of astronauts who have circled the earth for decades, and the airplanes we can ride in up to 36,000 feet as we circle the globe and see for ourselves the curvature of the earth, a significant portion of our population still thinks the earth is flat.

How can this be? Obviously, answering that question is beyond the scope of this book. Yet, as I write this chapter, this question rattles around in my mind and disturbs my thoughts.

When we hunker down, circle the wagons, and get tribal, confusing our beliefs designed around our sense of self-interest with larger independent truths, civilization falters. The dark ages were not the result of embracing truth and celebrating curiosity; the renaissance was.

Understanding how our bodies work to shoot our bows and arrows can help us develop better ways to shoot. It can help bring us out of the dark ages of our mediocre shooting.

I know that understanding (at least to some degree) why the swing-draw method works gives me the confidence to continue my practice on those days when things aren't going so well. By the same token, I hope this chapter may help someone else better endure a bad day of practice.

And I also realize that the theory outlined here could be nothing more than my version of an old wives' tale. But it does fit the facts and is, at least, a starting point for understanding why the method works.

CONVENTIONAL EXPLANATION

No matter the question, there is always an answer and someone ready to give it. We have heard the same answers to the same questions for so long that it may not occur to us to suspect that maybe the answer has outlived its usefulness.

In a sense, all answers are temporary. They are placeholders that allow us to make sense of our world and are regularly replaced by newer (and hopefully better) placeholders as our knowledge and understanding improve.

Take, for example, the number of planets in our solar system. For thousands of years, the answer to the question "How many planets are there?" was that there were five planets (besides Earth). That's what we can see with our naked eyes: Mercury, Venus, Mars, Jupiter, and Saturn.

With the invention of the telescope, we were able to see more, and eventually, the count increased to nine. Then, as our understanding of the solar system improved even further, that number was reduced to eight after we learned that Pluto was just one of many planetoids in the outer reaches of the system.

Now scientists have found gravitational evidence for a potential new planet, which means that, if and when it is discovered, the count will again go back to nine.

None of these answers to the question of how many planets there are is wrong. In fact, they were all correct in their time. The fact that the answer has changed simply shows that our understanding has improved.

As I think about the conventional explanation for why the swing-draw works, I wonder if it isn't time to improve our answer. The current understanding of how we can point our bows at something and hit it relies on the word *subconscious*. We say that through practice, we train our subconscious mind to aim the arrow.

We also talk about *muscle memory*. We say that repetitive practice trains our muscles to move in the same way without conscious thought.

We have used these words to name things we knew were happening but couldn't put our finger on exactly what was actually happening. We needed an answer to the question, "How can a person shoot so well without a conscious aiming mechanism?" The answer was, "The subconscious mind aims for us."

When troubles arise (like target panic), we explain that it is caused by our conscious mind interfering with our subconscious mind.

It's hard enough to understand the conscious mind. What is this subconscious mind? The various answers to this follow-up question (do an internet search on the phrase "what is the subconscious mind" to see what I mean) can get hard to believe. And then the idea of these two minds interfering with each other? It is a lot to contemplate without much supporting evidence.

I accepted these explanations of muscle memory and the subconscious mind as I began my swing-draw adventure. I had heard these terms used my whole life, and they seemed reasonable to me.

But as I continued to practice and experienced a slow but steady improvement in my form, I started wondering about it. I had no hint, caught no glimpse, of this subconscious mind at work. Surely, with all this practice aimed directly at the subconscious mind, I would catch sight of it for at least a moment?

I was thinking these thoughts on a hot summer day as we were canning beans.

I was standing by the counter (probably trying to look busy) as my wife reached across the stove for a pot of lids that had been boiled to sterilize them and soften the rubber seals. As she did this, she inadvertently touched her forearm to a canner that was approaching ten pounds of pressure and was thus superheated.

Her response was immediate. She quickly withdrew her arm. But it wasn't as simple as that. There were pots and canners on every burner. From her position, she could not simply pull her arm away from the canner, or she would have bumped into another. No, she had to bend her elbow, twist at the waist, and raise her hand all at the same time to move her arm away from the current hot spot and avoid touching any others.

It all happened in an instant.

There was no time to figure that fancy move out. Therefore, it must have been the subconscious mind at work! Absolute, irrefutable proof of its existence—or not?

This explanation is an example of the *post hoc* (correlation does not mean causation) logical fallacy.

We credit this untenable subconscious mind of ours with controlling our reflexes. The reasoning goes something like this: Our conscious mind didn't do it. The action showed purpose; therefore, a mind must have initiated the action. Thus, by the process of elimination, if our conscious mind didn't do it, our subconscious mind must have done it.

I think this idea of a subconscious mind rises out of our hierarchical western civilization. We organize everything in a hierarchical structure.

Corporations are hierarchical, as are governments, families, and every other structure we plan, build, or participate in. We impose this structure on nature as well.

We see our bodies as hierarchical in design. Lowly muscles, glands, organs, and bones sit at the bottom of the structure, while nerves lead to the spinal cord, which in turn leads to the brain, sitting atop the structure.

Until very recently, our computers were designed this way too. Our top-down approach informed our computer and software designs. However, over time, those designs were improved, leading us to the idea of neural networks and their surprising ability to learn, solve problems in unique ways, and evolve. The study of these computer neural networks has now started to reflect back on our own human neural network. Neural networks are not a top-down structure, and yet they are surprisingly smart and can mimic human intelligence. Maybe our neural system is not so hierarchical after all.

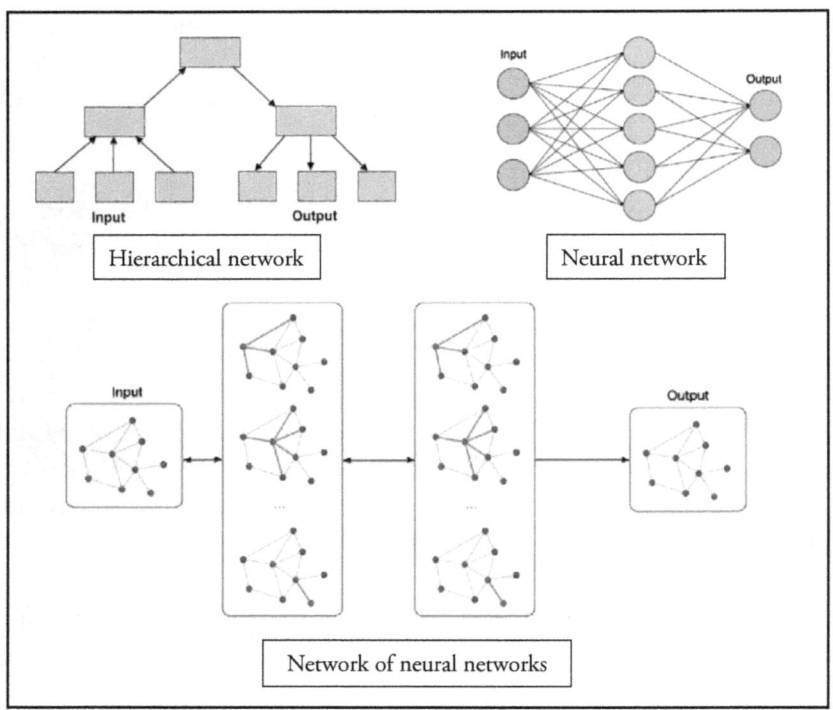

REFLEXES

After watching my wife's reflexive response to the hot canner, I did a little research and quickly learned that it is well known that the brain is not responsible for our reflexes.

In fact, the spinal cord is where the connection is made between an environmental stimulus and a physiological response. The speed at which a signal travels through our nerves is not fast enough to guarantee that a reflexive response would be effective in reducing or eliminating injury from some fast-occurring danger.

There is a nerve circuit (a neural pathway) called the *reflexive arc,* which controls our reflexive responses. When we do something that calls for a reflexive response, like touching something hot, a signal is generated by a somatic receptor. The signal is sent up an afferent nerve fiber (a neural pathway for input signals) to the grey matter column in the spine (yes, the spinal cord contains grey matter, just like the brain). The grey matter in the spinal cord processes the input signal and generates an output signal that is then transmitted down the efferent nerve fiber (a neural pathway for output signals) to the correct muscles needed to move the body away from danger. At the same time that the spinal cord grey matter is initiating this reflexive action, it is sending the original signal received from the afferent nerve up to the brain for further processing.

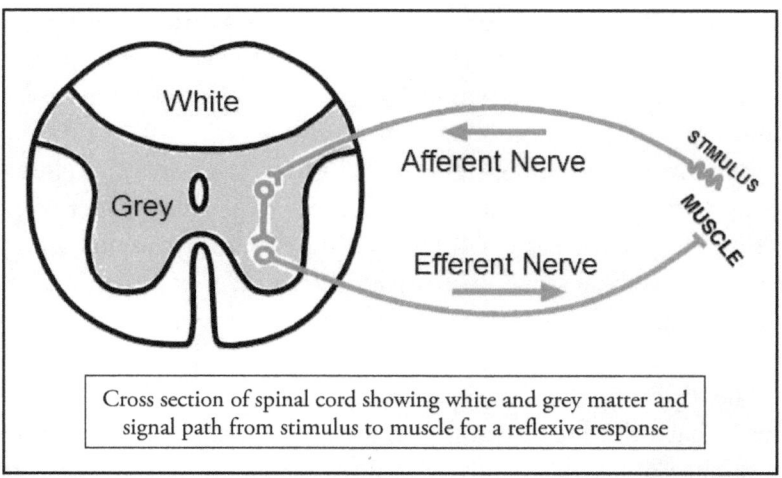

Cross section of spinal cord showing white and grey matter and signal path from stimulus to muscle for a reflexive response

This further processing by the brain allows us to initiate a more complex response, if one is needed, to permanently escape the danger.

As I digested this description of our current understanding of reflexes, I was excited because I had just learned something new. I had always assumed reflexes were initiated in the brain. It was very interesting to me that the response was instead initiated in the spinal cord. It was also very interesting to me that the spinal cord contains grey matter.

While the grey matter contains most of the neurons, the white matter contains most of the axons. Axons are the nerve tracks, or wires, that interconnect the neurons so that they can communicate. As is often the case with learning, the more we learn about white matter, the more we realize that it does more than we could have possibly imagined. Recently, we have learned that it modulates how the neurons in grey matter communicate, and it seems to have control over which parts of the brain can communicate with each other as well.

As I thought about my wife's reflexive response to the hot canner and our current state-of-the-art understanding of reflexes, I couldn't help but think that our current understanding of the spinal cord and its contribution to our daily lives might be lacking.

If the reflexive response is truly mindless, then my wife would have surely just pulled her hand straight back after touching the canner. Had she done this, the canner would have ended up on the floor and maybe blown open, scalding us both. No, her response was involuntary, for sure, but it was not mindless.

Her arm moved to the right, up, and back. Not only that, but she also twisted at the waist at the same time. This allowed her to pull her arm free of the stove while avoiding the front canners and the vent hood over the stove. It involved the muscles of her upper arm, shoulder, and back. Surely that complex motion was not a hardwired response.

The traditional example of a hardwired reflex is the patellar reflex. That's the kicking response our leg makes when the doctor strikes our knee with his rubber mallet. Simple, mindless, and fast.

While I cannot persuade my wife to repeat her performance at the stove to verify what I remember, I remember her moving instantly away from the stove. Her motion was just as fast as the aforementioned patellar reflex.

This tells me that whatever happened in her nervous system to make her body escape the danger of the hot canner must have occurred in the spine. There was no chance for the signal to make it all the way to the brain in time to save the day.

NERVES HEAL AND LEARN

It seems hardly a day goes by without some new discovery about how robust and adaptable our bodies are. And yet a theme that seems to play out over and over is our surprise that our bodies can heal from traumatic injury.

We used to think that the cartilage of the spinal disks could not heal if it was damaged. Now we know that with proper physical therapy, the disks will indeed heal.

We used to think that the brain could not heal from an injury. Now we know that it can heal and indeed has the ability to adapt to and heal from severe injury.

And, of course, it has been a bygone conclusion that if the spinal cord is damaged, well, that's it. It cannot repair itself.

However, starting around the beginning of the 21st century, this age-old assumption began to yield to a new understanding of the dynamic nature of the spinal cord. Along with this new understanding of the spinal cord's ability to heal came a new understanding of the contribution the spinal cord makes to our neural system.

An article titled "No Dullard, the Spinal Cord Proves It Can Learn" by science writer Erica Goode in the September 21, 1999 issue of the *New York Times* captured our dawning appreciation for what the spinal cord contributes:

> Spinal cord neurons, researchers are finding, are capable of learning... and show changes in response to environmental cues that many investigators interpret as a form of memory... These abilities remain even when the spinal cord is cut off from the brain.

It goes on to describe further our changing understanding of the spinal cord:

> It is now clear... that the whole nervous system changes continually in response to development, to learning, to trauma... There is plasticity and the capacity for change throughout the central nervous system, and that includes the spinal cord.

The article went on to give examples of people with spinal cord injuries who had regained function in their affected limbs through physical therapy designed around this new appreciation for what the spinal cord is capable of.

This article provided me some justification for my thought that the spinal cord was responsible for more than just a quick jerk to save my wife from the hot canner. I also found a slew of research papers on the subject that illustrated the potential for just how important the spinal cord might be beyond simply transmitting nerve impulses between the brain and muscle necessary to execute movement. One study, in particular, stands out for showing what the spinal cord can do on its own to control our movements.

The study conducted by Serge Rossignol and Laurent Bouyer (then medical researchers at the University of Montreal) was published in February 2004 in the *Journal for Integrative and Comparative Biology, Volume 44, Issue 1*. The subject was spinal locomotor plasticity. The researchers wanted to learn what potential the spinal cord had for controlling motion.

Obviously, finding out how the spinal cord works means that scientists have to study it. These studies are performed on animals. In the study referenced here, the researchers section the spinal cord of a cat. This means they remove a piece about half a centimeter long, paralyzing the cat's back legs.

The researchers found that after several weeks of physical therapy (harnessing the cat over a treadmill so that its legs were receiving stimulus to move), the cat regained its ability to walk. Some cats even learned to do so on their own without the harness.

If that isn't amazing enough, the researchers also discovered:

[The cats] can adapt their locomotion to the varying speeds of the treadmill, and if the progression of one leg is perturbed by contact with an obstacle, the limb can generate a coordinated hyperflexion to bring the foot up and around the obstacle.

These studies were done on cats because cats show a high aptitude for adapting to spine injuries. Humans may or may not respond to the same therapies that helped cats regain their motion.

What I found particularly amazing about the ability of the cat to successfully stumble over an obstacle and keep going is that it shows that the spinal cord is not only remembering the repetitive motion of walking but also adapting to its changing environment. It responds to the neural inputs from the touch sensors in the cat's feet.

The more we learn about the brain, the more we find out how adaptable it is. We have learned that it can change itself to adapt to new demands or to injury. The brain is plastic.

We are now finding out that the rest of our neural system, including the spinal cord, is just as dynamic as the brain. Should this really be a surprise? Are we surprised that our finger heals after we cut it? Are we surprised when our arms get stronger after chopping wood all winter? Are we surprised that the more aerobic exercise we get, the more efficient our heart and lungs become?

I think that our inclination to assume our neural system is static comes from our sense of self-preservation. We know that our sense of self resides in our brain, and so we worry that if our brain changes, that which makes us who we are may be lost. Thus, we desire a static brain. This inclination has extended to the rest of our neural system.

Here is where I make my leap of logic—where I go a bit beyond the evidence, where I combine my life experience, my understanding of the science that has led us to this point, and my intuitive sense of how things work.

The further we extrapolate beyond the known, the more likely we are to be wrong. While I think that the hypothesis I express here is probably true, I must acknowledge that the evidence supporting it is thin.

My hypothesis (my leap of logic) is that those aspects of our swing-draw that we don't consciously control, those that we attribute to our subconscious mind, are not controlled by something indefinable called the subconscious mind but instead are controlled by the spinal cord and the grey matter within it.

We make a conscious decision about what to shoot and when to shoot. Our brain propagates this decision to the spinal cord along with spatial information to orient the bow and arrow to the intended mark. From that point on, the bulk of the neurological control of the shot is carried out by the grey matter in the spine. There is no subconscious mind at work.

These cat studies show that the spinal cord can control the act of walking without input or direction from the brain and prove that the spinal cord is more than a nerve cable connecting the brain to the body.

The studies show that the spinal cord can act independently from the brain. It can remember. It can learn and adapt. Are these not the same qualities we have attributed to our subconscious mind?

Human studies have shown that people, too, can regain some functionality after suffering a spinal injury. This tells us that cats are not the only ones with smart spinal cords.

Seeing that the spinal cord is made up of grey matter and white matter (just like the brain) makes me ask why it would be so if not to provide control and memory.

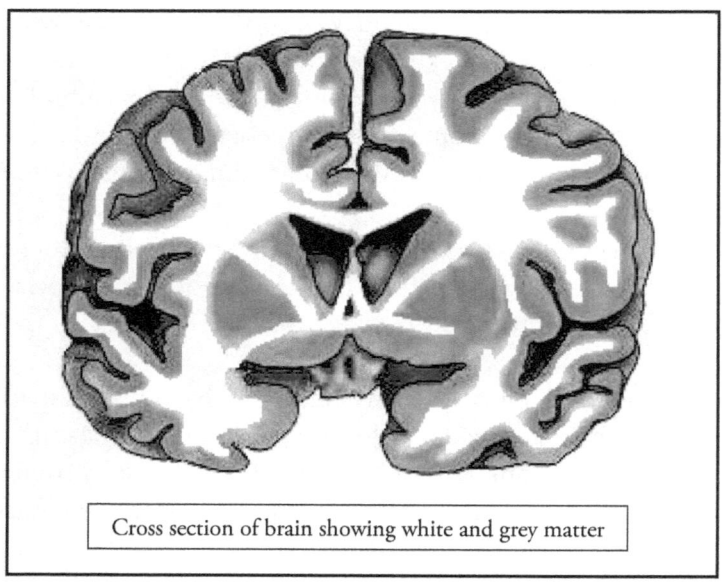

Cross section of brain showing white and grey matter

EXPLAINING OUR ACTIONS

We perform actions that are the direct result of conscious thought, and we also perform actions that are not the result of conscious thought. These actions can be divided into four categories based on how conscious we are of them. Let me explain.

When we clap our hands to applaud a fine performance, we are conscious of how hard we clap, how fast we clap, and how long we clap. We intend it to be so. This is an example of a voluntary action.

While I am typing these words, my liver is busy detoxifying my body and controlling my metabolism through the secretion of the perfect amounts of hormones. My pancreas is releasing insulin into my bloodstream to regulate blood sugar and bile into my small intestine to facilitate digestion. All these things (and many more) happen under the direction and control of my nervous system and without my knowledge or capacity to even sense them. These activities would happen in my body even if I were in a coma and brain dead. These are examples of involuntary action.

If I hold my breath as I type a particularly hard sentence, I can do so for a minute, but eventually, I am forced to breathe. Breath control is an example of a semi-voluntary action.

When I type these words onto this page, I am aware of what I want to write, but I have no conscious control over my fingers as they rapidly cycle the keys making the words appear almost as fast as I can think of them (which is not a testament to my typing speed). My finger motion is not controlled by me, yet because the keys pressed produce readable words instead of random symbols, the motion implies intent. And intent implies mind. I can find no name for this type of action. We simply attribute it to our subconscious mind.

Isn't it interesting that we have a name for a voluntary action that eventually becomes involuntary? The transition from holding our breath to having to breathe is an orderly transition from voluntary to involuntary. Thus, we name it semi-voluntary action.

But typing, like archery, is a hybrid action. It involves a conscious goal (type that word) with the unconscious action of pressing all the required keys in the correct order. If we are shooting with the same hybrid action, we focus our mind on hitting the mark and depend on the unconscious action of our body to get the arrow there.

Typing can be performed in two different ways.

We can hunt and peck to type the words. Anyone can take advantage of this method as long as they can see the keys and move their fingers. It is an example of depending on conscious thought and voluntary action to achieve the desired result. It can be done accurately, but the disadvantage is that it is very slow.

We can touch type the words if we learn to find the keys with our fingers and without looking at the keyboard. It can take up to a year of steady typing practice to become a touch typist. Touch typing can be done very quickly and very accurately, but the disadvantage is that it takes a while to learn.

Typists and archers have a similar choice. They can choose immediate success based on conscious motion (looking at the keys on a keyboard or aiming with a sight on a bow). Or they can choose delayed success based on developing a hybrid skill (finding the keys by touch or shooting a bow accurately without visual or mechanical aid).

I wonder if we couldn't call this hybrid action (this action that takes advantage of all that our neural network has to offer) a fluid action?

In our compartmentalized western way of thinking, there must surely be a department of conscious thought (our conscious self) and a department of unconscious thought (our subconscious self) to explain these four groups of actions.

And in our old model of understanding our neurological system, the only place the mind could exist was in the brain. Every other element of the system served simply to provide input or execute commands.

By changing our neurological model of understanding from a hierarchal system dependent upon a subconscious to explain some unexplainable behaviors to a neural network (or even a network of neural networks), we can explain all our actions from simple mindless reflexes to complex fluid actions without the need for a subconscious mind.

With our recently acquired technology to study the character of the living human neurological system in real time (magnetic resonance imaging, or MRI), and our rapidly advancing artificial intelligence and computer networking technology, we have begun to understand and appreciate the benefits of neural networks and how the science of neural networks may help explain the human mind.

It is important to note that MRIs measure blood flow, not neural activity.

We make an assumption that active working nerves need more blood flow than inactive nerves. Therefore, we conclude that areas in the brain that show greater blood flow must be more active.

Nerve impulse transmission is measured in milliseconds, and the hemodynamic response (blood flow) is typically about two seconds. Thus, we must conclude that blood flow can be a useful proxy, but we must also realize that there are all kinds of opportunities for bias and misinterpretation of MRI studies.

Consider the example of the dead salmon MRI study that Craig Bennett (then a neuroscientist at Dartmouth University) performed to calibrate their new machine. He and his students performed an MRI on a dead salmon while showing it pictures of human faces and asking the salmon to think about how the people felt.

The students, seeing the humor of it all, wanted to maintain the "integrity of the calibration" and, therefore, asked the salmon the same questions they would ask a human subject. To everyone's surprise, when the data was analyzed, it showed some brain activity that correlated to the questions.

As Bennett said in an interview with *Wired Magazine*:

> By complete, random chance, we found some voxels (3-dimensional equivalent of the 2-dimensional pixel) that were significant and that just happened to be in the fish's brain. If I were a ridiculous researcher, I'd say, "A dead salmon perceiving humans can tell their emotional state."

Studying the nervous system with MRI technology can lead to some wonderful discoveries, but we must cautiously remember that even though increased blood flow to some region of our nervous system implies neural activity, the dead salmon story illustrates that it's not proof of anything other than blood flow.

Even after considering the aforementioned limitations of our technology to truly show us how our neurological system works, I don't think it's too much of a stretch to begin to think of our human neurological system in terms of a neural network. We have bundles of nerves in our head, our spinal cord, and our stomach that behave more like members of a network than links in a causal chain.

Indeed, the recently discovered network of hundreds of millions of neurons lining the stomach has been described as practically another brain. Emily Underwood (science writer for the journal *Science*) highlighted the importance of such a cluster of nerves when she wrote about them in the September 2018 issue of *Science* and observed that: "This new discovery may shed light on why conditions like depression and autism are linked to a malfunctioning gut."

Instead of splitting ourselves into different minds to manage these conscious and unconscious actions, it might be more accurate to think of an integrated self. Our consciousness is an emergent property of our entire neurological system.

As we struggle to shoot our bows well and wonder what value there could be to all these repetitive exercises, it helps to understand that we are actually training our entire neural network to perform our desired task.

What has been attributed in the past to muscle memory or a subconscious mind might more accurately be attributed to the neurological functioning of the spinal cord and its grey matter.

In a network, different areas of the neurological system can specialize in different functions. Those neurological regions can then interact through the network in ways that optimize our ability to function.

Neuroscientists have boiled down our memory into three categories.

Declarative memory is the memory of facts. We remember things like a pound is sixteen ounces, but we don't necessarily remember how we learned that fact.

Episodic memory is the memory of events. We can remember talking to a friend, but we may not remember what we talked about.

Procedural memory is the memory of action. We can ride a bike, but we can't explain exactly how to balance it. Procedural memory is what we think of as muscle memory.

There have been many studies that show changes in the brain and how white matter and grey matter interconnect as we learn new skills. Ainslie Johnstone (then a research student in the Wellcome Centre for Integrative Neuroimaging) summarizes these studies in an article she wrote for Oxford University Press called "The Amazing Phenomenon of Muscle Memory":

> Changes in white matter, grey matter, and in motor cortex representation all appear to be important for skill learning and memory. The brain of a person who is very good at a particular skill, such as lindy-hop dancing or playing a certain video game, might have stronger white matter connections between the different brain areas needed for each task, more grey matter in some of these regions, and might have larger motor cortex representations of the muscles needed. However, there are probably many other types of structural changes that occur when we learn a new motor skill that is yet to be discovered.

Thinking about Johnstone's observation that there is likely more to discover about how we learn skill memories and thinking about how efficient nature is, I can't help but wonder why the spinal cord would be packed with grey and white matter if it was simply a conduit for nerve impulses.

Seeking the truth is a noble journey. Sometimes, we can accidentally bind ourselves to an idea in our search for truth and make it a part of our sense of self when it should have remained just an idea.

Science is about seeking truth. If an idea cannot be falsified, it is not science. By this, I mean that if we learn to state an idea in such a way that it can be tested and proven true or false, we are participating in science. We can move our thinking forward and understand ourselves and the world a little better.

Maybe one day the idea that the spine stores procedural memories (and is actually responsible for the automatic parts of the swing-draw) can be tested. Until then, it remains a theory.

In the end, it really doesn't matter if my theory is true or false. While this theory may not serve to expand our knowledge of how our nervous system works, it can serve to get us thinking about and being mindful of the complexity of everything that makes up our body and our ability to control it. It should give us reason to be patient with ourselves as we learn the swing-draw.

And maybe it can remind us to keep an open mind and refuse to internalize and defend ideas that cannot be proved one way or the other.

As I have worked to improve my automatic swing-draw skills through endless blank bale practice, I have found that my sense of consciousness has improved as well. If we see ourselves as a complex neural network instead of just a brain and some other bits, it should come as no surprise that improving some aspect of our neurological system would improve our consciousness.

When we think of our consciousness as an emergent property, it becomes clear that it is intangible and, thus, hard to explain. But at least it also becomes clear that we should be wary of any characterization of the mind that separates us from our bodies. Christof Koch (then chief scientist of the Allen Institute for Brain Science), in his article titled "What is Consciousness?" in the June 2018 issue of *Scientific American*, observes that consciousness is:

> Everything you experience. It is the tune stuck in your head, the sweetness of chocolate mousse, the throbbing pain of a toothache, the fierce love for your child, and the bitter knowledge that eventually all feelings will end.

In other words, consciousness results (emerges) from our memories, knowledge, and experience. I think it is even more fascinating to consider the possibility that the memories, knowledge, and experience that make up our consciousness reside not only in our brain but also, quite possibly, in our spinal cord and maybe even in our gut.

Just as a weightlifter benefits from understanding how lifting weights makes their muscles grow larger and stronger, an archer benefits from understanding how shooting endlessly into a blank bale (with little sign of improvement) makes their shot more accurate.

After a hard day at the gym, a weightlifter will probably be weaker than they were at the start. Yet they will still be happy and content in the knowledge that, over time, they will indeed get stronger because they understand that forcing muscles to strain against heavy weights will make them stronger. It just takes time.

By the same token, an archer can be happy and content in their practice even if they don't see improvement because they understand that unending blank bale practice will train their neurological network (from brain to fingertips) to shoot arrows gracefully and directly into the mark. It just takes time.

And by these exercises, we increase the complexity of our neural network and thus the complexity of the emergent property that we think of as our self.

Maybe the opportunity that archery affords us for self-improvement explains why its practice is held in such high esteem by so many cultures, ancient and modern.

Chapter 10

BOW TILLER – PART 1

A Historical Perspective

Good design is a matter of balancing priorities. The trick is to know what qualities make for a good bow and, of those qualities, which ones are the most important. In short, to know your priorities.

Bows are such simple things, and yet, their design has eluded our full understanding for all the ages that have passed since someone shot an arrow from the first bow.

Is it any wonder, then, that a full understanding of how to shoot a bow has eluded us as well?

As we learn to shoot a bow, I think it can be helpful to develop a basic understanding of how bows work, like knowing how a car works helps us become better drivers.

Nothing is more fundamental to the workings of a bow than its tiller. Tiller is the word we use when we attempt to describe how the bow bends and how it behaves as it shoots an arrow. It can function as both a noun and a verb.

This chapter and the next are dedicated to exploring what a bow tiller is from a historical perspective, as well as from an ergonomic perspective.

The most obvious quality of a bow that comes to mind, and the one we most eagerly try to improve, is the *profile* of the bow. Robert Elmer reliably distills the options available to us in his book *Target Archery*:

> One of the most important features of design that bowyers of all times have investigated is the curve that a bow should assume when fully drawn. By appropriate tillering, the traditional bow may be made to bend in any of the following curves: the arc of a circle for the whole bow; two arcs of circles of the same or different radii; two such arcs separated by a straight handle; forms similar to the preceding but with elliptic arcs; two parabolic curves; two hyperbolic curves; irregular curves with whip ends; wide variations in the length of the central stiff portion; stiff center, stiff ends, and flexible mid limbs; various modifications and combinations of these principal forms.

How our priorities stack up informs our choice of basic bow configuration and the materials from which it is made. In my case, that means a straight wooden longbow with a belly and back of fiberglass.

While I like to shoot wooden longbows with fiberglass on the back and belly (just my personal fancy) and want to make and shoot them well, I am also curious: How do these particular bows relate to other bow designs?

GENERALIZING

Are there some general truths that apply to all bow designs?

Obviously, there are a few. All bows have a string and shoot an arrow. All bows shoot lighter arrows faster than heavier arrows. All bows eventually break.

But are there some truths that can be found common to all bows that may help me shoot my bow better?

Learning to generalize what we know is a powerful skill that can help us to see past the specific to the universal. Generalizing what we know has led to some of the greatest achievements of humankind and the most important advancements in society.

One of the most important generalizations that comes to mind is Einstein's general theory of relativity. It generalized Newton's law of gravity.

Isaac Newton was able to give us a law of gravity that is specific to our frame of reference: being on our earth, viewing the universe from our place in the solar system. Newton's law of gravity relates the force between objects to their combined mass, the distance between them, and the gravitational constant. Newton's law of gravity explains everything from why boats float to where a cannonball will land to when the next solar eclipse will be. Newton's law of gravity is one of the greatest advancements in human knowledge and certainly improved our lives, and yet, even Newton himself was uncomfortable with the limits of his law, as he expressed in the second edition of his book *Philosophiae Naturalis Principia Mathematica*:

> That one body may act upon another at a distance through a vacuum without the mediation of anything else, by and through which their action and force may be conveyed from one another, is to me so great an absurdity that, I believe, no man who has in philosophic matters a competent faculty of thinking could ever fall into it... I have not yet been able to discover the cause of these properties of gravity from phenomena, and I feign no hypotheses... It is enough that gravity does really exist and acts according to the laws I have explained, and that it abundantly serves to account for all the motions of celestial bodies.

It was left to Albert Einstein to coax more truth from the universe and theorize that gravity was not so much a force acting between bodies ("without the mediation of anything else," as Newton put it) as it was a warping, or curvature, of space-time caused by the bodies themselves.

The mass of an object causes space-time to warp around it, forming a well into which other objects can fall. This explanation is rudimentary and flawed, but it allows a person to develop an initial understanding of space-time and gravity and allows them to begin to understand how two bodies could act upon each other at a distance through a vacuum.

Space-Time warped around
a planet and a moon

The better understanding afforded to us by Einstein's general theory of relativity has again improved our lives through new technologies (GPS location, for example) and furthered our understanding of the universe we live in. Yet it, too, falls short.

There is another equally strong and well-tested theory called quantum mechanics, which has yielded many new technologies (smartphones, for example) and furthered our understanding of the universe.

Quantum mechanics helps us understand the building blocks of the universe, quantum particles. Quantum particles are the smallest particles in the universe, and everything else is made from them. It turns out that there are many different kinds of quantum particles. By finding them and studying them, we learn about matter and the forces that hold it together. It turns out that there are only three forces in the universe (besides gravity) that hold everything together and account for all pushes and pulls: the weak nuclear force, the strong nuclear force, and the electromagnetic force.

These two theories, the general theory of relativity and quantum mechanics, conflict in several consequential ways that tell us they both can't be exactly right. Or, more accurately, the conflict tells us that they are incomplete. The resolution to this cosmic riddle might constitute the next great generalization in human knowledge—the famous yet elusive Grand Theory of Unification.

The Grand Theory of Unification, if it is ever developed, would reconcile all the conflicts between gravity (as we understand it from Einstein's theory) and the three nuclear forces (as we understand them from quantum mechanics).

I was thinking about the power of generalization to improve our understanding of things while, at the same time, I was thinking about learning to better shoot my bow.

What generalizations can I draw about tillering my bow? Will they help me shoot better?

One of the best ways I have found to start organizing my priorities is to first try to understand how others have organized theirs. Studying the tillering strategies of others is a good way to understand their bow-making and shooting priorities.

Tillering. The act of shaping bow limbs so that they bend together in harmony. A simple definition that really doesn't convey much. What is this harmony of which I speak?

Again, I can't help but think about purpose and priorities. Our purpose drives our priorities. And again, I realize that studying the purpose and priorities of others will help me discover my own.

Until very recent times, most bows were made of a single piece of wood or, at most, a few layers of wood glued together. The uppermost concern in the mind of bowyers and archers who used these bows was how long the bows would last. A second concern would have been how accurately they would shoot and, finally, how fast they would shoot.

It would be interesting to know how the English came to the design for their longbows or how the Japanese came to the design for their yumi bows, or how the Mongols developed their horse bow. None of the craftsmen of these bows thought to leave detailed designs and theories to history. About all we know of their thinking is what Ascham said about the profile of the English longbow when he wrote that it should "come around full compass" in his book *Toxophilus* published in 1545.

Then in the 1920s and '30s, there was a trio of scientist-engineers—Hickman, Nagler, and Klopsteg—who took a shine to archery and set about trying to define what exactly constituted a good bow.

We learned a lot from their efforts. They were not trying to make a living from their archery studies, so they freely shared their findings with us.

The most important thing we learned from their studies is that a bow limb with a rectangular cross-section is the most efficient and, thus (unlike the highly stressed "D" cross-section of the English longbow), least likely to cause structural bow failure.

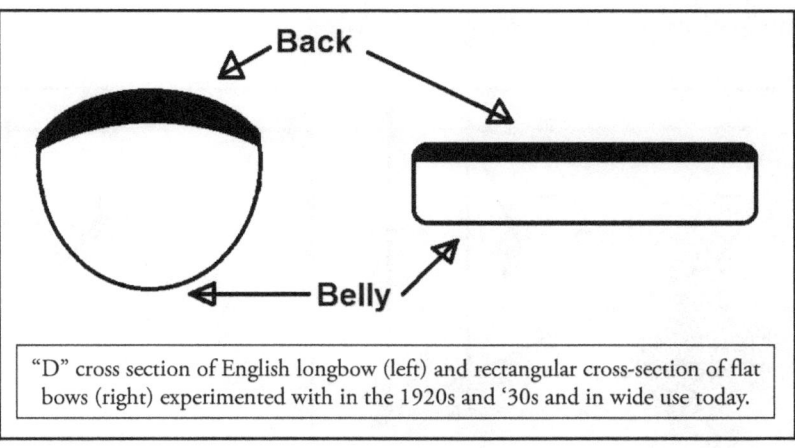

"D" cross section of English longbow (left) and rectangular cross-section of flat bows (right) experimented with in the 1920s and '30s and in wide use today.

Another thing they did for us was express (in mathematical terms) the fact that a limb bent in the arc of a circle carries uniform stress through its entire limb length. Uniform stress is good because it means no part of the limb is working too hard, and likewise, no part of the limb is slacking off.

In my opinion, bow durability (along with arrow speed) drove most of the effort to understand and improve the bow tiller. Understanding their priorities and their frame of reference helps me benefit from their work. It helps me develop my understanding of the tiller.

Over the years, I have found several notable strategies in addition to those of Hickman, Nagler, and Klopseg that come at bow tillering from different perspectives. I will share them here.

TILLERING STRATEGIES

A simple graphical approach to designing and tillering a bow based on more than bending the bow to make it come round full compass was presented by Paul Klopsteg in the June 1939 issue of *Ye Sylvan Archer*. The design Klopsteg published was the result of almost ten years of study and experimentation. They began with C.N. Hickman's initial articles published in 1930 that showed that a rectangular cross-section was more efficient than the "D" cross-section almost universally employed up to that time.

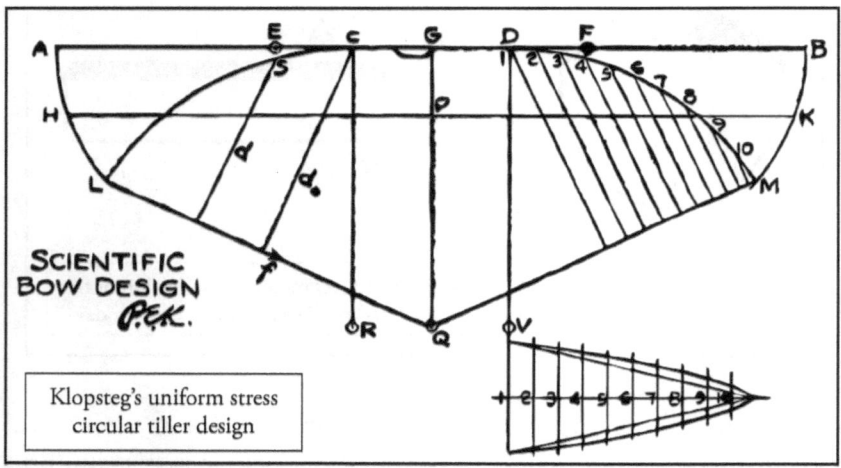

Klopsteg's uniform stress circular tiller design

It took Klopsteg ten years to produce the graphical design that relates the fact that the length of a perpendicular line drawn from the string to the limb is proportional to the stress in the limb at that point. It is such a simple relationship. Yet, it took three of the sharpest minds interested in archery ten years to find it. This easy example shows how hard it can be to suss out a simple truth—a generalization.

The power of Klopsteg's strategy is that it provides a graphical method for determining the cross-section of a bow limb based on maintaining uniform stress along its entire length. Anyone can use this method to design a bow of any length and any poundage. This design surely does approach a general solution.

An interesting quality of this design is that it is based on shooting the arrow from the middle of the string. Klopsteg makes a point of pointing this out in his article but also says: "If momentum of custom or difficulty of making a break with tradition should decree limbs of unequal length, the principles of construction outlined apply in precisely the same manner."

Oh, Klopsteg has my hackles up now! I have experimented with bows that have a bottom limb one inch longer than the top limb all the way to bows that have a top limb four inches longer than the bottom limb (which allows an arrow to be shot from the center of the string as Klopsteg advocates). And I always come back to bows that have a top limb two inches longer than the bottom limb.

Dean Torges, in his book *Hunting the Osage Bow*, has put words to the vexation Klopsteg caused me:

We have grown skeptical of well-intentioned scientific claims and are no longer optimistic children of the technological revolution. With worshipful faith, we followed a bread trail through the first half of the [20th century], a bread trail that promised a scientific utopian society but led instead in the opposite direction to nuclear terror.

But I am afraid that maybe Torges is throwing the baby out with the bathwater. As we listen to what people tell us, we are in danger of getting the wrong message, of learning the wrong lesson, if we are unaware of their priorities.

This means that the lessons we learn may not actually be the lessons that science had to teach us. Is the nuclear terror Torges speaks of the result of bad science or bad politics?

Science is about the discovery of truth. It's about learning how the universe works. Newton and Einstein teaching us how gravity works is not to blame when the gunner uses that knowledge to shoot a cannonball into a city he cannot even see. Science gives us knowledge, but it is up to society, and the politicians it produces, to use that knowledge wisely.

Klopsteg's work got me thinking about how the string nock-set travels (in a straight line or in a curve?) as the bow is drawn and released and how it can affect the trajectory of the arrow.

A different approach to finding a good tiller was put forth by Edward J. Wendell. Another engineer, he studied both the bow tillered to bend in a circle and the bow tillered to bend in an ellipse at full draw. What he discovered was that, as Dr. Elmer relates in his book *Target Archery*:

> A whip-ended bow (elliptical tiller) just resting under brace is under a stress of 65 percent of capacity all day... When shot, it takes a shock load of about 130 percent in the outer quarter of the limb... In a bow of circular bend, these values are slightly reduced... In other words, a bow should not be stressed uniformly at full draw but with a gradual and considerable decrease towards the tips.

This is a new observation. Up to this point, it was assumed that the highest stress a bow would see was when it was pulled to full draw. Yet, with a little more consideration, it is easy to understand how a bow may face even higher stresses as it returns to brace and casts the arrow since it is at this moment that the limbs are left to deal with all the energy remaining after the arrow has left the bow. The catastrophic results of this stress can be seen when a bow is dry-fired (shot without an arrow).

While I appreciate this new perspective, I can't help but wonder how the numbers were derived. There was no accommodation made for variations in arrow weight, brace height, or bow length in the shock load value of 130 percent.

Yet still, his experimental results are interesting. Wendell made an array of bows that demonstrated a spectrum of conditions from uniform stress at full draw to uniform stress at brace. What he discovered is that bows on one end of this spectrum showed uniform stress at full draw, following the string towards the tips. Bows on the other end of this spectrum showed uniform stress at brace height and followed the string at the fades.

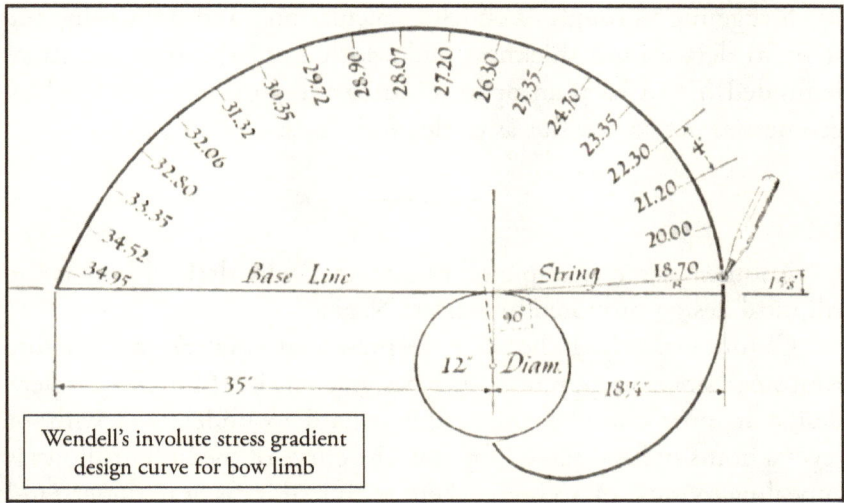

Wendell's involute stress gradient
design curve for bow limb

To solve the problem, Wendell made use of an involute curve. Engineers love involute curves because they solve problems and look good doing it.

An involute curve can be created graphically by first wrapping a string around a geometric shape and then unwrapping it. As the string is unwrapped, the end of it traces out the curve. Involute curves created by wrapping a string around a circle have been the most useful.

Involute curves have been used successfully to design mechanical devices in many engineering disciplines.

Involute gears in our automobile transmission, for example, run quietly because they are in constant contact with each other. By contrast, the reverse gear set is made of spur gears, and it clacks, rattles, and whines as we back up because the gears lose contact with each other as they rotate.

Another example is the involute air compressor used in air conditioners. Called a scroll compressor, it's used because it requires no reciprocating parts and so is more efficient.

Bows made so that the thickness and width of their limbs are proportional to an involute curve generated by unwrapping a string from a twelve-inch circle show stiffness near the fades and tips and bend mostly in the middle.

Struggling through Wendell's calculations and following the steps to derive limb thickness and width from the involute curve reminded me to keep an open mind to the possibilities offered by geometries not so obvious as circles and ellipses.

—◦◦◦—

Another prime example of a mathematically derived bow is the elliptical design proposed by Forrest Nagler.

Chronologically, I should have presented Nagler's work before Klopsteg's since his graphical limb design came in 1933. But Nagler's design is more complex (his graph is hard to understand without several hours of head scratching, but the curve of the limb it shows is appealing to my eye), so I put it here because it is easier to understand Nagler's design after studying Klopsteg's.

Klopsteg kept the limb thickness constant and varied only the width of the limb to arrive at a circular shape for the profile of the drawn bow. Nagler varies both the thickness and width to arrive at an elliptical shape for the profile of the drawn bow.

In his book *Archery, An Engineering View*, Nagler summarizes his motivation for designing an elliptical bow as follows:

> I am not an advocate of the circular arc, but there is no getting away from the fact that we must try to approach uniform stress over as much of the limb length as possible. On the basis that a bow weak in the middle is inefficient, a whip-ended bow is in the right direction. The "circle" bow separates these two classes. A whip-ended bow may be bent somewhat in the form of an ellipse having its minor axis about in line with the arrow.

Further on in the work, he finishes his justification for preferring an elliptical shape over a circular shape:

The reasons [for the elliptical shape] are that the shape looks better, both in the limb and in the drawn position, and because a very slight elliptical form outside of the circle theoretically demands widths of limb greater than the thickness near the tips. Instability, or the tendency to turn over, as well as excess weight are thereby avoided without departing from the correct design.

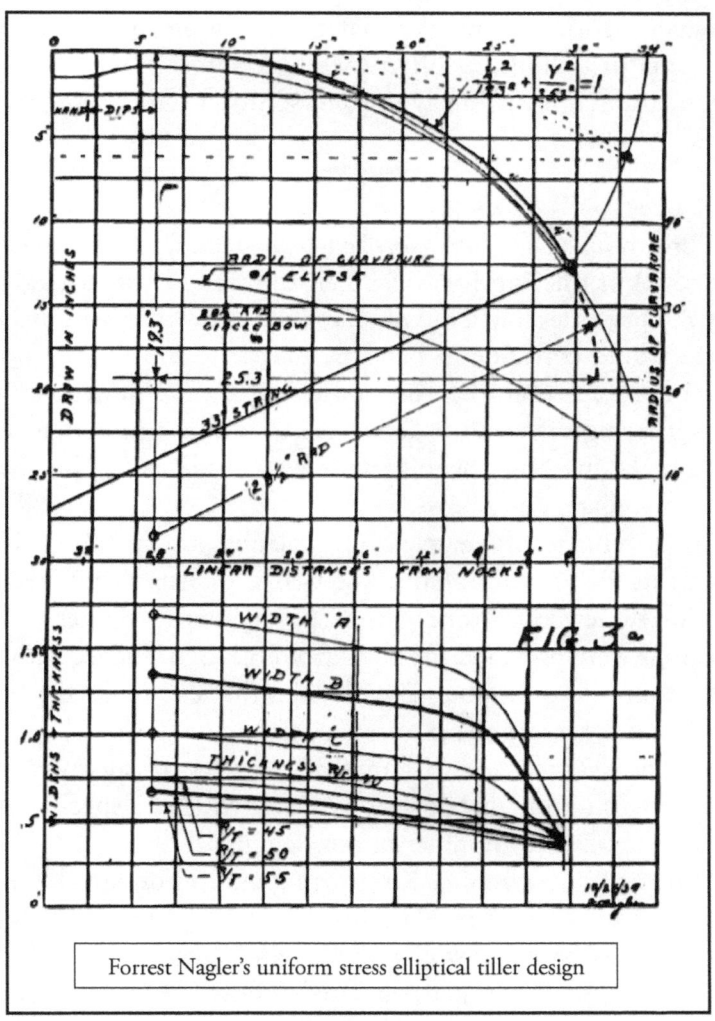

Forrest Nagler's uniform stress elliptical tiller design

I think the real bee in Nagler's bonnet regarding a circular tiller is expressed in the last part of the last sentence: "…without departing from correct design."

The Klopsteg circular design graph shows an ideal width of zero at the nock. Obviously, this is impossible, so the bowyer must cheat the dimensions and leave some width. Nagler's elliptical design does not yield a zero result at the nocks, so it can be built exactly to theoretical dimensions (no "cheating"). Engineers (like me) like that.

Nagler's work reminds me that there is more than one way to peel a potato. I think we often forget that we are searching for *a* solution and that it isn't likely the *only* solution.

—◦◦◦—

In my book *The American Longbow*, I endeavored to explain the method of tillering I was using at the time. I was struggling to clarify my priorities, but I did observe that a bow that bent in a circle at brace would continue to bend in a circle at full draw. Knowing this to be true, I could then use some simple rules of geometry and my engineering software to derive sketches and numbers to which I could make my bows bend. The bows I made using this method were, and still are, good bows.

The advantage of the method explained in that book is that anyone can use it without the knowledge or experience necessary to derive dimensions from graphs or geometric figures. All the dimensions were provided for bows from 62 to 70 inches with draw weights from 45 to 60 pounds with rules that can be used to adjust any parameter to the bowyer's preference.

The disadvantage of this method is that, because it's not a generalized solution, the bowyer is stuck with the specific curves provided for a limited number of bow lengths.

While I was researching Klopsteg's graphical design, I used my engineering software to recreate his drawn bow graphic. I did this out of curiosity to see how closely his hand-drawn graphical results would match my computer-generated results. As it turns out, the hand-drawn results are spot on.

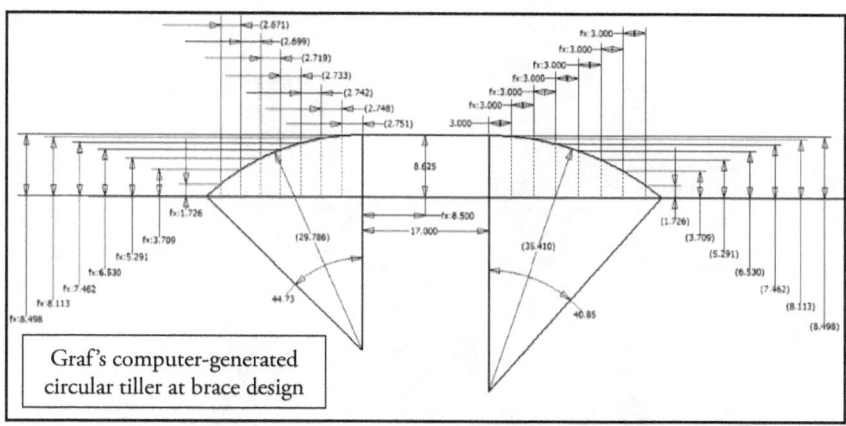

Graf's computer-generated circular tiller at brace design

While I was at it, I took Klopsteg's advice and generalized his graph for bows with uneven limbs to see what would happen. As it turns out, his design is as robust as he claimed and did indeed adapt itself to a longer top limb. Additionally, I was also able to match my circular tiller curve to his for the specific cases I had modeled.

———

One of my favorite tillering sketches comes from a 1930s *Popular Science* magazine article, which was reprinted in the *Amateur Craftsman's Cyclopedia of Things to Make* in 1937. It accompanied a clear instructional article written by Jack Hazzard about making what he called the American flat bow. His design shows a bow that varies in both limb width and limb thickness.

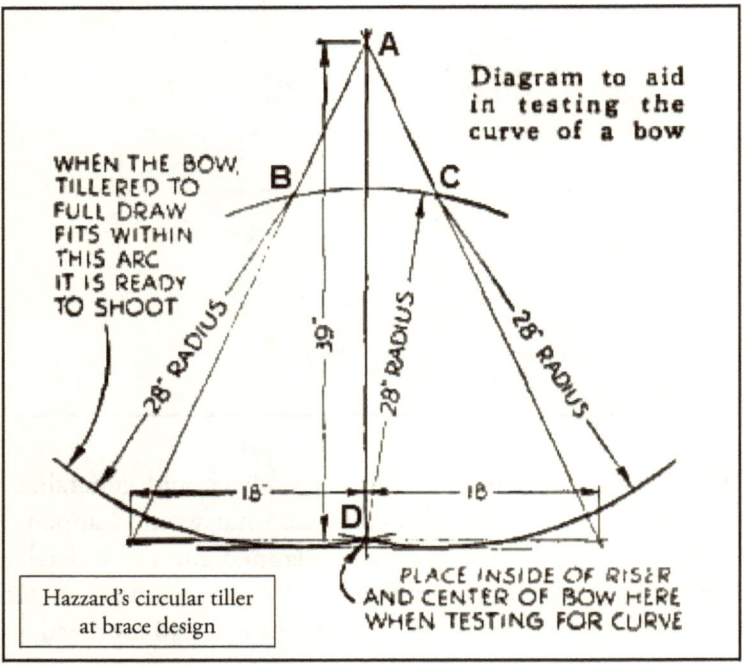

Diagram to aid in testing the curve of a bow

WHEN THE BOW, TILLERED TO FULL DRAW FITS WITHIN THIS ARC IT IS READY TO SHOOT

28" RADIUS

39"

28" RADIUS

28" RADIUS

18"

18

A

B

C

D

18

Hazzard's circular tiller at brace design

PLACE INSIDE OF RISER AND CENTER OF BOW HERE WHEN TESTING FOR CURVE

All that Hazzard has to say about his tillering curve is that:

Flat bows bend in a different arc than ordinary long bows—practically a perfect arc, slightly flattened in the center opposite the grip. So slight is this flattening that the radius of the curve of each limb should be the same as the length of the draw—in this case 28 inches... [by using this sketch] you are practically sure to produce a bow which will give flat trajectory, good distance, and little jar.

I have looked long and hard for any information about Hazzard and how he came up with (or where he acquired) this tillering graph, but I am afraid its history may be lost to the fog of time.

Looking the graph over yields some understanding of its character and the priorities of its maker, but one dimension remains mysterious to me: the 39-inch-long construction line AD at the center of the drawing. Why is it 39 inches?

As I did with Klopsteg's sketch, using my engineering software, I recreated the sketch to see how closely the computer version would appear to match the hand-drawn one. Again, they matched well.

Then I started to play with the 39-inch construction line to see what would happen.

I shortened it to 28 inches and verified that the two limb arcs would then form parts of the same circle, and vertices A, B, and C would become one point.

I shortened it further and found that vertices B and C swap sides, but the shape holds its geometric definition.

I lengthened it up to 60 inches and watched the limb circles open like a clamshell about vertices D.

I even forced the triangle formed by vertices A, B, and C into an equilateral triangle (all sides the same length). I found this yielded a length for the central construction line AD of 31.177 inches, but the limb curves folded closed and looked terrible.

While I think this curve probably makes a good approximation for tillering a bow with a stiff handle section, it can only be an approximation as the curves don't come tangent to a flat handle section in the graph.

I love the simplicity and easy nature of Hazzard's sketch. I drew up the sketch and taped it behind my tillering tree and pulled my bow across the sketch. It didn't miss the lines of the sketch by much. Hazzard's sketch reminds me that I don't need a micrometer to get a tillered bow. Simple tools and a sketch will do.

I have saved the best for last.

Anyone who has played with making bows long enough will eventually come across the four-volume *Traditional Bowyer's Bible* series. In volume 1 of this series is an article by John Strunk in which he relates his method for making the yew longbow.

While Strunk goes into detail about the construction of his bow, his remarks about tillering are just this:

The correct tiller between the string and belly surface of the stave should be as follows: The distance from the string to the belly surface of the upper limb should be 1/4 inch greater than the measurement at the same location on the lower limb because the lower limb is slightly shorter. This will allow both limbs to bend equally as you draw the bow while shooting... Once the tiller and weight are correct, the bow is ready to be shot.

When we measure the tiller of a bow, we usually measure the distance from the string to the bow at the end of each fadeout. Normally, the upper fadeout is further from the string than the bottom fadeout.

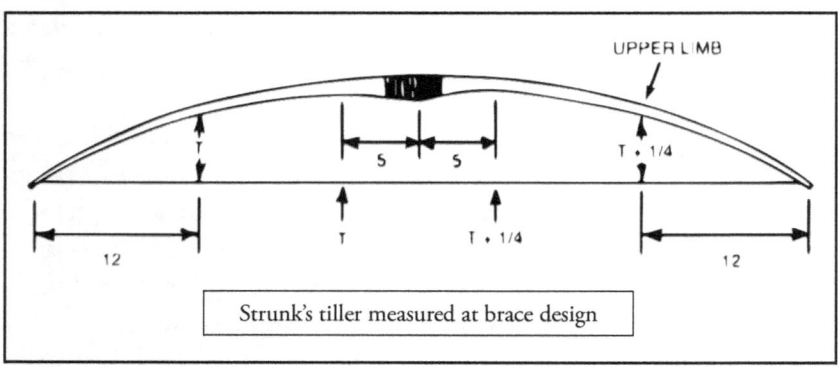

Strunk's tiller measured at brace design

What I found interesting about Strunk's sketch is that he measured the distance not at the fadeouts but from two points equidistant from the center of the bow handle. And he didn't settle for this one measurement; instead, he measured a second point in from the string nock.

I suspect that since self-bows don't have distinct "fadeouts" like laminated bows do, his points of measurement were chosen for convenience and consistency. That said, I think looking at the bow from Strunk's perspective might give a clearer picture, a more balanced view, of what is happening, rather than relying on the obvious geometry at the end of a laminated fadeout to tell us the story.

If you think of making a bow as a dance between the bowyer and the stave, then you will see that the stave leads the dance. If the bowyer fails to follow the stave's lead, then it is likely to end the dance in a huff (shower of splinters). The laminated bow is not so loud in its desire to lead. In fact, it will follow the bowyer. But if the bowyer takes time to notice, he may see that his laminated stave is just limping along.

While Strunk makes no mention of what geometric shape he thought the limb profile should assume as the bow is pulled to full draw, he does specify a limb shape that tapers in width and thickness. Based on what we know from Klopsteg's and Nagler's work, this suggests a bow that may have limbs that approximate an elliptical curve.

Strunk's sketch reminds me that if a bow is well made and holds true to its layout dimensions, then just a few checkpoint measurements will yield a good bow.

I will circle around again to Strunk's tillering sketch in the next chapter.

Chapter 11

BOW TILLER – PART 2

An Ergonomic Perspective

Reading this chapter isn't necessary to learn the swing-draw method of shooting the bow and arrow. This chapter gets into the weeds of what I have learned about making bows work. My shooting informs my bow-making, and my bow-making informs my shooting. The more I do both, the less I can separate them in my mind.

While I was helping a friend put together a half dozen arrows tuned to his bow and shooting style, he remarked that he had many hobbies and asked me if I had any other hobbies aside from archery. Seeing that I am retired, he figured I should have plenty of time on my hands to pursue other hobbies.

It took the rest of the afternoon to get his arrows put together and flying right and to give a short summary of the different facets and plentiful ways that the hobby of archery can consume all your spare time.

Aside from helping other people get their gear in order, one of my favorite ways to spend my archery time is by trying to figure out how it all works. I find that I can better use a tool if I can better understand how it works. My longbows are my favorite tools to think about.

When I started playing with building and shooting longbows, the only information I had to work with was what I read and what I knew from my engineering work. From this foundation, I was able to build some pretty nice bows (in my opinion, anyway).

As I built my firsthand knowledge gleaned from making and shooting bows, I was able to tune up my ideas of what constitutes a well-tillered bow.

I have come to think of tillering as more than just how the limbs bend and work together as the string is pulled. It's really how the whole bow works together with the archer to shoot the arrow.

The more I fool around with bows, the more I have come to think that there is no one right way to tiller a bow. I think the real secret to making a good bow is in knowing all the different ways a bow can be adjusted and all the different ways to measure and compare those adjustments.

Another part of the secret to good tillering hides in the layers of experience gained by building many bows for many people. There is no substitute for experience. While I was visiting with John Schulz and taking his swing-draw class, we talked some about making bows. He told me that looking back on his life (and long unbroken career as a bowyer that few have equaled), he figured it takes about forty years of steady bow-making to really get the hang of it, to develop a deep understanding of the art.

I don't mean art as in a painting or a statue or a vase of flowers. I mean art as in state of the art. That all-encompassing notion of taking a thing to its highest technical and aesthetic level.

Another requirement that is important to the process of becoming a good bowyer is the development of good listening skills. The tiller of a bow is really a form of communication between the bowyer and the archer. In my case, it's usually a conversation with myself.

That said, I find making bows for others is the most fun. And I am usually impressed (and a little frustrated) by how good they look and how well they shoot in the hands of other archers, as compared to my own.

Making a good bow for oneself requires that we are honest about our limitations. I find the effort to be honest about my archery limitations good practice, as I think we are better at recognizing other peoples' limitations before recognizing our own.

I have a sneaking suspicion that making bows is a lot like shooting bows. No matter how good a person gets at it, they likely feel that there is still room for improvement.

Whether we are making a bow for ourselves or shooting one that was made for us, it is important to understand how the bow will respond to its tillering so that we have some idea of how it will shoot for us.

This brings us to the real point of the chapter. The information in this chapter will give the reader a general understanding of how tillering the bow will affect its nature. Its personality. This chapter differs from other discussions of tillering because it does not specify a single set of parameters as correct but instead explains in general terms how the performance of the bow is affected by its geometry.

I don't think it is possible to really master a skill or feel the joy of learning it until one develops at least a basic working knowledge of the tools used in performing that skill. If you never learn to tune your guitar, you will probably always play off-key.

GENERAL THEORY OF TILLERING

Understanding how the properties of a bow can be changed and how they interact with you (the shooter) will allow you to know if the bow in your hands is right for you.

There are a few measurable qualities of the bow that affect its forgiving nature, and I have generalized them into what I like to think of as a general theory of tillering.

In simple terms, the theory states: If the centers of balance, pressure, and mass are coincident, if the bow limbs are balanced across the sagittal plane, and if both limbs bend to the same arc, then the bow will shoot more consistently, and be more forgiving, than if built otherwise.

Let me explain.

I called this subsection "General Theory of Tillering" because I think that the principles I list apply to all bows, whether they are straight-limbed, recurved, all wood, or backed with fiberglass. But, of course, these principles have been derived based on my shooting priorities.

My priorities in understanding the bow tiller have (while occasionally wandering toward speed) focused mostly on forgiveness and comfort. Ergonomic design. Forgiveness and comfort are important to me, as I am a decidedly mediocre shot. Arrow speed, on the other hand, has not been that important to me as I stick with the highly elastic fiberglass laminated bows that shoot pretty fast no matter what their design.

I like to think of this general theory of tillering as a stool upon which a bowyer could sit and think about how to make an even better bow. This stool would have three legs, and each leg would represent one of the postulates of the theory. If the three postulates are sound, then the theory will be sound, just as if the three legs of the stool are sound, then the bowyer is safe to let his mind wander while resting his weight after a hard day of bow-making.

Let me list the three postulates here for the sake of clarity. Explanations of each will follow:

1. The center of balance, pressure, and mass are coincident (Traditional Tillering)
2. The bow is balanced side-to-side (Sagittal Tillering)
3. Both limbs bend to the same curve (Synchronization)

POSTULATE 1 - TRADITIONAL TILLERING

I have already raised the idea that learning to shoot the bow well depends on learning to balance the bow. When we learn to balance the bow, what we are learning to do is to eliminate all parasitic forces and torques so that when we drop the string, the arrow flies true.

The balance I speak of implies a fulcrum.

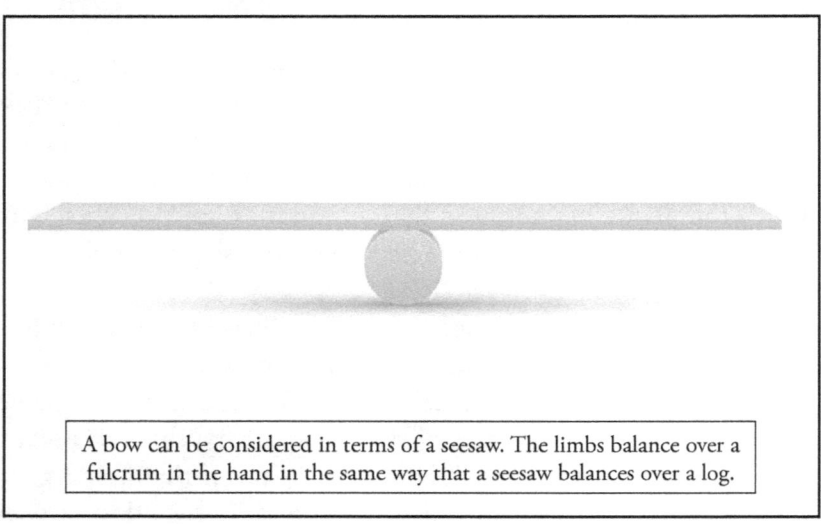

A bow can be considered in terms of a seesaw. The limbs balance over a fulcrum in the hand in the same way that a seesaw balances over a log.

If we incorporate this idea of a fulcrum into our effort to understand and measure bow tiller, several properties of the archer-bow-arrow machine emerge that we can then seek to combine in a beneficial way.

- Center of Mass - The bow will have a point somewhere in the handle upon which it can be balanced on a fulcrum.
- Center of Balance - The bow will have a point somewhere in the handle upon which it will balance on a fulcrum as the string is pulled to full draw by the archer.
- Center of Pressure - The archer will have in their palm a point upon which the pressure of the bow is applied. This point will be the average of all the pressure taken by the hand as a result of drawing the bow, the bow grip style (straight, locator, high-wrist, etc.), and the morphology of the archer's hand.

If a bow is ideally tillered, then the center of mass and the center of balance will occupy the same point in the handle of the bow and will coincide with the center of pressure in the archer's hand. This is the first postulate (leg of the stool) of the theory and constitutes one-third of the requirements of an ideally tillered bow.

I say ideally because there are physical limitations imposed by the shape of the bow that make it nearly impossible to get the center of mass and the center of balance to coincide. Additionally, I find it nearly impossible to identify (even in myself) an exact point where a hand takes the pressure of the bow as it is drawn.

The hand doesn't take all the force at one point. The force is, of course, distributed across the palm. But it can be thought of as all acting at a single point located somewhere in the area of the palm where the bow is held. That point will be different for each person and moves up and down according to how we address the grip (more pressure toward the heel or more toward the web between the thumb and index finger). I have given up trying to deduce where exactly that point lies in my hand and have adopted a point 1.5 inches below the arrow shelf as my balance point. It works well enough for me.

So why is it important that these centers be coincident?

Because aside from any other priority, desire, or perceived advantage of one tillering strategy or another, there is one basic truth that supersedes them all. And that truth is this: If a force is applied at the center of mass of an object, the object will move in the direction of force without rotation. Similarly, if a force is applied at a point other than the center of mass of an object, the object will rotate and move in a direction that is not in the direction of the applied force.

This is a simple truth with a long history. Simple truths and simple designs seem obvious once known. But simple does not mean easy. The simplest truths are often the hardest to learn.

In this particular case, Archimedes was the first to observe (sometime in the 2nd century BC) that a rigid body (like a seesaw or bow) responds to gravity and other forces as if all of its mass is concentrated at one point, the center of mass. Some seventeen centuries later, Leonhard Euler reformulated Newton's laws of motion around the center of mass to arrive at what we know as Euler's laws.

Euler's laws state that Newton's laws of motion can be applied to the center of mass of an object, and the results will apply to the whole object.

In the time, between Archimedes and Euler lived at least a dozen mathematicians and scientists that refined our understanding of the universe and this simple idea known as the center of mass. It is such a simple and powerful tool for understanding the universe we live in that it has been ingrained in all science and engineering. We (engineers, mathematicians, and scientists) are so familiar with the idea that we often take it for granted. Remembering that simple ideas and designs don't come easily is yet another lesson my longbow has to teach me.

Simple truths like this, illustrated by my bow, are the result of centuries of deep thought by some of the greatest minds humanity has produced. It is a triumph of the human spirit that those truths have lasted in our cultural memory for more than twenty centuries.

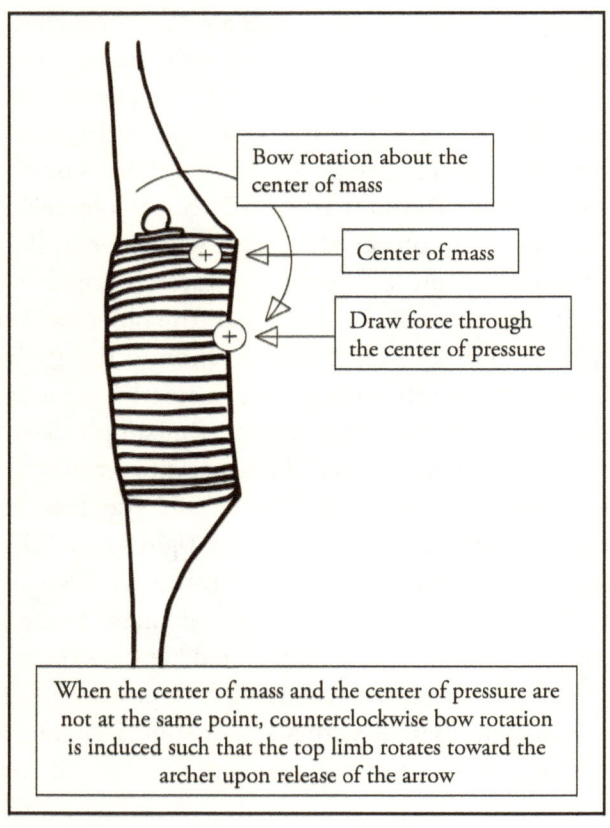

Bow rotation about the center of mass

Center of mass

Draw force through the center of pressure

When the center of mass and the center of pressure are not at the same point, counterclockwise bow rotation is induced such that the top limb rotates toward the archer upon release of the arrow

What this simple truth that Archimedes gave us means to the archer is that if the center of mass of their bow is coincident with the center of pressure of their hand, then when they release the string, the bow will move directly toward the target without rotation. This will improve the stability and forgiveness of the bow.

The reason that the bow moves toward the target after release is in response to the force applied by the bow arm and its compressed muscles, tendons, bones, and cartilage. The archer can't help but push the bow forward when the string is dropped. To minimize the effect of this forward push on the trajectory of the arrow, it is ideal to have that push directed through the center of mass of the bow.

This is why having the center of pressure of the hand coincide with the center of mass of the bow is important. The center of pressure is the place where the force of the hand acts on the bow.

This desire to have the force of the hand act through the center of mass to avoid rotation also drives the desire to have the center of balance coincide with the center of mass.

The center of pressure of the hand on the bow will move to the center of balance no matter what. If it didn't, then the bow would rotate until the points were forced together.

To prove this to yourself, take your bow in your bow hand the normal way and draw the bow. The bow will remain stable in your hand as you come to anchor. Now take the string six inches above or below the nockset and draw the bow. See how the bow rotates uncomfortably in your hand until all the forces come to equilibrium.

It is best for that equilibrium to occur when the center of pressure and center of mass are at the same point. We can help make that happen by tillering the bow so that the center of balance occurs at the desired center of pressure.

POSTULATE 2 - SAGITTAL TILLERING

I call it sagittal tillering because it is tillering, or balancing the limbs, in a plane different from the plane in which the limbs are typically balanced in the traditional effort to tiller a bow.

When we think about mechanical systems like the universe or seesaws, bows, or people, it often helps to visually subdivide those systems with an imaginary plane. A plane is nothing more than a surface with no depth, like a sheet of paper with no thickness.

Mathematicians, engineers, and designers have labeled the imaginary planes that subdivide people about a line of symmetry. It seems appropriate to use the same planes to identify the lines of symmetry that are important for tillering a bow, since we already use the anatomical names *back* and *belly* to identify the front and back surfaces of the bow. Adding to the appropriateness is that the word *sagittal* is based on the Latin root word sagitta, which means arrow.

Traditional tillering balances the bow about a plane called the transverse plane that slices through the center of the bow from side to side. Sagittal tillering balances the bow about a plane that slices through the center of the bow from limb tip to limb tip, called the sagittal plane.

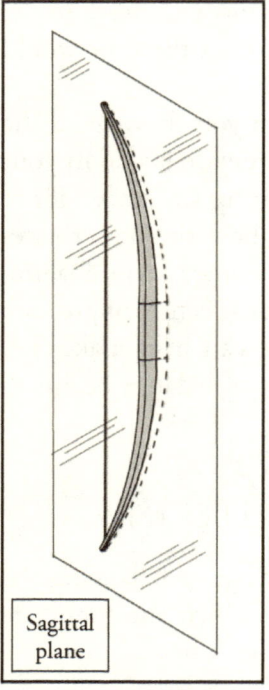

Sagittal
plane

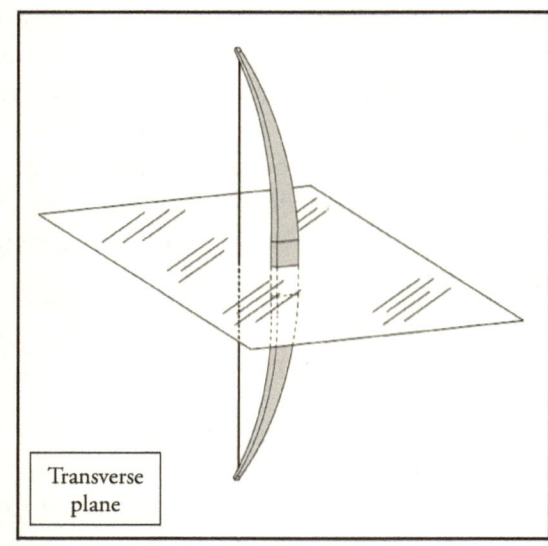

Transverse
plane

On a side note, I could refer to traditional tillering as transverse tillering to remain consistent with identifying what tillering action is being taken based on the plane about which the tillering balance is sought. The engineer in me wants to affix the plane of symmetry to specify which type of tillering I would be referring to, but I will refrain from doing so.

To keep it simple and to honor the terminology as it has been used historically, I will use the terms sagittal tillering to describe tillering about the sagittal plane and tillering to describe tillering about the transverse plane.

Fundamentally, sagittal tillering is nothing more than making the bow meet a common specification mentioned by most bowyers—to ensure the string passes over the center of the handle. But there is more to it than initially meets the eye.

There are (at least) two causes that can move the string away from the center of the handle and are visibly obvious: If the limbs are bent to one side or the other, or the string nocks are not evenly cut into the limb tips, the string may not pass over the center of the handle.

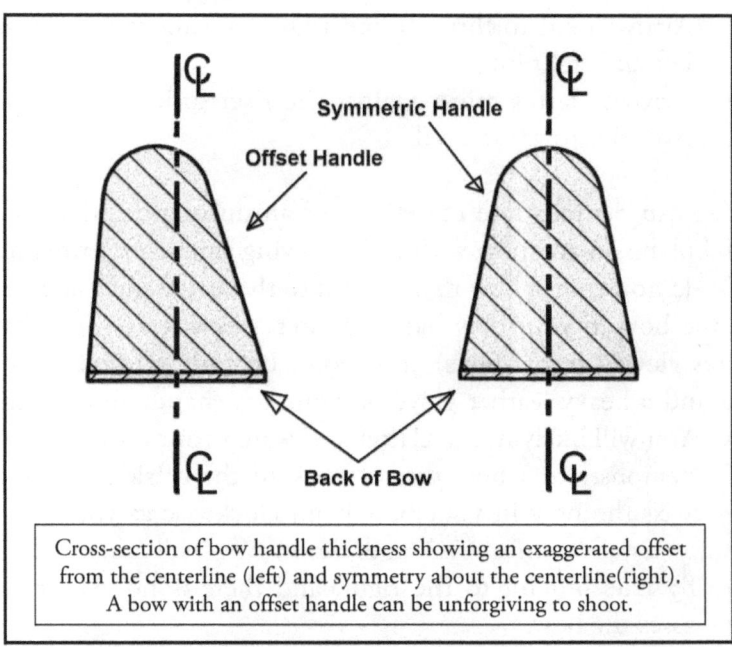

Cross-section of bow handle thickness showing an exaggerated offset from the centerline (left) and symmetry about the centerline(right). A bow with an offset handle can be unforgiving to shoot.

There are at least two causes that can move the string away from the center of the handle that are *not* visibly obvious: If one side of the limb is stronger than the other or the handle thickness is not perpendicular to the back of the bow, the string may not pass over the center of the handle.

Some of us have a better eye for balance, symmetry, style, and maybe even beauty than others of us.

Those of us who lack the natural ability can make up for this deficiency through the use of tools. Where a good bowyer can simply hold a bow in his hands and look down the string to establish whether a bow is symmetrical about the sagittal tillering plane, I need a tool. So I made one I call the bow-bob (see Appendix B for a full discussion).

The bow-bob is nothing more than the plumb-bob Egyptians invented millennia ago adapted for use with a bow.

Before we get to the bow-bob, let us ask: What are the consequences of shooting a bow that is not balanced about the sagittal plane? There are two I have noticed:

- Arrows tend to flirt left and right, causing the unexplained left and right hits.
- Arrows clatter more against the riser unless under-spined (weak) arrows are used.

You can demonstrate the effects of an unbalanced tiller on the sagittal plane on any bow with the following simple experiment.

To demonstrate a bow that is weak to the arrow shelf side, gently twist the bow in your bow hand counterclockwise as you draw the bow (as viewed from above) and shoot. Be careful to wear an arm guard and a heavy leather glove on your bow hand, and use sturdy arrows. You will likely hear a clatter and watch your arrow fly poorly.

To demonstrate a bow that is weak to the offside of the bow, gently twist the bow in your bow-hand clockwise as you draw the bow (as viewed from above) and shoot. You will notice that the arrows fly true but hit to the right, and there is no clatter as the arrow passes the bow.

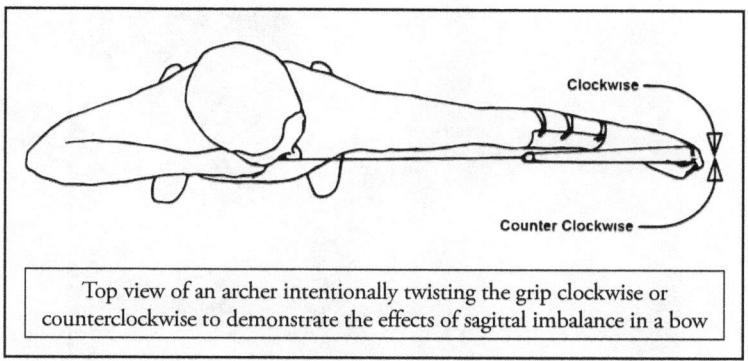

Top view of an archer intentionally twisting the grip clockwise or counterclockwise to demonstrate the effects of sagittal imbalance in a bow

In my experience, it is best to balance the sagittal tiller of a bow so that the string runs true down the center of the bow or just slightly to the offside of the bow.

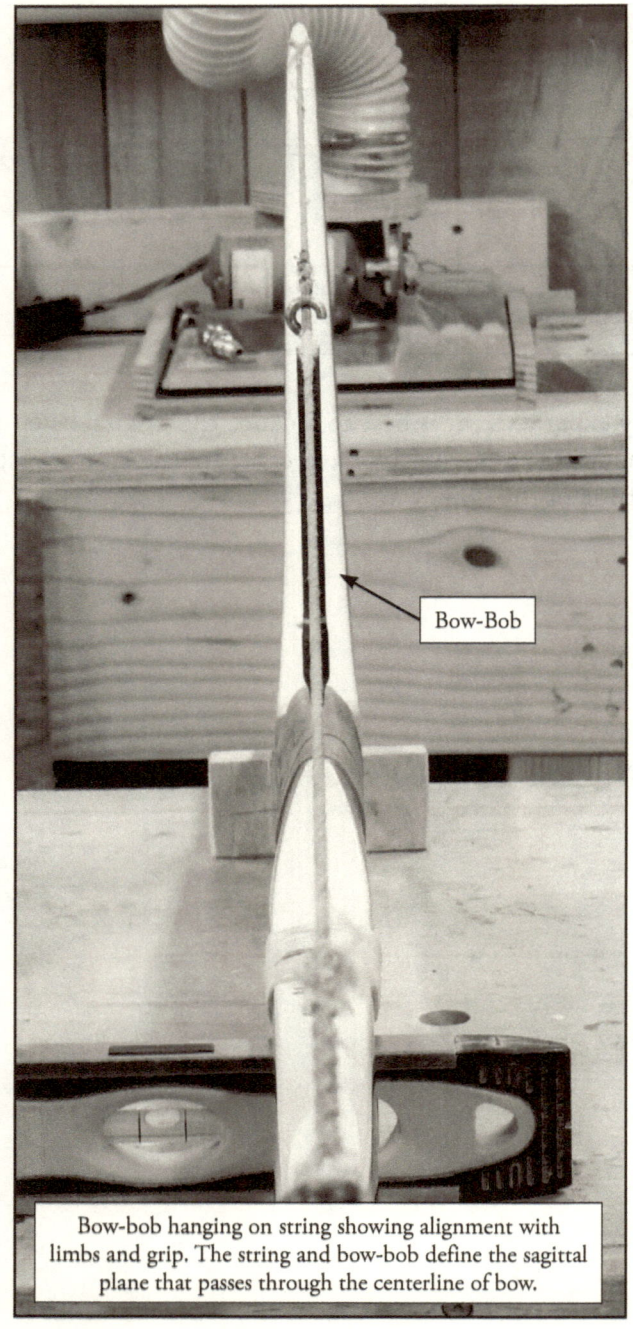

Bow-Bob

Bow-bob hanging on string showing alignment with limbs and grip. The string and bow-bob define the sagittal plane that passes through the centerline of bow.

What this accomplishes is to make the arrow side of the bow limb the stronger side, and thus, as the bow relaxes from full draw to brace, the limbs will pull the string more in line with the arrow shelf and allow the arrow to clear the bow with less paradox (flexing around the handle).

You can use the bow-bob to study your bow if you feel it shoots especially well, or maybe not so well. The bow-bob will allow you to see not only whether the string tracks down the center of the grip but also whether it tracks down the center of the limbs.

I have found that by holding the bow just so, I can usually trick myself into thinking that the string does indeed track down the center of the handle and limbs. But by using the bow-bob, I have to face the facts.

To test a bow for a sagittal tiller, you will need a bow-bob, a level, and a small block. The bow is set upon the level and the block, and the bow-bob is suspended from the string over the handle area.

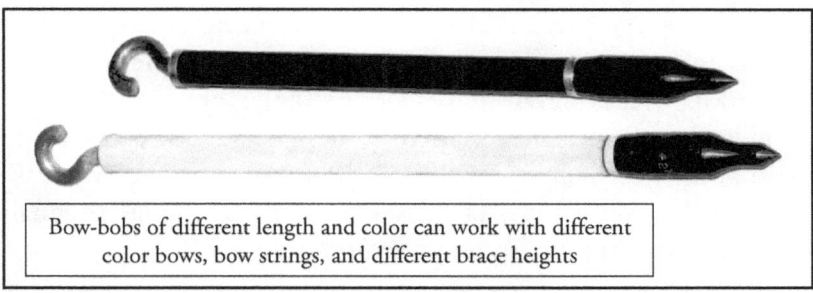

Bow-bobs of different length and color can work with different color bows, bow strings, and different brace heights

Making sure the level reads level will ensure that when the bow is set upon it, the bow back will be perpendicular to the sagittal plane. Thus, the bow-bob will hang in the sagittal plane.

Once the bow-bob comes to rest, you can look down the bow from one limb tip toward the other. As you do this, subdivide the bow-bob with the string. As you do that, take note of how the string lays in the limbs.

If the bow is perfect, then the string will subdivide the bow-bob, both limbs, and the grip exactly in half.

My preference is to have the string subdivide the limbs and bow-bob exactly in half but for the point of the bow-bob to be just slightly to the offside of the centerline of the grip. This makes the arrow rest side of the limbs the slightly stronger side.

POSTULATE 3 - SYNCHRONIZATION

You cannot time a bow like you can time an engine. There are no spark plugs, ignition points, or timing lights. A bow is a simple thing, and yet, the subtleties of its dynamic nature are securely hidden from us. We know implicitly that the limbs must move together in harmony. But what does this really mean? It means the limbs must be synchronized.

Synchronization is a subtle twist upon the observations that the founding fathers of our scientific appreciation of bows made back in the 1930s.

Klopsteg et al. observed that uniform stress in a bow limb meant that every part of that limb was working equally hard. It logically follows that if every part is working equally, then no part is overworking (breaking) or underworking (dragging).

This observation allowed them to design the improvements we saw in bow performance in the first half of the 20th century.

More than six decades later, Ray Axford made another equally powerful observation in his book *Archery Anatomy*:

> Failure to achieve a symmetrical stress distribution simultaneously in both limbs causes them to move out of synchronization, a form of instability resulting in inconsistency and reduced efficiency.

What does this mean in simple terms? What is the sturdy leg that we add to our bowyer's stool? It means that not only do the limbs need to bend in a uniform curve like a circle (as Klopsteg and Hickman advocated) through the entire length of the limb, but both limbs also need to bend in the *same* curve.

The meaning of Axford's observation is subtle. I don't mean that the limbs bend to a circle with the same radius. No. I mean that they bend to the *same* circle. The same circle can be drawn around both limbs. Both limbs have the same center of curvature.

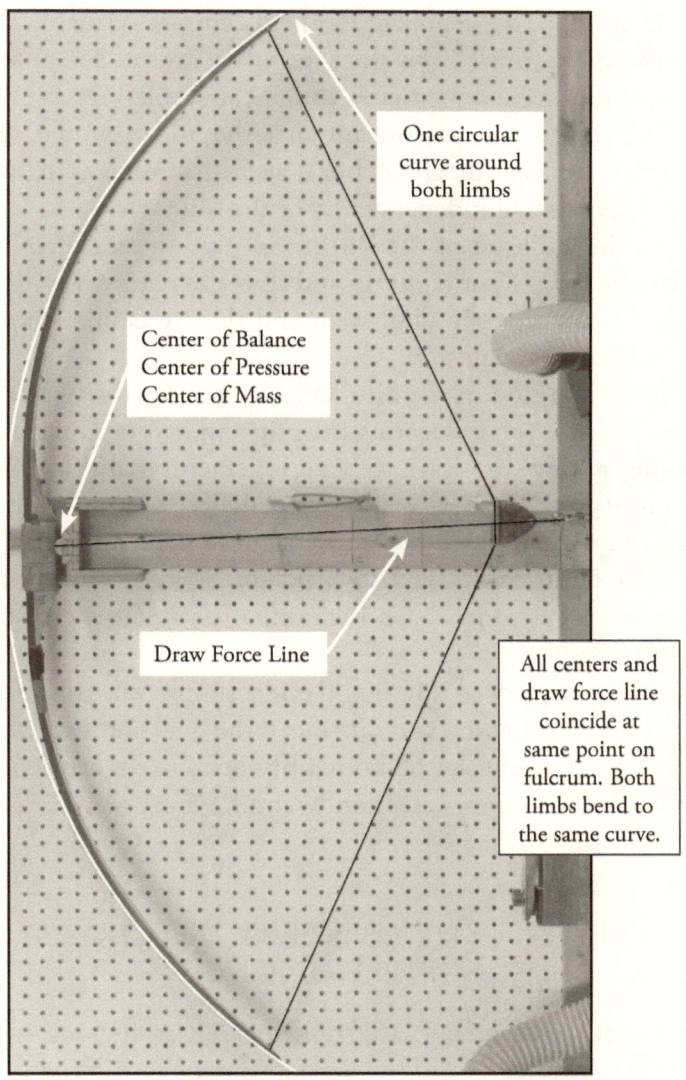

One circular curve around both limbs

Center of Balance
Center of Pressure
Center of Mass

Draw Force Line

All centers and draw force line coincide at same point on fulcrum. Both limbs bend to the same curve.

Limbs bending to the same curve was the automatic outcome in the days before we had a stiff handle in the middle of our bows. When Ascham advised tillering the bow so that it came "full compass," the bow bent in a single arc from one limb tip to the other. There was no stiff handle, so the bow bent as one curve.

Things got complicated after Buchanan added a stiff handle and his dips (fadeouts) to the bow in the 19th century. Arguably the first real improvement to self-bows since they were invented in prehistoric times, these dips have nonetheless complicated tillering.

Adding the stiff handle meant that the archer would feel less shock from the bow at the loose, but it also meant that each limb was now capable of acting independently of the other.

Before the addition of the Buchanan dips and stiff handle, the archer would move their hand up and down as required to find that sweet spot where the bow shot well, and there was little shock felt. That spot became the grip.

With the addition of the dips and stiff handle, the bowyer takes upon themself the job of locating the grip and herding (like cats) the limbs along so that they learn to bend together in harmony.

The results of my bow-making experience indicate support for Axford's claim that the limbs must achieve a "symmetrical stress distribution simultaneously" and bend to the same curve with the same center of curvature. This is the final postulate of the general theory of tillering.

My general theory of tillering, then, is simply this: If the centers of balance, pressure, and mass coincide; if the bow limbs are balanced across the sagittal plane; and if both limbs bend to the same arc, then the bow will shoot more consistently and be more forgiving than if built otherwise.

APPLYING THE GENERAL THEORY OF TILLERING

I made the case in my last book that I was sticking with the circular tiller because I could see no advantage to a more complex curve, and I could find no one who had made the case empirically or mathematically for the superiority of any other shape.

Bowyers Tillering Stool Postulates:

- <u>Leg 1</u> – Centers of Balance, Pressure, and Mass coincide (Traditional Tillering)
- <u>Leg 2</u> - The bow is balanced side-to-side (Sagittal Tillering)
- <u>Leg 3</u> - Both limbs bend to the same curve (Synchronization)

I still feel the same way.

That said, no matter what curve you choose to chase, it's important to keep sturdy the three legs of the bowyer's stool. And while I still keep chasing a simple circular limb, I have modified how I test bows.

As already mentioned, I test the sagittal tiller of a bow using a bow-bob and a level.

To test the coincidence of the center of pressure with the center of bending, I have modified my tillering tree so that the bow sits upon a radius support. I also made the pulley anchor point adjustable so that I could move it left and right in order to get the limb tips to bend to the same level.

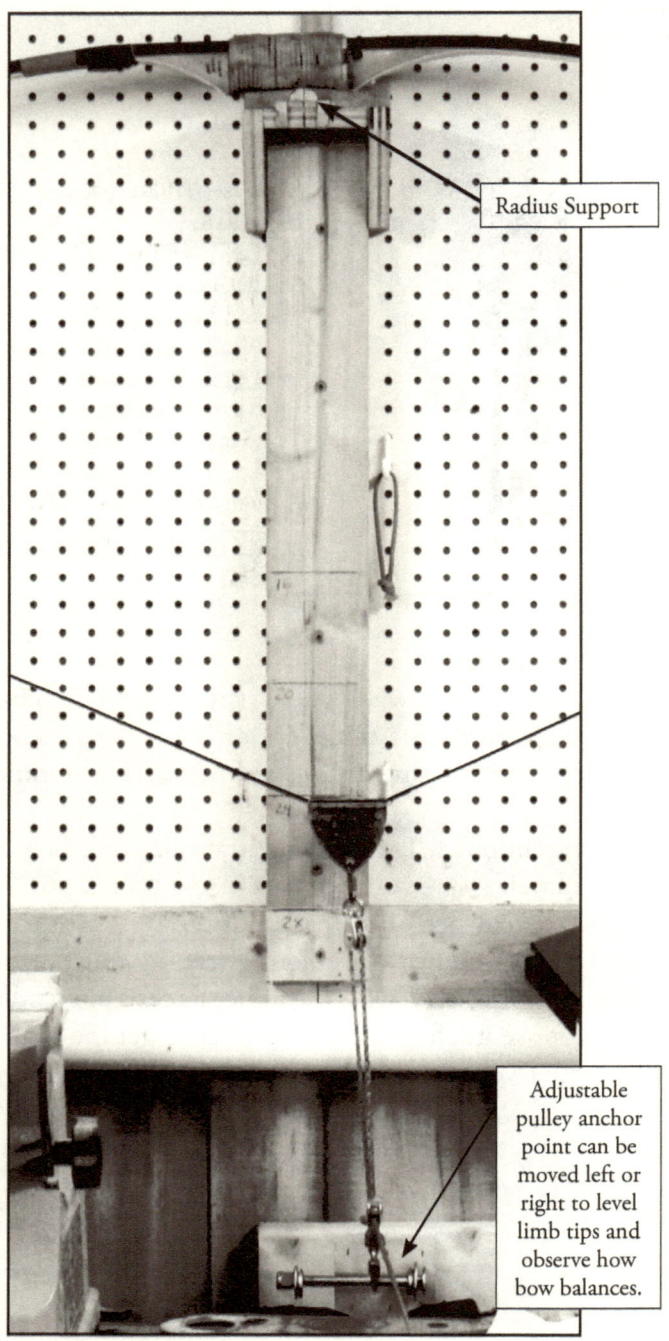

Radius Support

Adjustable pulley anchor point can be moved left or right to level limb tips and observe how bow balances.

The center of mass is another matter altogether. The center of mass will move around based on the relative limb length (even limbs, longer top limb) and how much material is removed from each limb as required to persuade them to bend correctly. Thus, it can't be designed into the bow ahead of time.

I think one of the reasons that bows with longer tops have fallen out of favor is that people feel that they are heavy-chested. After having shot bows with even limbs, the archer shooting a bow with a longer top limb can feel that, by comparison, the center of mass is near to (or above) the top of their bow hand, and this makes the bow rock at the shot and feel unstable.

I like a longer top limb for the simple fact that the more closely we nock the arrow to the center of the string, the more evenly we can work the limbs. I keep experimenting with bows that vary from one-inch-longer bottom limbs to four-inch-longer top limbs (that result in shooting from the center of the string). In the end, I keep coming back to my bows that have a two-inch-longer top limb.

Living a good life in harmony with family, friends, and the earth is about compromise. Most often, good design is also the result of good compromise. I have found this to be absolutely true with good bow design.

A two-inch-longer top limb has allowed me to make the three legs of the bowyer's stool equally stout and equally long. This doesn't mean that a bow with a two-inch-longer top limb is better than a bow with even limbs; it's just what I have found works for me. The compromises I make in constructing a bow this way are good compromises for me.

I have found that using a version of John Strunk's tillering method on longer top limb bows will get me most of the way to a good tiller without a lot of fiddly measurements. I use Strunk's method with just two changes:

- Instead of locating the inside tillering marks (T) by measuring an even distance out from the center of the handle, I measure them an even distance out from my chosen center of pressure. I do it this way to comply with the third postulate of my theory as best I can. I find that changing the center of the inside tillering marks from the center of the handle to the center of pressure makes a surprising difference in the readings. If I measure the distance to the string at my usual six inches from the center of pressure, I get a tiller reading of positive 1/4 inch. If I take the same tiller reading but instead measure from the center of the handle, I get a tiller reading of positive 5/16 inch. Results will vary based on bow geometry and set brace height.

- I make the distance measured at the outer station (T1) equal between limbs (even tiller). I do it this way because I think that having a positive tiller reading out here makes the bottom limb too stiff and straight as compared to the top limb. It also seems to shoot better for me.

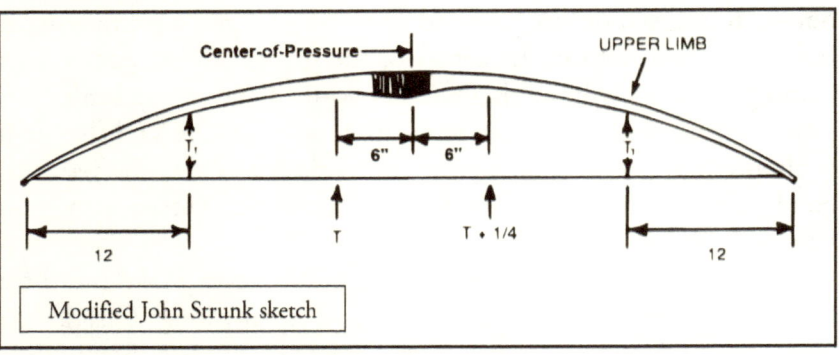

Modified John Strunk sketch

Once a bow is tillered in the traditional sense so that two of the three centers coincide and are tillered in the sagittal plane to balance the limbs side to side, I have just one thing left to do: adjust, if I can, the center of mass so that it sits with the other two centers.

Adjusting the center of mass can be problematic to our sense of fair play. One easy way that we adjust a bow's center of mass is by affixing a stabilizer to it. But stabilizers can be seen as offering an unfair advantage to the archer. Archers who pursue competitive shooting are understandably concerned with the rules and regulations put in place to keep things fair and find that stabilizers are often deemed out of bounds.

If you are not held to such constraints, then you may enjoy experimenting with moving the center of mass of your bow around. It's fun and will do no permanent harm to your bow.

People have been adding stabilizers to bows (whether they knew it or not) ever since the first bow quiver was made. Anything you attach to the bow changes its center of mass. The point of a stabilizer is to change the center of mass in a beneficial way.

Watching tournament archery, you will see recurve bows with long stabilizers sticking out all over the bow. Some out front, some towards the back, and sometimes even ones that point up and down.

Stabilizers are found on that slippery slope of compromise. Every good effect on shooting that a long stabilizer promises must be counterbalanced for those detrimental effects that come along with it.

A long stabilizer out front, for example, gives good stability side to side, but it pulls the bow over, making it want to point at the ground instead of at the target. More stabilizers must then be added to the rear to pull the bow back up and back on target. Games with long stabilizers can be played on the field of tournament archery, but they have no place in the woods that hunters and rovers inhabit.

That said, we wood folk can still benefit from the judicial placement of a little extra weight on our bow to gently move the center of mass to a more comfortable point under our hand.

To do this, I add a little lead weight to the bottom limb until the bow balances at a point on the handle 1 1/2 inches below the arrow shelf.

To find the correct amount of lead and the correct location for it, I string my bow and balance it on my index finger to find the initial center of mass. I then set weight on the limb close to the fadeout to move it to my desired balance point.

Once I find the correct amount of lead and the correct location, I wrap some painter's tape around the limb to protect the finish. Then I cut a small piece of leather to set the lead on to cushion it from the limb. Finally, I place the leather and lead on the belly side of the fadeout, and I wrap electrical tape around them to secure them to the bow.

After I have shot the bow this way for a while and am happy with how things are working, I may wrap the whole mess with some leather lacing to hide my indiscretion.

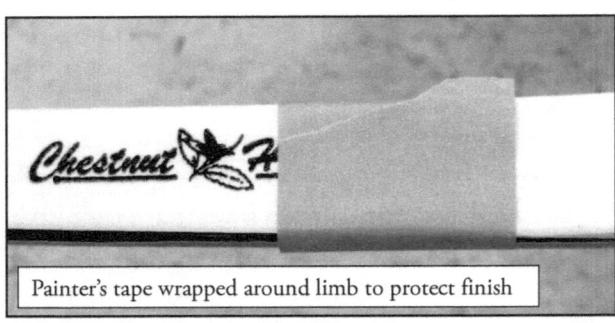

Painter's tape wrapped around limb to protect finish

Lead resting on leather to cushion it from limb

Electrical tape wrapped to secure lead to limb

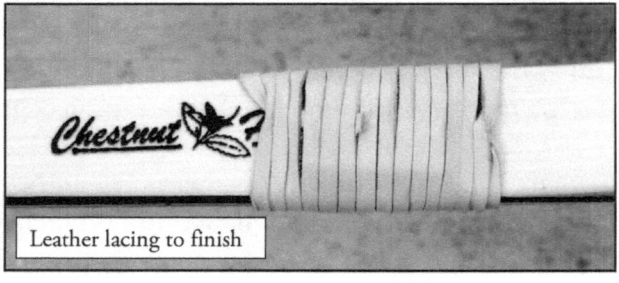

Leather lacing to finish

Chapter 12

GONE A-ROVING

Archery is a quiet sport. Its language is spoken in hushed tones, uttered in the calm between important moments. The beauty and dignity of archery are found in its whispering shafts, humming bowstrings, deep forests, shadows on a nearby deer, and (of course) a quiet archer.

When the weather is right, when the sky gives that certain light and the wind makes that certain sound in the leaves, the archer knows it is time to go a-roving. If he or she is near a fellow archer, nothing more than a nod and a certain look are needed to convince the other to go.

To go a-roving.

The Merriam dictionary defines roving as being "inclined to ramble or stray." Indeed, those of us who love roving best love it for the freedom that comes with it—the freedom to ramble and stray any old way that seems fine (at the time, anyway).

Roving can be an antidote to our serious nature. Our serious nature can, among other things, muck up our archery fun. Roving can help us recalibrate our sense of what is important. The catch is that we must be good at roving.

So, how does one get good at roving? In my experience, the same one-word answer suits here just as well as it suits in answer to any question of improving skill—practice. That's right; the more time spent a-roving, the better one gets at it. And while it may appear to the casual observer that there isn't much skill involved in roving, that is hardly the case.

The first skill needed for roving is the ability to recognize when it is time to go. I call it the first skill because if you don't practice this skill, you will find that an entire year goes by, and you haven't gone a-roving once, which means all your other skills have gone rusty as well.

You must develop a keen sense for the perfect moment to slip out. The ideal moment can be when you notice that the weather has been just right, and therefore, the woods should be full of toadstool targets. Or maybe it is the realization that the day is headed in the wrong direction, and you need a course change. Recognizing either of these moments when they happen shows improving skill.

Another skill the keen rover develops is the ability to keep the adventure fresh. While we naturally tend to take the path well trod, it is the knowing rover that steps off the trail and heads over the hill they have not crossed before. Who knows what stumps or clods of clay lie that way?

Taking to parts unknown sometimes makes the next skill easier to practice, and that is the skill of finding a target. We common archers likely walk by all sorts of suitable targets without noticing them. How much more exciting would our roves be if we improved our ability to find a target? Finding a likely mark involves a keen eye and a sense of imagination while at the same time avoiding the fault of becoming uptight or worried that a target hasn't been found.

The next skill is more of an ability to give a nod to good etiquette while at the same time learning to let go of unimportant things. It is the skill of practicing the rule: They who find the target shoot first.

At first glance, it may seem more polite to allow your roving partner to have the first shot; however, upon further consideration, it will be observed that hitting the found target with your arrow may, from time to time, produce unfortunate consequences.

Take, for example, the target that at first appears to be a beech leaf resting upon the bank but is later deduced (from the splintering action of your arrow) to be a hefty chunk of stone. It shows better roving etiquette if the splintered arrow is yours if you have picked the target.

And by extension, should your arrow end up in more pieces than you might like, it shows good form not to make much fuss about it or of your fellow rover's decision to pass on the shot.

Another important skill a good rover develops is the ability to shoot just once (or, at most, twice) at a chosen mark. Take your shot, and then let that be that. It is ever so tedious to stand by while a person empties their quiver at a mark, missing each shot wider and maybe clouding the air with some untoward words about how things are unfolding.

This unpleasant scene is often followed up by another one, equally awkward: The fit of frustration brought on by trying to find the mark with multitudinous arrows is extended by the additional frustration of trying to find those same arrows, now hiding under the leaves or grass. How many shots was that, exactly?

In the end, more fun is had shooting once at a mark and then finding the next target, rather than spending prime roving hours bent over in the weeds looking for hidden arrows.

That said, a good roving partner always goes the extra mile to help their friend find a lost arrow. It is up to the owner of the missing shaft to call off the search.

The final rule that helps ensure a good rove is to refrain from worrying too much about the outcome of a shot. It's important to remember that what makes for a good time is not so much how close your arrows come to the mark, but how much fun (and how much exercise) you had in the process.

While these rules have been laid out in the context of going for a rove with at least one friend, I have found they apply equally well when I am out alone. And I'm sad to say that I have found if I want to practice my roving skills often, then I likely have to do it alone.

We live in a busy world filled with ever-increasing responsibilities. It is often hard to remember to practice the first skill, and when we do manage to, it's even harder to coordinate schedules with others to go out for a rove.

Despite all the forces holding us back, if we manage to practice our roving skills on a regular basis, there are several improvements we may experience.

Spending a few hours in the vertical position and tromping over a hill or two will surely do a body good. It's well known that exercise, especially walking, is good medicine for what ails you.

In fact, I think going for a rove might just be about as complete an exercise as can be had, especially if taken in the company of good friends.

An extended walk is good for just about every part of the body and mind. It has long been known that walking helps keep the cardiovascular system fit. But now studies are piling up that show a regular walking routine also helps keep the brain fit and has even been shown to be the best overall treatment for a bad back.

There are five words that can summarize the gist of all these studies: "Use it, or lose it."

What better way to use it than to spend some time afield with your bow and blunt-tip arrows? Maybe throw in a friend or two with which to talk and enjoy the day?

It can be hard to justify so much time spent in a seemingly profitless activity like roving. But when we consider the effect such healthy exercise and friendly society (amongst rovers) has upon our health and lifespan, how can we not go a-roving at every opportunity?

Practicing all the skills associated with a good rove is practicing all the same skills associated with a good shot. If you show me someone who shoots calmly at their mark and then smiles while accepting the results (good or bad), I'll show you someone whose arrow likely landed near (or in) the mark.

If you show me someone who makes it a habit of emptying their quiver at every mark, I will show you someone who struggles with their form and has likely forgotten to enjoy the moment.

Being a decidedly average archer myself, I spend most of my time with my bow and arrow in front of the blank bale. Spending all this time in this way has changed my life for the better. But I have found that taking a rove is equally important. It is the glue that cements everything I have learned in front of the blank bale to how I shoot in the rest of the world.

Shooting into the blank bale allows me to improve my form, both mental and physical. The blank bale is such an effective tool for learning form because the variables that affect a shot, such as unknown range, a mark to shoot at, and the stress of failure, are removed.

Going for a rove is a good opportunity to put back into my shooting those things that make shooting fun while working to keep out those things that are not.

Slipping through the woods and finding something new to shoot at gives us a mark at an unknown distance to focus on. By shooting at the leaf or the mushroom, we are adding a target to our shot.

The main skill we get to practice while roving—not worrying overly much about where our arrow falls—is a skill that can help us be more successful hunters and target archers. It is a hard lesson to learn that how much we worry over where our arrow falls has little to do with affecting the outcome of this shot (or the next) in a positive way.

It is no small accomplishment to develop the ability to watch your arrow fly far from the mark and not feel discouraged. Feeling no worry about the outcome, or discouragement in the results, is not a sign that we rovers care not where our arrows fly. It is the result of patience and confidence in ourselves that we will eventually hit closer.

Going for a rove is not just for fun, then. Going for a rove is a way in which we can start to fine-tune our archery form learned in the empty environment of the blank bale. It helps us to build context around our basic skill set.

When we began learning our swing-draw form, we needed the context of the blank bale to help focus our mind and body on the act of balancing the bow without the confusion of our eye focusing on a mark.

As we gain experience and develop our automatic swing-draw shot, we can add complexity to the experience by adding something fun to shoot at while keeping the stress level low.

One of the traps we might fall into while thinking about going for a rove is the idea that we need some gigantic and unexplored bucolic landscape in which to wander. While such an area is surely an ideal location for our sylvan adventures, it's not essential.

Most of my roving happens on my farm, every inch of which I have been over countless times. Still, it is possible to find new things to explore and new objects to make into fun targets.

Sometimes, I combine activities. If I have some farm chore that needs attending, I might take the long way around and cast a few arrows as I go.

A favorite combined activity of mine is to walk the summer woods looking for new deer signs to help me judge the prospects for the coming hunting season.

It's also fun to stop next to a particular tree and remember the time a few seasons ago when that little buck stepped out in front of me, and I shot an arrow right over his back. He was right over there next to that little pinecone stuck in that bush. I can't believe I missed that easy shot. Of course, that was before I started really practicing on my blank bale. I wonder, *Let's make that pinecone hop!*

Hmm. Whether that pinecone did indeed hop out of that bush when I shot my blunt arrow at it is neither here nor there.

As I walk past the bush with the pinecone (still) in it to pick up my arrow, I think to myself that had the little buck been standing here just now; he surely would be mine. And that's a fine outcome for this decidedly average archer. Besides, the pinecone will likely be there tomorrow.

It is a hot day. I've cleaned the rubber blunt of dirt and returned the arrow to my back quiver. I take off my straw hat to wipe my forehead and notice that my glasses are covered in spider webs. This is getting complicated, so I lean my bow against a tree and commence getting myself back in order.

These are my favorite moments in the woods. Stopping, standing, taking a break, looking around, and putting myself back together. I feel connected to the squirrel that stops his nut hunt to groom his face and hands. Like him, I know it feels good to get things just right, even if it doesn't last too long.

I've cleaned my glasses and donned my hat again. I take up my bow and recommence my slow walk, feeling the sweat building again on my brow. It is surely summer now.

I am thinking about the squirrel and the deer that inhabit these woods and how they have made their place. I wonder about their sense of agency just as I wonder about my own. *Do squirrels feel in control? Does it ever occur to a squirrel that it may slip and fall? Is a squirrel even capable of a miss-step?*

I wonder these things, of course, within the context of my struggles with target panic. When we let go of the string before reaching anchor, a voluntary action becomes involuntary. *When* we let go of the string should be under our control, determined by our will. When we let go early, it is a sign that our agency has devolved.

Did I somehow give up my agency? What caused my target panic? How can it be so hard to control an action so voluntary as opening my fingers? While I will likely never get answers to these questions, I am happy with the thought that I have found a way forward.

I have always enjoyed a good walk in the woods with my bow. As I walk through these summer woods, thick and still with humidity, I am keen to hear the sounds of katydids in the trees and their first cousins, the common crickets, in the duff. When they begin their relentless daytime songs, I know that fall is just around the corner. There is no singing today.

As I walk, I remember other roves. When my kids were younger, and I had more say over how they spent their time, a friend and I would take our boys to the mountains for a few days of relief from the summer heat. We would take long roves through cool mountain ravines with our boys and our bows. Many good hours were logged, and much good practice was had.

As I look back on my past roving adventures, I can see the pattern develop as my shooting went south. While I always had fun a-roving (who doesn't?), I grew increasingly frustrated at my declining self-control. As my target panic finally took over my shooting, I remember almost dreading the idea of finding something to shoot.

I missed more than a year of roving as I focused on the blank bale, ironing out my relationship with my target panic. Sometimes, relationships are hard to define, especially when we are not even aware that there is a relationship. I am reminded of one of our chickens, Gimpy.

Gimpy was a chick that came to us with a broken leg. The leg healed, but it pointed out to the side and never supported his weight. The fact that his leg would never support him was a truth that Gimpy just never seemed to learn.

Gimpy didn't have the advantage of years of therapy to iron out his relationship with his bum leg. If he had, he might have learned to hop efficiently on his good leg instead of losing time and energy stumbling around on his bad one.

I think of my blank bale practice as therapy for what ailed me. During the period when I focused on the blank bale entirely, I learned not only to improve my form but also to understand my relationship with my target panic. I learned to hop around despite my ailment.

When I committed to blank bale practice, I thought the purpose was to help me eliminate my target panic. But as time passed, I realized that the real purpose was to help me live with it.

I don't guess I will ever really shake off my target panic completely, but that's okay because it doesn't control my shooting anymore—not much, anyway. I still feel the compulsion to drop the string before I am ready, but I don't. I have found that target panic is not an ailment that can be cured. Instead, it is an ailment that can be managed.

Since my kids have flown the coop, I can no longer compel them to take those long, cool mountain roves with me. But I still have my roving fun. Indeed, as I look back in time at all my roving adventures, I think I enjoy my time a-roving in meadows here and there even more now.

I have come to the place where the little creek on our farm joins up with the big creek. The creeks compete here at this joining to decide who is boss and who gets to pick the course. As a result, there is a large shifting sandbar serving as referee, deciding which stream shall lead the way.

As I stand on the sand and wipe my brow again, I look down to see what tracks have been left by the other residents of these woods.

I try to cipher how their day has been going by the marks they left behind.

I see the ever-present raccoon tracks, the sometimes-present bobcat tracks, and the just-made-this-morning deer tracks. As usual, the raccoon looks like he has been earning his living along the water's edge while the bobcat had his eye on the horizon and was just passing through. The doe and her fawn appear to have stopped by for a drink. I guess it's been just another day without any big news.

The shadows have grown deep this time of year. The air smells of brand-new oxygen, let free from its chemical bond to carbon, courtesy of these woods. And here I am to breathe it in and bond it again to carbon before I breathe it out. It feels good to stand here with my bow, breathing in and out, feeling the vibration of life all around me.

It reminds me of the good vibrations I feel in my bow after a well-made shot. Vibrations are life. In fact, the only things that do not vibrate are dead things.

This is not to say that all vibrations are good vibrations. A note well played on a guitar is a good vibration. A note sung off-key is a not-so-good vibration.

I think of my bow and how I shoot it in the same terms. After I brace my bow, I am often inclined to pluck the string, to hear the note and gauge how my bow is tuned this morning. If the note is a bit low and sluggish, I might look to see if the string needs a twist or two to bring the fistmele up a bit.

I listen to the bow and feel how it moves as I shoot. I have no string silencers or big padding on the arrow shelf. I want to hear and feel the bow because that is part of how we communicate. If I balance myself with the bow, then when I drop the string, the bow will speed the arrow on its way while gently nuzzling its grip into my hand and voicing a quiet hum.

If I don't quite achieve this desired balance before dropping the string, the bow is apt to kick in my hand like a spooked mule and bray at me.

Standing here on this sandbar, I take a shot at the mushroom growing out of the dead beech tree. The sound of the shot is sweet, and I can't help but feel that it belongs in the woods. I see the arrow clip the mushroom and bury itself in the rotten wood. Nice. No birds fly off; no squirrels get upset. I have no intent to kill today, and the animals know it. They are content to let me play in their woods, and they don't seem to mind my bow.

I hop the creek (though not as spritely as the bobcat did) and retrieve my arrow from the rotten tree. As I clean the muck off the rubber blunt and drop the arrow into my back quiver, I can't help but think about the many times I've performed this simple motion. I reminisce happily over the improvements I have made in my shooting form, as well as the freedom and joy I have found in learning to shoot naturally.

The freedom comes from realizing that how I shoot—my form—is individual to me. Trying to parrot the form of some more successful shooter is a waste of time.

There are certain commonalities to walking. We all put one foot in front of the other and try not to kick ourselves in the ankles. By this method, we can get from here to there, and we accept that we all have a different look and a different cadence while doing it.

By the same token, as long as I exercise some basic shooting fundamentals, I can shoot my bow as surely as the next fellow. I have made my peace with the fact that I cannot run as fast as an Olympic athlete, but that knowledge doesn't stop me from moving fast enough to hop this creek. And I know my arrows will probably never fly as true as those of Howard Hill or the Wilhelm brothers, but that doesn't stop me from taking my best shot.

The day is starting to get a little long in the tooth, and I think that a big glass of cold water would be good right about now. I look around at "my" beautiful woods and inhale the tree air deeply. As I turn toward home, I feel my trusty longbow in my hand, always ready for an adventure, and savor the anticipation of the next time I will go a-roving.

There is no greater joy than the joy we find in simple things. For me, the joy of walking a simple path while holding a simple bow is made sweeter still because I finally beat the worst archery fault of them all: getting in my own way.

I take in one more deep, long breath and feel my connection to this earth made stronger by it. At the same time, I am thankful for my simple bow and my arrows and for this land upon which I have been a-roving. I let my breath out.

It's time to go home.

~Appendix A~

HOW TO MAKE A SHOOTING GLOVE

Continuing education is the buzz phrase used to convey the idea that even after we have received our formal education, we can continue to learn new ideas and skills.

It is a well-recognized truth that continuing our education has many benefits aside from the usefulness of our newly acquired knowledge and skills. Learning new skills and exploring new ideas helps keep our brains healthy and our minds open to new ways of thinking.

One of my favorite things about archery is that it continues to provide me with opportunities for advancing my education. In the case of making my glove, it gives me the opportunity to learn about leather craft.

I had always thought that leather craft was a mysterious skill I would never acquire, and maybe that's why it took me so long to think about making my own shooting glove. I have a couple of shoeboxes full of tabs and gloves that I have accumulated over the years.

Looking back at it now, it seems to me that making our own shooting glove (or tab) is the neglected opportunity we traditional archers miss out on most often. How we address our hand to the string is at least as important as how we address our hand to the bow.

Tuning our gloves to suit our hands and shooting styles is at least as important as tuning our arrows to our bow.

And while we constantly play with our arrows to get them to fly right by adjusting their spine, length, material, point weight, fletching, etc., we are content to blindly buy a glove, give it a try, and then toss it in the drawer when it doesn't work right. And then eagerly buy another to repeat the process.

Early on in this book, I quoted Byron Ferguson's observation that any bow will do, but good arrows are a necessity for good shooting. I have found the same relationship to be true with our chosen glove or tab. I would rather switch bows than use a glove that doesn't fit me correctly.

The main purpose of this appendix is not to debate whether a glove or a tab gives a better loose. The purpose of this appendix is, instead, to convey the idea that the best loose can be had if the archer employs a glove or tab that has been tuned to their way of shooting and their physical morphology.

Another purpose of this appendix is to show that working with leather is not actually that hard and can be accomplished with the help of just a few tools. Once you get the hang of it, you will be surprised at how many opportunities there are to make something useful.

Leather craft is a hobby that has the potential to, at least in a limited way, pay for itself. In the case of shooting gloves, enough leather can be purchased for the price of a commercial glove to make at least a dozen custom gloves yourself. There may even be enough scraps left over to make a cell phone case and a knife sheath.

Exploring a new aspect of archery gives me that same sense of excitement as exploring some new woods. What possibilities lie around the corner? What will I find? I encourage you to consider making your own glove or tab. You may find that through the process, you will learn things not only about leather craft but also about how you shoot.

The design of the glove I show here evolved from my experience with several "Hill Style" gloves, and it suits my fancy. By illustrating why I like it, and how I make it, I hope the reader will be encouraged to explore their ideas and figure out what they fancy.

IMPORTANT FEATURES

I think of my glove as a hybrid Hill glove. I combined several features (of the Hill glove and others) into what has become my favorite glove. The basic components of this glove are:

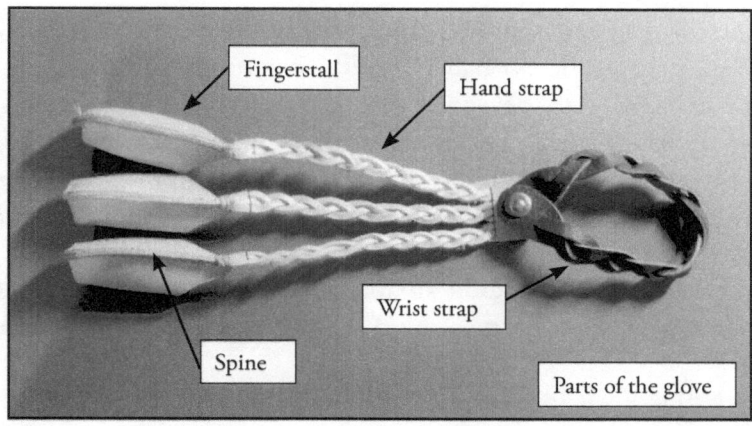

Parts of the glove

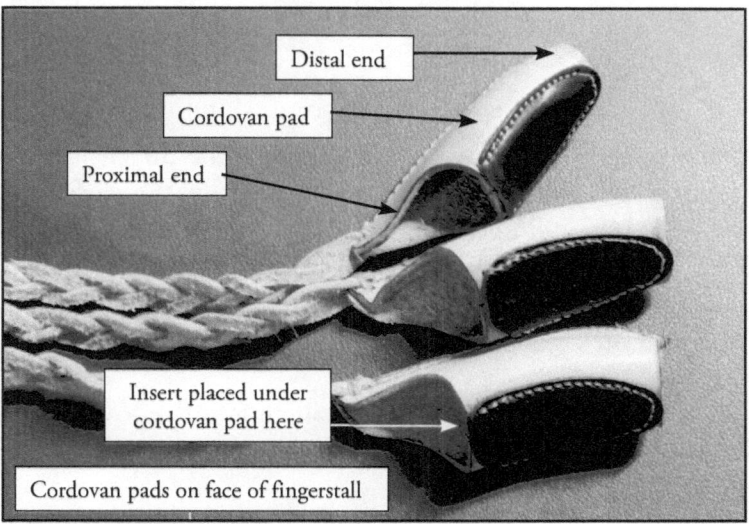

Cordovan pads on face of fingerstall

A cordovan pad is sewn on the face of the glove. Cordovan leather is the toughest natural material I know of. It never seems to wear, and it won't take a set or wrinkle like other leathers will. Cordovan provides the slickest and cleanest string loose I have found. But making the whole glove from cordovan would be much more expensive and difficult. Having a pad sewn onto the stall keeps the cost down and provides an extra layer that increases stiffness and adds tunability to the glove.

A nylon insert is placed under the cordovan pad. The cavity under the cordovan pad is readily accessible, and any number of materials can be experimented with. My all-around favorite is 0.030-inch thick nylon. That said, I have experimented with turkey quill, leather, rubber, Polyvinylchloride (PVC), and high-density polyethylene (HDPE), to name a few. They each have their pros and cons. The insert augments the function of the cordovan pad by adding an additional layer of stiffness to keep the glove from kinking around the string as the bow is drawn.

A stiff spine is built into the back of the fingerstall. By virtue of how it's sewn together, it will have a spine along the back. I have found that the natural stiffness of this spine can be enhanced by gluing the leather together before sewing the spine seam.

An open distal end is built into the fingerstall. I have found that if the fingerstall is closed over the end of the finger, it is harder to make the glove comfortable. Additionally, the closed fingerstall's longer length doesn't allow the string to pass as close to the face. The end can be left open while still keeping the finger fully contained within it. This is a feature that can only be reliably obtained on a custom-made glove.

Some elective features that still add functionality but also add additional work are:

A braided hand strap. While this is obviously not a required feature, I have found it worthwhile because the shape allows for more ventilation as compared to a flat leather strip and because the shape keeps the stalls from spinning and/or twisting around each other as the archer dons the glove.

A braided wrist strap. As with the hand strap, if the wrist strap is braided, it is easier to manage, and it provides more ventilation. I have to admit that I like the look of the braided strap as well.

A liner is sewn into the stall. I have found that a liner helps to stiffen the stall, makes the stall feel more comfortable, and reduces the long-term overstretching of the stall. However, I have found that it adds significant time to the break-in period for a glove and makes sizing the glove correctly more critical.

A magnetic snap is used to close the wrist strap. Because my glove is custom made, I can size the wrist strap correctly and so do not need adjustability in the strap. This is helpful because there is no tag end to catch on sleeves or branches, and I am free to use a magnetic snap as a fastener. I have not found an adjustable strap with a magnetic snap fastener for sale (like the mechanical snap fasteners that are available from leather craft suppliers), but since I don't need to adjust the strap, I can take advantage of the magnetic snap. Magnetic snaps close more easily, do not need periodic lubrication, and are as reliable as mechanical snaps.

TOOLS AND MATERIALS

The tools required to make a shooting glove are the same tools you can use for a variety of leather craft projects. Not only that, but the leather you buy for making gloves can be used for any number of other fun do-it-yourself projects. You will need the following:

- 1/8-inch diamond chisel set – Used to punch holes for hand stitching.
- Hand stitching needles – They should have round tips, so the needle won't cut or split the thread. I prefer the John James Saddlers' needles because they are finer and have a smaller eye so that they are easier to pull through the leather.

- Waxed thread – Any thread will do, but waxed thread designed for hand stitching makes the job easier and the final product nicer. I prefer Ritza Tiger thread in 0.6-millimeter thickness. This is an expensive thread, but it lies in the diamond holes nicely, threads the needle easily, doesn't fray, and is strong and UV light resistant.
- Edge beveller – This is a tool used to cut a chamfer on the edge of the leather. Its use improves the utility of the glove by smoothing the edge of the fingerstalls, which reduces finger irritation.
- Dividers – A tool used to transfer the edge line some desired distance into the work. I use them to trace a line about 1/8 inch in from the edge, which I use to punch a stitch line.
- Hammer – You can spend a lot on a hammer specially designed to work with leather craft punches and chisels. I just use my light-peening hammer.
- Razor knife – Any style razor knife or box cutter will do. Be sure the blade is sharp.
- Stitching pony – You need something to hold the work while you stitch it together. For a long time, I used two pieces of 1/2-inch scrap plywood clamped in my table vice to hold the work. Eventually, I made a stitching pony that also gained its clamping action from my table vice. It, too, was made from scrap materials. There are many styles for sale from leather craft suppliers.
- Cutting board – You can get fancy with your choice of cutting board for leather craft. That said, I just keep a cheap plastic kitchen cutting board in my shop and use it for many tasks outside of leather craft. It does work well to cut on, and it absorbs the chisel punch abuse.
- Pencil – I find a sharp pencil works for most of my leather marking needs. The pencil hardly ever actually marks the leather. Instead, it just leaves a fine indentation line. If it does leave an unintended mark, it is easily removed with an eraser.
- Leather craft cement – I use white PVA-based leather glue to affix the pigskin liner to the fingerstall leather. I think PVA

leather craft glue gives a more permanent and stronger bond than rubber cements.

- Barge rubber cement – Any rubber cement will do, but I use Barge for bonds that I don't want to clamp.
- Light-duty glue stick – I use a nonpermanent bond glue to affix the cordovan pad to the fingerstall so that it will stay in place while sewing but will easily separate so that an insert can be placed under the pad.
- Four-to-five ounce vegetable-tanned leather – This is a stiff leather that runs about 0.060-inch thick. I use this weight leather if I am making a glove without fingerstall lining. I also use it for the hand strap. I have found cow-belly leather a very economical choice as it is cheap and ideal for small parts. Save the thicker parts of the cow belly for the wrist strap.
- Two-to-three ounce vegetable-tanned leather – This is a stiff leather that runs about 0.040-inch thick. I use this weight leather if I am making a glove with a fingerstall lining. The only way to get vegetable-tanned cow leather this thin is if the supplier thins the leather. I have found Herman Oak Craft Leather panels work very well. They are more expensive than the cow bellies.
- Cordovan leather – This is the most durable (and expensive) leather I know of. It is made from the hide of a horse and comes from the top of the haunches. Each horse hide provides two pieces roughly 8 inches by 18 inches. One piece of cordovan can run upwards of $200. Thankfully, it can also be acquired from old shooting tabs or even an old pair of shiny men's dress shoes found at the Salvation Army.
- Pigskin leather – This is a thin leather that averages about 0.020-inch thick and makes a fine liner for the fingerstalls. Goat leather will work as well, but my supplier had pigskin. At first, I really wanted goat leather, but I have found that the pigskin is even more durable than the goat and much cheaper.

MAKING THE FINGERSTALLS

When I started making these gloves, I made unlined versions. While I have made many of both the lined and unlined gloves, I am still on the fence as to which is better. I encourage you to start with the unlined version, as it requires less work and can be made in less time. This is important since your first fingerstalls will probably not fit how you want them to, and you will need to modify your template. No sense in wasting time and materials while adjusting your template so that your glove fits you just so.

That said, the instructions provided here are for making a lined glove. I trust you can back out the information needed to make an unlined glove.

The first thing you will need to do after obtaining all of your supplies is to make a template (or pattern) for the fingerstalls. At the end of this appendix are two drawings showing the shape of the fingerstalls and the wrist strap. While the drawings were made full scale, the images in this book are undersized. Use them simply to guide your efforts in making a template for each finger. You will likely need to make several templates as you test and refine your fingerstalls for fit.

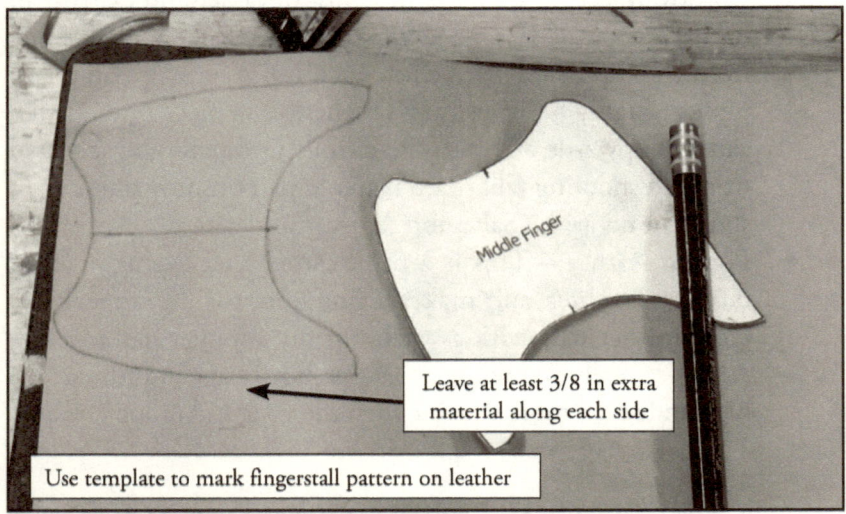

Leave at least 3/8 in extra material along each side

Use template to mark fingerstall pattern on leather

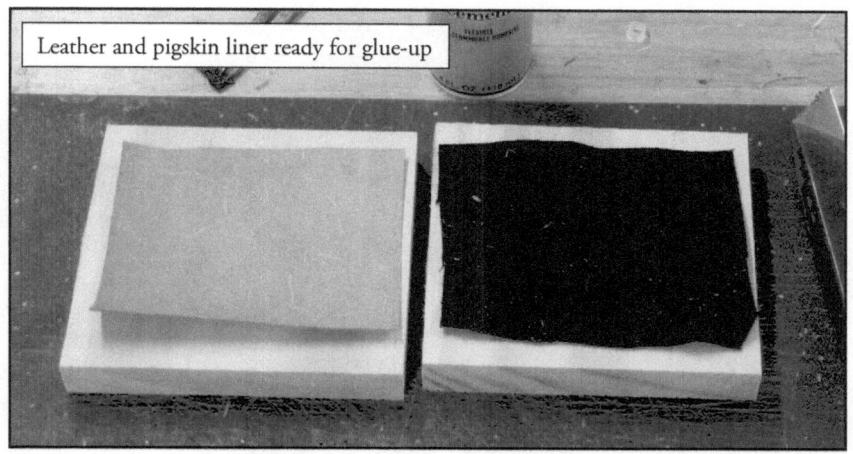

Leather and pigskin liner ready for glue-up

Make your first templates from paper. As you gain confidence in the sizing of your pattern, you can then make your final patterns from cereal box cardboard or any other suitable material that will allow multiple use and easy tracing.

Use your template to trace a fingerstall pattern onto your leather. Then cut out a rectangle of leather around your pattern, leaving at least 3/8-inch extra on each side. This extra leather is used to help in the stitching step and will be trimmed later.

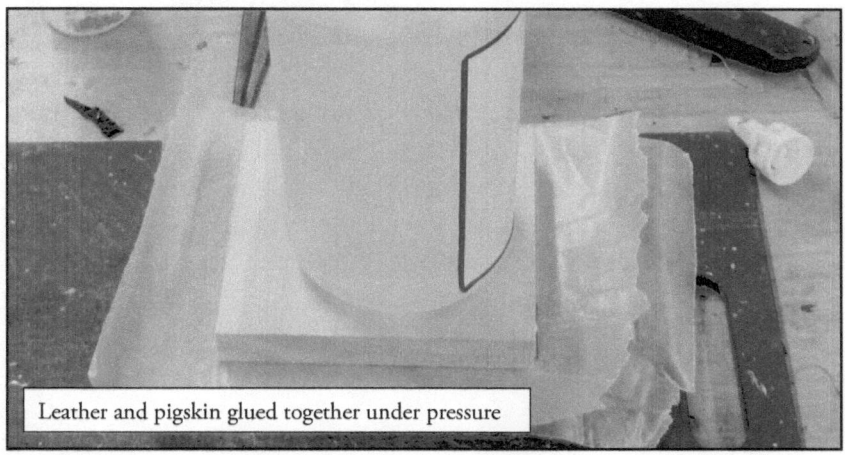

Leather and pigskin glued together under pressure

Cut a similarly sized rectangle from the pig leather liner. These will then need to be glued together. To facilitate a good bond, I press the leather together between some scrap wood after gluing. I usually leave the project alone, at least overnight, to allow the glue to cure.

Cut the curves that will form the openings of the fingerstall. Scissors can be used (or a sharp razor), a knife, and a cutting board. I prefer the razor knife. While not strictly necessary, I chamfer the edges of the openings at this time. I find that it helps to make the edges smoother and less irritating to my bent fingers.

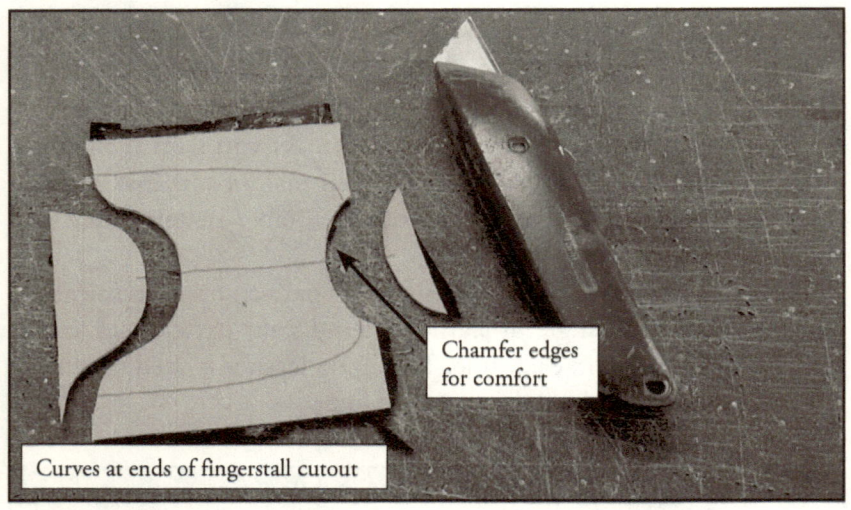

Chamfer edges for comfort

Curves at ends of fingerstall cutout

The next task is to make a stitch line along each edge that becomes the spine of the fingerstall and along each curve that become the finger openings. I use my dividers to make a series of marks about 1/8-inch in from the spine line. Then I use my template to mark the stitch line. I use my dividers, still set from making the last line, to scribe a line along the opening curve.

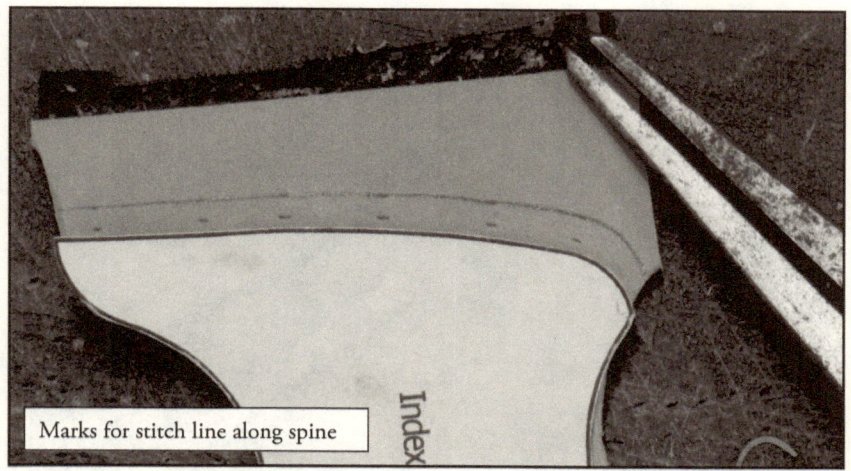

Marks for stitch line along spine

Next, I punch a single stitch at the four intersections of the spine stitch line and the openings stitch line. Then I will use my two tang punch to lightly mark where the rest of the holes go. When I am satisfied that I have the spacing correct, I will use the single tang punch to make the holes. I use the single tang punch because the stitch lines are so curvy that it would be impossible to get the holes to line up correctly with a punch with more than a single tang.

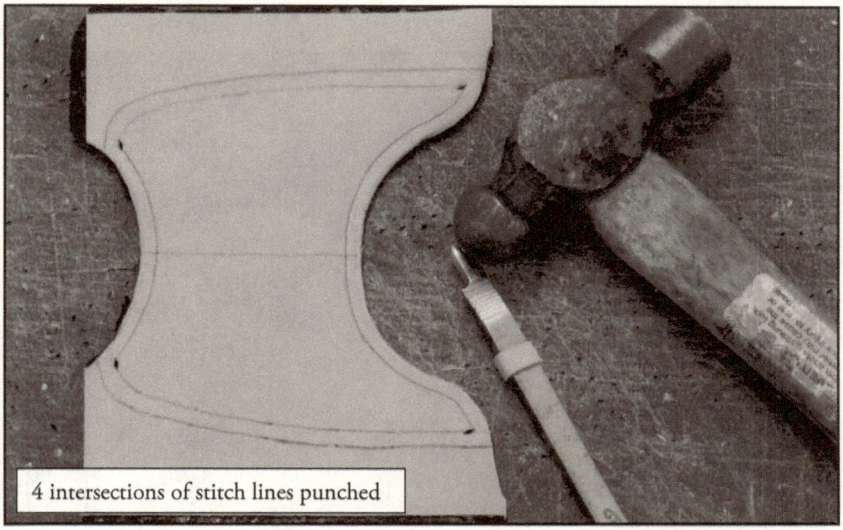

4 intersections of stitch lines punched

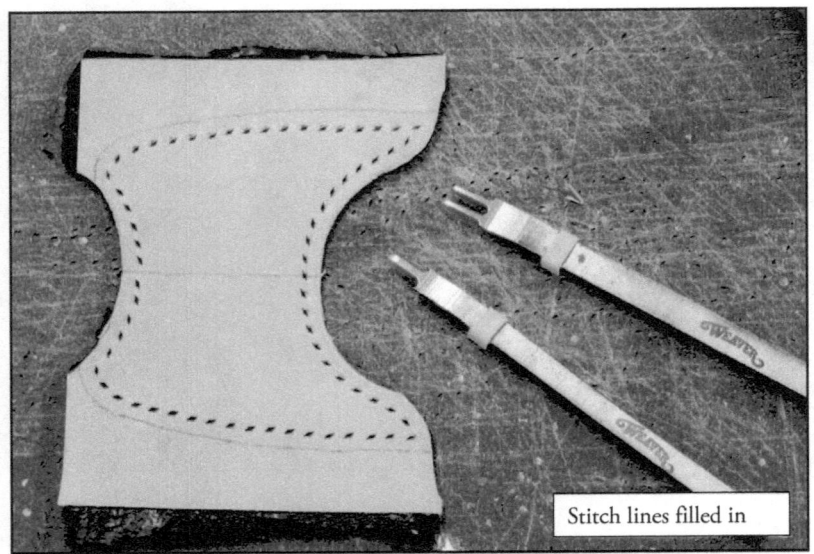

Stitch lines filled in

Now it's time to begin stitching.

It would suffice to stitch the opening curves with just a saddle stitch. I chose to add a crossover stitch so that the liner would not pull away from the edge. I found, with my standard Hill gloves, that over time, the liner pulled away and bunched up against the stitching. Not a fatal fault, but it bothered my aesthetic sensibilities.

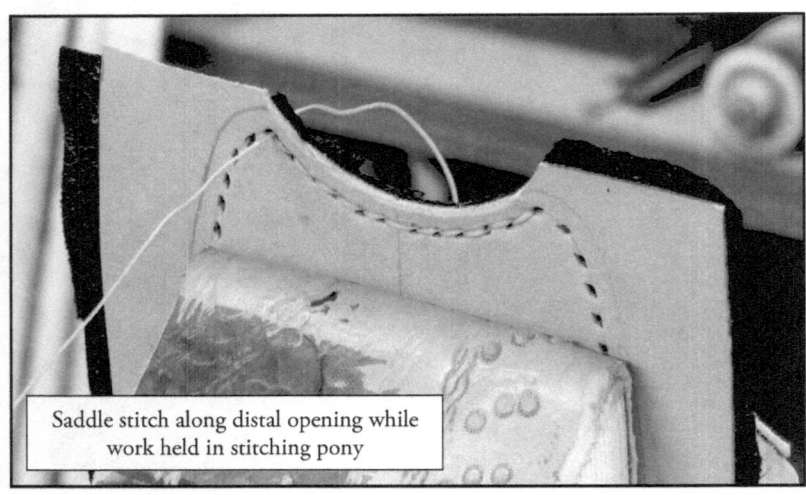

Saddle stitch along distal opening while work held in stitching pony

Start at one end of the opening curve and sew a saddle stitch to the other end. Then return to the starting point by sewing the crossover stitch. Finish with three back stitches.

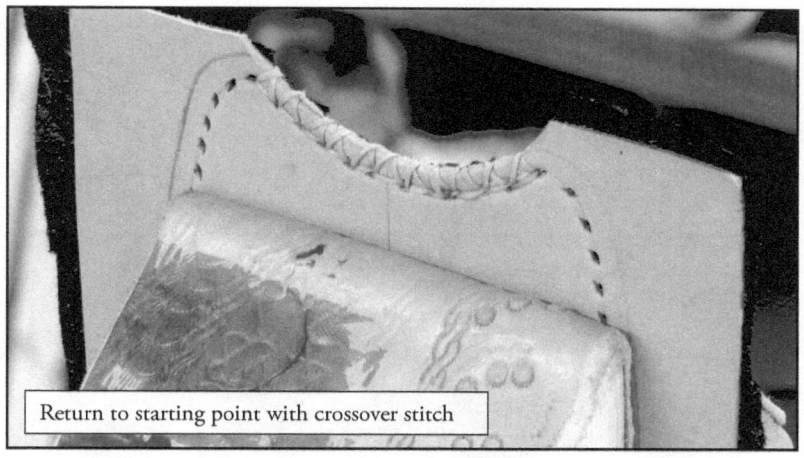

Return to starting point with crossover stitch

Next, stitch the cordovan pad to the fingerstall. To keep things from shifting on me as I do this, I glue the cordovan to the fingerstall using a temporary, or light-duty, glue stick. I sew the pad using a sewing machine and upholstery thread. It can be hand stitched as well, whichever you prefer. After stitching the pad on, I apply leather

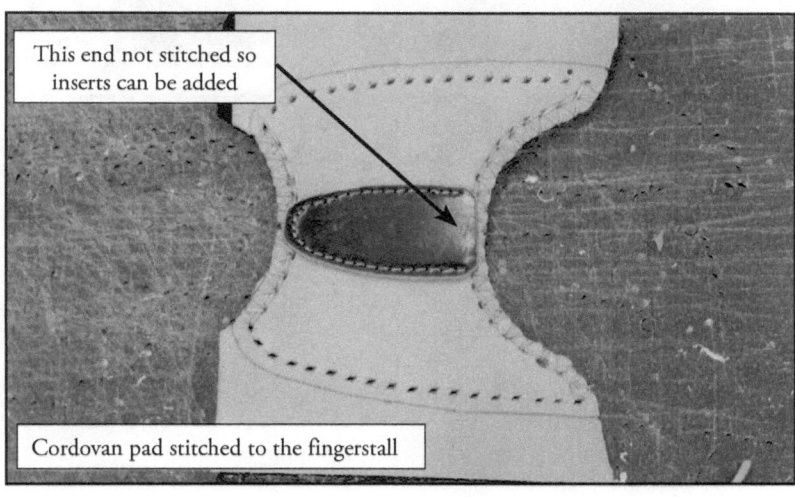

This end not stitched so inserts can be added

Cordovan pad stitched to the fingerstall

glue to the stitching on the liner side and work it into the stitching holes. This helps ensure that if a stitch fails, the pad will remain secure. This stitching would be hard to fix without opening the fingerstall, so I try to make sure I won't ever have to. And I never have.

Once the cordovan pad has been sewn in place, it's time to close the fingerstall. I have found that using contact cement to glue the spine together helps with the sewing process and also helps make the spine as stiff as possible. Apply contact cement on all the extra material along the spine, down to the stitching line that you punched

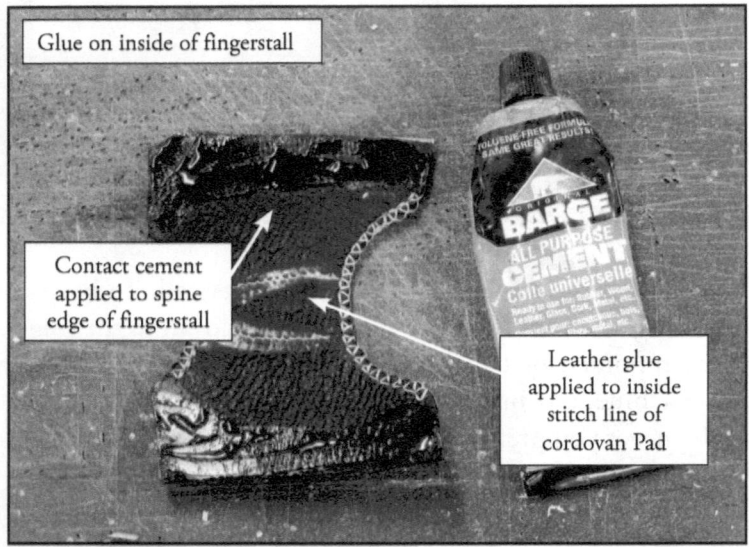

Glue on inside of fingerstall

Contact cement applied to spine edge of fingerstall

Leather glue applied to inside stitch line of cordovan Pad

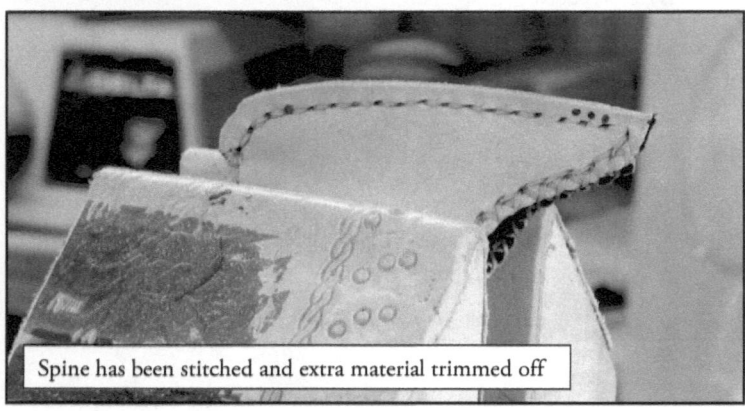

Spine has been stitched and extra material trimmed off

earlier. Once the glue has dried, close the fingerstall, making sure that the stitch holes line up. I usually put a needle through a couple of holes to help with this alignment process.

In the picture of the spine stitching, you will notice that there are three holes left open. These holes are left open to accommodate the hand strap stitching. I start my stitch in the fourth hole and proceed toward the distal end of the fingerstall.

You will also notice in the picture that there are three ink dots above the holes. I marked the fingerstall with three dots to indicate it is for the third finger (ring finger). This is how I know which fingerstall to affix to each braid of the hand strap.

MAKING THE HAND STRAP

The hand strap needs to be nothing more than a piece of leather that has been partially slit lengthwise to accommodate the three shooting fingers and provide a solid place for the wrist strap to connect.

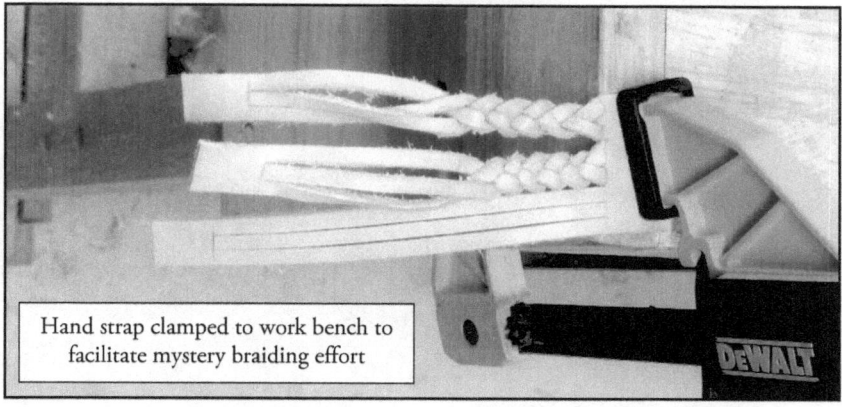

Hand strap clamped to work bench to facilitate mystery braiding effort

I have found that taking it a step further helps to make the glove easier to don and keeps the straps from sticking to me during hot weather. I have found that braiding the strap serves these useful purposes. The braiding process I use is called mystery braiding because there is no open end to the braid, and it appears mysterious as to how such a thing could be done.

With some practice, it's not hard. There are several tutorials in both written and video forms to be had. A search on the internet of the phrase "mystery braid" will provide a variety of instructions.

Once you have made your hand strap, you will need to affix it to the fingerstall. A single hole and stitch will suffice. I have taken to using my four tang punch to put a set of holes at the end of the strap that will match up to the holes on the spine of the fingerstall. I then saddle stitch the hand strap to each stall.

Double-check that you have identified the correct stall for the correct strap before stitching. This will save you from the unpleasant task of removing your nicely made stitch line.

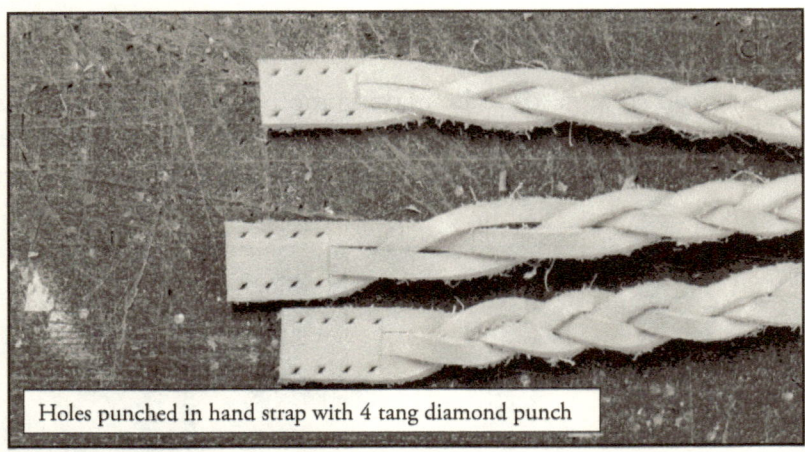

Holes punched in hand strap with 4 tang diamond punch

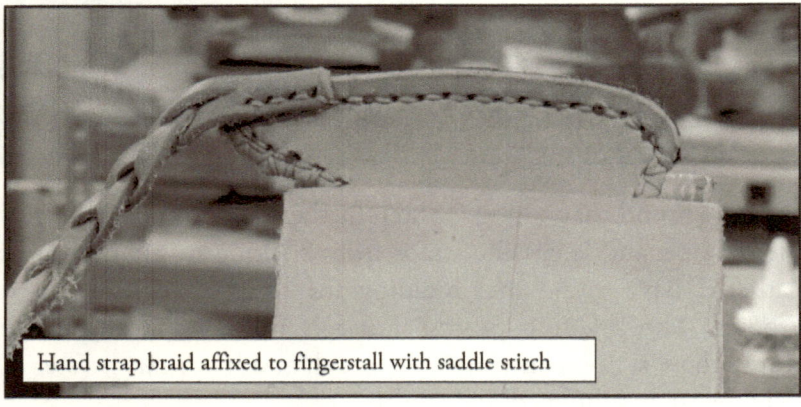

Hand strap braid affixed to fingerstall with saddle stitch

I have found that wetting the end of the braid with water allows it to stretch and form around the spine of the fingerstall as it is stitched in place.

MAKING THE WRIST STRAP

Making the wrist strap can be done in the same manner as the finger strap. A flat piece of leather will suffice, but as stated at the beginning of this appendix, the braiding makes the strap easier to manage, improves ventilation, and gives the glove a nice look.

A significant benefit to making your custom glove is that you can size it perfectly (admittedly, a trial-and-error process). Doing so will allow you to avoid the need for an adjustable wrist strap snap and the inevitable tag end that always catches on clothing.

MAKING THE INSERTS

Experimenting with insert material can be fun. That said, nylon is the old standby and always a reliable choice. I bought a small sheet of nylon that is 0.030-inch thick and have cut lots of inserts from it.

Another choice is high-density polyethylene, otherwise known as HDPE. Coffee can lids, soda bottles, and most other containers are made from it.

Horace Ford talked of using turkey feather quills in his book *Archery - Its Theory and Practice*. I have used them, and they do work well.

I have also used rubber. A 1/16-inch-thick sheet of rubber (at least 80 on the Shore A Hardness Scale) has worked well for me. The rubber makes it easier for the string to find its place in the finger joint, gives a clean release, and does not take a set.

One of the advantages of the glove described in this appendix is that you can change the inserts and mix and match thickness and materials until you find exactly what suits you.

BREAKING IN THE GLOVE

If a glove of the type that I describe here has an Achilles heel, it would be the time it takes to break the glove in and the decrease in accuracy and fun that can accompany the break-in period.

I have found that (depending on the season) it generally takes about two months of daily shooting to get the glove fitting like a second skin. It can go faster in summer due to the heat and moisture generated by sweaty fingers. The moisture helps shape the leather.

It's good to plan ahead if you anticipate needing a new glove by hunting season. Get it made and start using it after the new year so that it is in prime condition by the time Orion graces the early morning sky.

Get some leather cream to preserve the leather and make it more supple so that it will mold to your hand. When the glove is new, it should be so tight that you cannot get your dry finger all the way into the fingerstall. Apply some leather cream to your fingers each time you don the glove for the first week or so. This will allow your fingers to get all the way into the fingerstall without too much trouble. That said, the fit will be too tight, and it will be uncomfortable to shoot the glove for more than fifteen minutes or so.

Notice when your fingers start to hurt or get cold from lack of circulation. Take the glove off and go back to your old one for the rest of your practice.

Be patient.

TUNING THE GLOVE

We think nothing of the amount of time we spend tuning our arrows and our bows. The same is true about the time we spend talking and arguing over what is the most important aspect of arrow tuning: Point weight? Arrow length? Shaft spine? Feather length? Helical? Straight? Or bow tuning: Brace height? Bow length? String material? Arrow shelf depth? String silencers?

We are mostly mum on the topic of tuning our gloves. Most likely, we have never considered the merits of tuning our shooting gloves. Yet how many of us have a box full of old gloves and tabs that we never use? How many look like they are worn out?

This doesn't mean we lack favorites. It is just that we take the glove or tab as it comes and use it as is—a generic fit.

I have noticed that our hands tend to be more unique than we might at first suppose. Our fingers are not all the same length, nor are the relative lengths of those first three fingers, the string fingers, the same for every person. This should come as no surprise when we consider the fact that the very pattern of our fingerprints is so unique that it is used for personal identification.

Byron Ferguson argues that the arrow is more important than the bow. I would take a page from his way of thinking and add that I believe that the shooting glove (or tab) is also more important than the bow.

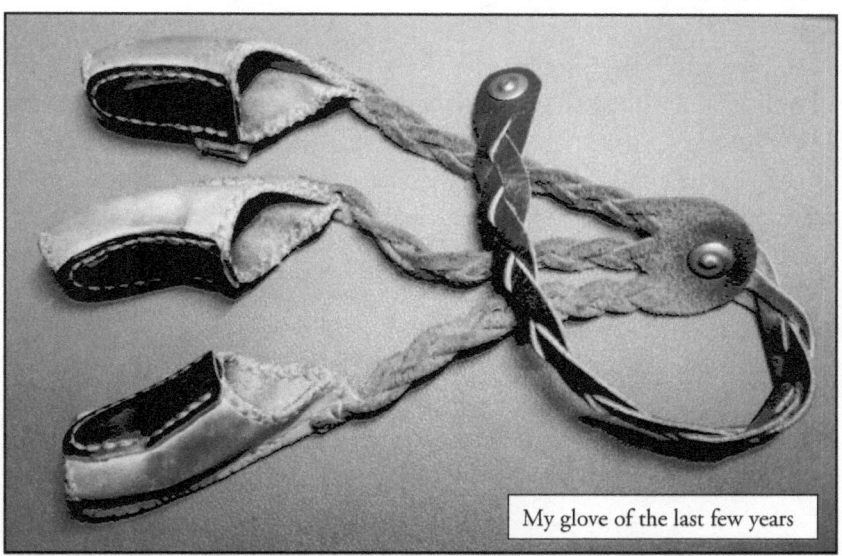

My glove of the last few years

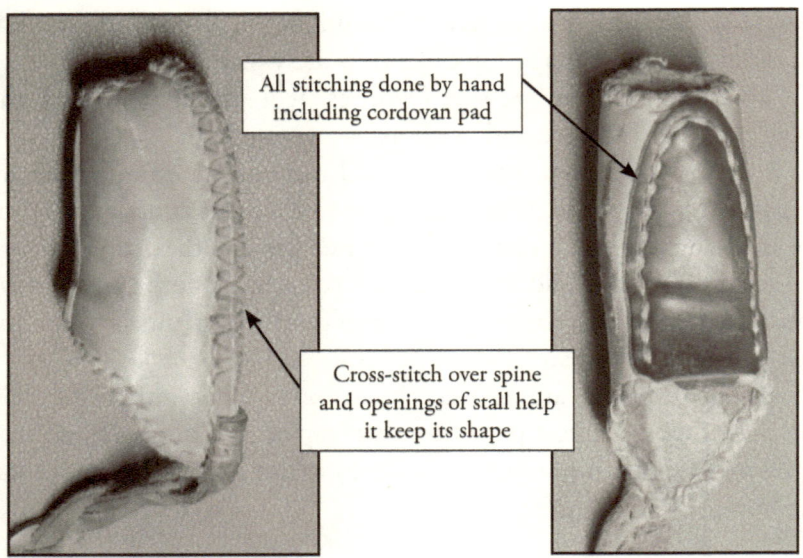

All stitching done by hand including cordovan pad

Cross-stitch over spine and openings of stall help it keep its shape

I love my bow. However, if I had to make one shot count no matter what and had to pick a generic bow or a generic glove to make it, I would keep my tried-and-true glove and risk the generic bow.

My glove of the last few years has been further customized to my needs. I've glued a patch of leather to the index fingerstall to act as a no-pinch on the arrow. I also have two nylon inserts under each cordovan pad, and I added a crossover stitch to the spine of the stall. None of these are essential or would necessarily prove helpful to other people. They just work for me. What might work for you?

The bow is the center of the archer-bow-arrow machine. It is the thing our eye is most naturally drawn to and arguably the most beautiful part of the machine. My intuition would lead me to believe that it was the most important part if not for my experience confirming Ferguson's point about the arrow and my point about the glove.

Making my gloves, and tuning them to fit so that I can hold the string with the least effort, and release it without fault, is another challenge my longbow has offered me. Having used gloves of my own making for several years now, I cannot imagine returning to a generic glove.

It's not the quality of the leather craft (far from it) that gives a self-made glove its lead over a generic glove. It's the custom fit, and the experience gained (by trying this-and-that material for inserts, and adjustments here and there for size, etc.) while on the path to finding that perfect custom fit.

What you will have in the end is a glove that you would not part with for any price. Though I am sure you will make one for a friend if they ask.

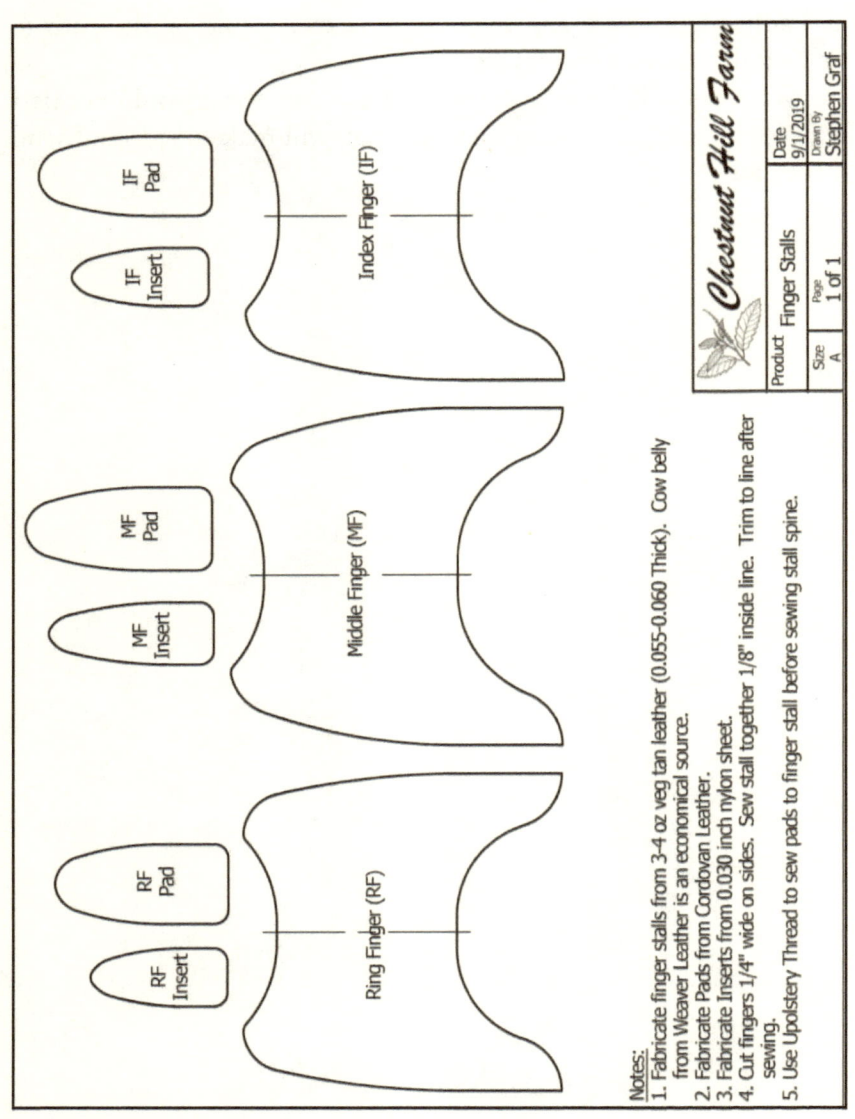

Chestnut Hill Farm

Product	Finger Stalls	Date	9/1/2019
		Drawn By	Stephen Graf
Size	A	Page	1 of 1

RF
Insert

RF
Pad

MF
Insert

MF
Pad

Ring Finger (RF)

Middle Finger (MF)

IF
Insert

IF
Pad

Index Finger (IF)

Notes:
1. Fabricate finger stalls from 3-4 oz veg tan leather (0.055-0.060 Thick). Cow belly from Weaver Leather is an economical source.
2. Fabricate Pads from Cordovan Leather.
3. Fabricate Inserts from 0.030 inch nylon sheet.
4. Cut fingers 1/4" wide on sides. Sew stall together 1/8" inside line. Trim to line after sewing.
5. Use Upolstery Thread to sew pads to finger stall before sewing stall spine.

238

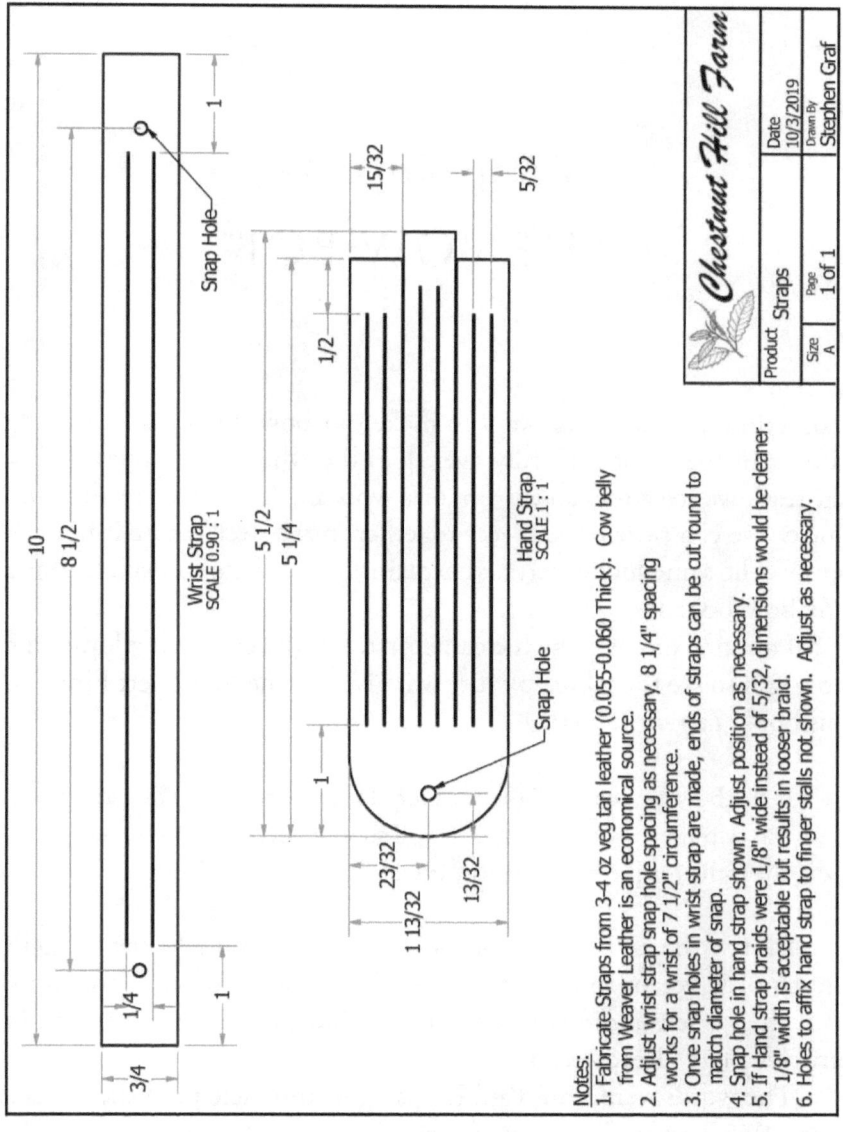

Wrist Strap
SCALE 0.90:1

Snap Hole

10
8 1/2
1/4
3/4
1

Hand Strap
SCALE 1:1

Snap Hole

15/32
5/32
1/2
5 1/2
5 1/4
1
23/32
1 13/32
13/32

Chestnut Hill Farm

Product	Straps	
Date	10/3/2019	
Drawn By	Stephen Graf	
Size A	Page 1 of 1	

Notes:
1. Fabricate Straps from 3-4 oz veg tan leather (0.055-0.060 Thick). Cow belly from Weaver Leather is an economical source.
2. Adjust wrist strap snap hole spacing as necessary. 8 1/4" spacing works for a wrist of 7 1/2" circumference.
3. Once snap holes in wrist strap are made, ends of straps can be cut round to match diameter of snap.
4. Snap hole in hand strap shown. Adjust position as necessary.
5. If Hand strap braids were 1/8" wide instead of 5/32, dimensions would be cleaner. 1/8" width is acceptable but results in looser braid.
6. Holes to affix hand strap to finger stalls not shown. Adjust as necessary.

239

~Appendix B~
THE BOW-BOB

Sometimes, hunting for ways to make our bows better is like seeing a deer in the woods. Hardly ever does the whole deer appear to us. Instead, we see a toe, an ear tip, or a whisker. And if we are alert and lucky, we can puzzle the pieces together into a deer before it bounds away. The same lucky alertness explains how I came to make and use my bow-bob.

I am not sure which clue came first, but the clue that allowed me to begin to see the whole picture was given to me by Robert Elmer in his book *Target Archery*:

> If the bow be given a light counter-clockwise torque... The arrow will slap the bow so hard that it will soon be marked and scarred... but if the torque be clockwise, it will fly off clear and clean.

I knew this to be true from my experience, but I hadn't thought much of it except to note it was another example of my poor form. But then a few more words came to mind of hints given to me in articles I had already read.

The words were from Paul Klopsteg in an article published in the July 1935 *Archery Review* magazine:

To reduce the impact between the bow and the arrow as the latter is loosed, two expedients are worth adopting. The first is to make the handle as narrow as practicable... The second is to put a slight intentional twist into both limbs such that, as the bow is drawn, its handle tends to rotate [counter-clockwise]... It is easily embodied in the bow by leaving the limbs somewhat thicker on the [arrow rest] side... The combination of narrow handle and correctly scraped limbs has the effect of decreasing very considerably the horizontal dispersion of ... arrows.

Then Klopsteg shared his patient wisdom with me even more in a chapter of the book *Archery, The Technical Side* that he cowrote with CN Hickman and Forest Nagler:

The manner of holding and the action of the bow seem especially important. Thus far, we have considered a [symmetrical bow]. Suppose such a bow is drawn and aimed [while] the handle is given a deliberate clockwise twist. What is the effect on the arrow when loosed? The general direction of travel of the string will [more closely] coincide with the axis of the arrow so that the impact between bow and arrow will be greatly lessened or eliminated. If the handle could be twisted the same amount every time, lateral errors might be eliminated.

He goes on to talk about how impossible it is to twist a bow perfectly every time, so then he explains how to build such forgiveness into the bow:

Make the limbs unsymmetrical, so that when the bow is drawn, they move towards the right [twisting away from the arrow shelf side] with respect to the plane of symmetry.

Then finally, in a footnote at the bottom of page 113 of the same book, he spells it out:

[One] way to accomplish [this twist] is to reduce the belly on the side away from the arrow plate.

This last quote tells me succinctly what I must do to relieve the arrow slap caused by a poorly balanced bow. But nowhere could I find an answer to my question, "Yeah, but how much do I scrape off?"

Sometimes, to find the answer to a question, we must experiment. Other times, to find the answer to a question, we must sacrifice something. In the case of answering this question of how much, I had to do both.

I took an old bow and looked it over the best I could to make sure it looked okay. The tiller looked okay; the limbs seemed to bend well, and looking down the centerline of the bow, it appeared that the limbs were not twisted. A fine bow.

I shot said bow for a while to get a feel for it and what I could expect to see accuracy-wise.

Then I started "reducing the belly on the side away from the arrow plate," as Klopsteg suggested, and shot the bow some more. It did seem to shoot in a quieter, more forgiving manner.

I looked the bow over and could discern no change in its appearance. I sanded the offside of the belly a few more times, shot more, and looked the bow over more. Eventually, I found that the bow started shooting more poorly.

Obviously, I was affecting the bow somehow. While I could see the effect of this belly scraping on my accuracy (both good and bad), and I could hear the difference in the arrow slap against the bow, I could not see any change in the bow's appearance.

If I could not see a change, how could I measure it and learn what the optimum unsymmetrical shaping should be? The answer to this question came in an ah-ha moment, similar in feeling to the moment when that whisker, shining in the morning sun, turns into a deer.

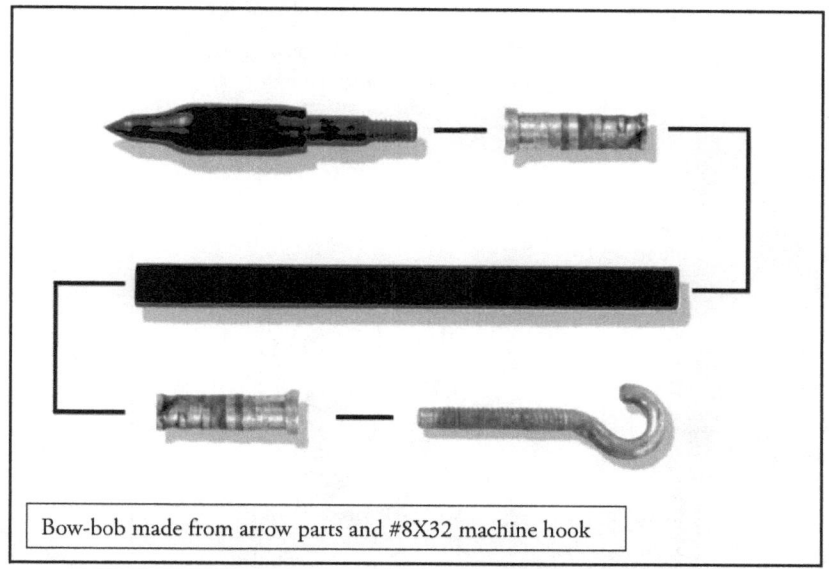

Bow-bob made from arrow parts and #8X32 machine hook

I knew that whatever the effect scraping one side (or the other) of the belly would have on the bow, it would be across the sagittal plane of the bow. My ah-ha came in realizing that if I could level the back of the bow and then see how the rest of it was twisting, I could measure the effects of unsymmetrical scraping on the limbs.

Taking a lesson from our Egyptian ancestors, as described in Chapter 11, I deduced that what I needed now was a plumb-bob.

Gathering together parts I had lying around resulted in the construction of a plumb-bob, now referred to as a bow-bob, at no cost. My bow-bob is constructed from a piece of carbon arrow with an insert installed on each end. A field point is installed in one end, and an 8-32 threaded hook is installed in the other. The threaded hook allows me to adjust the length of the bow-bob based on the brace height of the bow I'm testing.

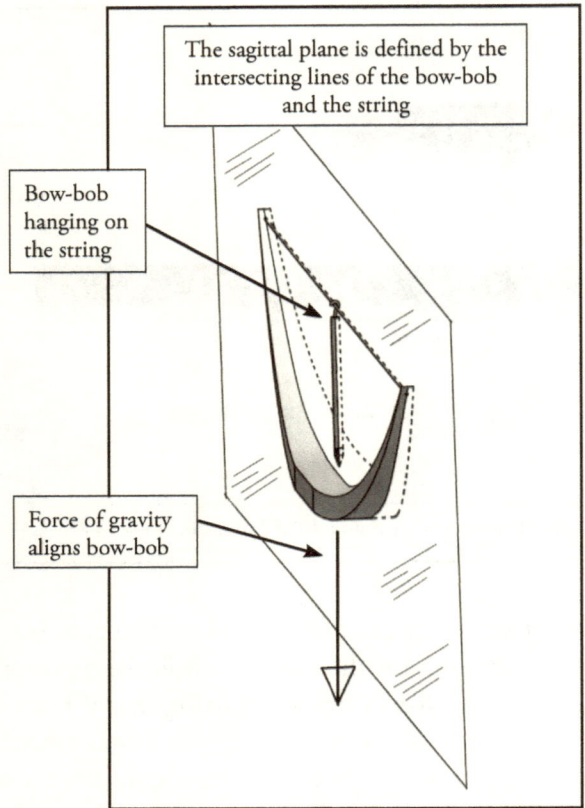

The sagittal plane is defined by the intersecting lines of the bow-bob and the string

Bow-bob hanging on the string

Force of gravity aligns bow-bob

An even simpler version of the bow-bob could be made from a broken wooden arrow. Using a short piece of arrow shaft, a point, and a nock will result in a fully functional bow-bob of fixed length.

So now I could take the bow I had been scraping on and actually see what it looked like perched on a level with a bow-bob hanging on the string.

Two intersecting lines define a plane. In this case, we have the line of the bowstring and the line of the bow-bob. By perching the bow upon a level, we orient the back of the bow perpendicular to the gravitational field of the earth.

By placing the bow on the level, we have guaranteed that the plane defined by the bowstring and the bow-bob is now perpendicular to the back of the bow. The question is, does it pass through the center of the handle and limbs?

And if not, how can we move the plane so that it does?

ADJUSTING AN UNBALANCED BOW

Before we can talk about adjusting an unbalanced bow, we need to know what qualifies as a balanced bow. And by balanced bow, I mean balanced, or tillered, across the sagittal plane.

The first thing I check is that the limb tips do not appear twisted with respect to the sagittal plane. If you look down the bow from a limb tip towards the center with the sagittal plane bisecting the nock, an imaginary line drawn through the center of the nock should appear perpendicular to the sagittal plane.

A limb can be twisted if the nocks are not cut evenly deep or if one side of the limb is stronger than the other. I have found that if I do my best to make the nock look symmetrical and if the string lies in each nock evenly, the problem usually lies in the limb.

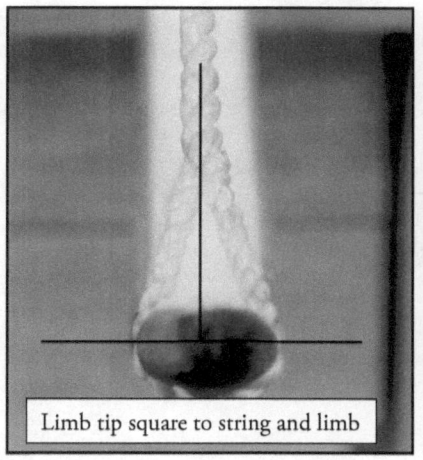 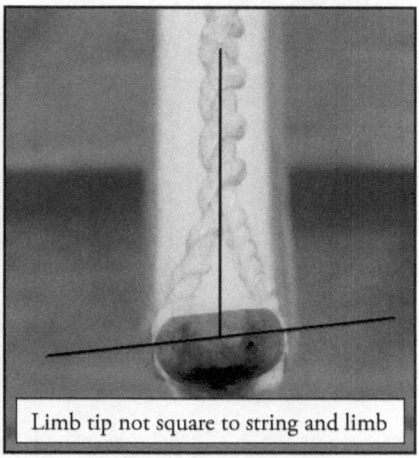

Limb tip square to string and limb   Limb tip not square to string and limb

I put my first effort into making the nocks look as symmetric as possible. If they look good, I have found that they are good.

The next step in the process depends upon whether I am making a new bow or trying to fix an existing bow.

If I'm making a new bow, I will shape the limbs and get them roughly bending correctly, sometimes referred to as floor tillering. At this point, the handle area has not been worked at all. I will then set the bow upon the level and, using my bow-bob, see how evenly the sagittal plane divides the limbs and how square to the string the limb tips appear to be.

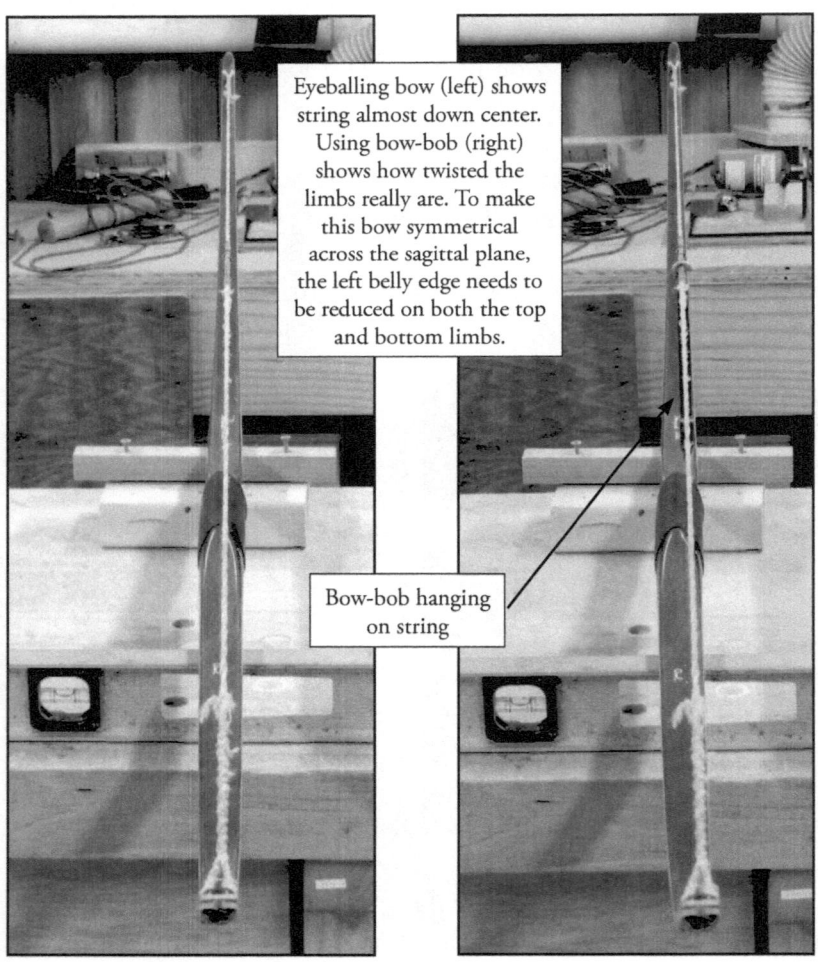

Eyeballing bow (left) shows string almost down center. Using bow-bob (right) shows how twisted the limbs really are. To make this bow symmetrical across the sagittal plane, the left belly edge needs to be reduced on both the top and bottom limbs.

Bow-bob hanging on string

When looking at the bow resting upon a level, the golden rule for adjusting the bow with respect to the sagittal plane is as follows:

Reduce the edge toward which the string should move.

The observant reader may ask, "What happens if the bow is reduced on the sides of the back instead of the belly?" I wondered that as well and sacrificed several bows to discover that the answer is not much. This result is consistent with my understanding that the belly controls the nature of the bow. It's also consistent with the eastern philosophical view that our strength and spirit come from our belly. Maybe that helps explain our use of the words belly and back to describe the two bending surfaces of the bow.

The limbs on this bow twist to the left (left picture). The bottom limb has a big twist in the outer third. After sanding the right side of the belly, the sagittal plane is centered in the limbs and handle (right picture). Bottom limb twist is mostly gone.

Through experience, I have found that the bending of the bow is controlled by the belly, and the power of the bow is controlled by the back. This should be no surprise, as bowyers of the past have instructed us to tiller self-bows by removing wood from the belly. They go on to suggest that if we want to make bows faster, we can do that by adding something elastic, like sinew, to the back.

Once I have the bow limbs bending correctly and symmetrically about the sagittal plane, it is time to address the handle.

The bow-bob can be used to mark the sagittal plane at the top and bottom of the handle

The first thing I want to do is find the centerline of the handle. At first, this seems easy enough. Just run a line down the middle. But if we stop and think about how the bow has arrived at its current state, some doubt as to the accuracy of this method may arise. Did I hold the bow exactly flat when running it through the band saw to cut it out? Did I cut exactly the same amount of material off of each side? Did the bow blank come out of the oven a little warped, so the handle wasn't located exactly in the middle?

By perching the bow upon the level and using my bow-bob, I can let the bow tell me where the centerline of the handle should be. I place the bow-bob at each end of the grip and make a mark on the handle. Then I connect the marks using my pen and a straight edge.

As you can see in the picture, the centerline of the grip does not follow the center of the handle area.

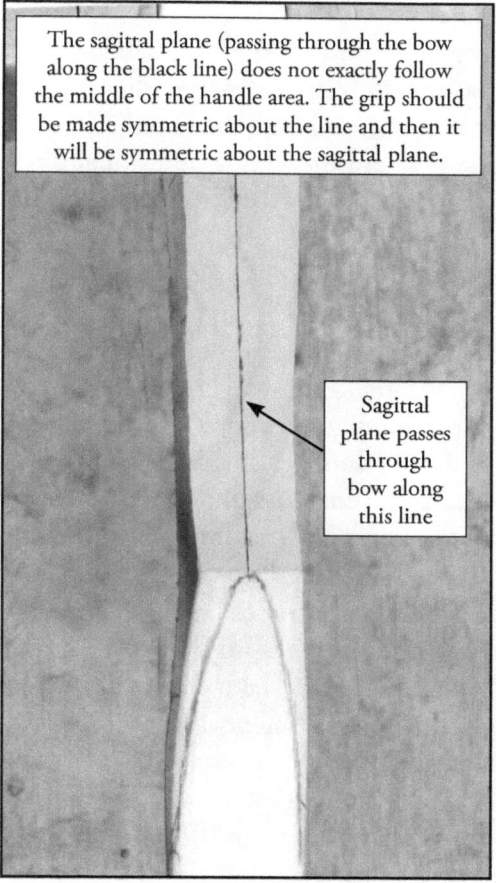

The sagittal plane (passing through the bow along the black line) does not exactly follow the middle of the handle area. The grip should be made symmetric about the line and then it will be symmetric about the sagittal plane.

Sagittal plane passes through bow along this line

Once I have a bow mostly finished, the last thing I like to do is to move the sagittal plane just a little to the offside of the centerline. I find that this does indeed make the bow a little more forgiving to shoot, just as Klopsteg and Elmer suggested it would.

When I finish out a bow, I usually leave the handle centerline in place and apply finish over it. That way, if there is ever a problem with the bow, I can set it upon a level and, using my bow-bob, determine if the bow has twisted out of alignment over time.

If I am looking over a finished bow to check its sagittal tiller and see that it is not balanced, I can follow the same basic steps laid out above to correct it, save the final shaping of the handle around the correct center line.

Adjusting the limbs so that they are balanced across the sagittal plane and so that the limb tips are perpendicular to the bowstring is not difficult. Sometimes adjusting the handle so that it is bisected by the sagittal plane may require gluing additional wood to it and can be challenging. That work is beyond the scope of this appendix.

ARRIVING IN BALANCE

The closer one gets to finishing a bow, the trickier the choices for the next step can become. At least, it may seem so.

As I shape a bow and get closer to that final moment when I say to myself, "I think it is done," I am aware of the shape of the limbs as they come around full compass, the sagittal tiller, the draw weight, and the look of the bow's lines as they transition through all of its parts.

I try to proceed in steps. I try to achieve plateaus where everything seems to be about right and in proportion. When the bow arrives at one of these plateaus, I can take a measure of its draw force to appraise my progress toward the goal of a balanced bow that I can pull to my draw length.

If I am just beginning to work on the bow and have been addressing its surface with rasps and files, then I will likely use the same to nudge the bow towards the correct sagittal tiller.

If I have made more progress and am now addressing the bow's surfaces with, say, 150-grit sandpaper, and I notice that something is a bit out of whack, I will correct it with the same 150-grit sandpaper.

And if I am giving the bow its last finish sanding with 400-grit paper and notice that I have again caused the bow to drift out of balance, I will nudge it back with the 400-grit paper.

As with all things archery, a large measure of patience will assure the best results.

Some of us are better at catching those fleeting glimpses of deer in the woods. While those of us with more practice will notice the tip of the deer's ear sticking out from behind the oak tree, others will not see a thing until the deer snorts and makes for parts unknown.

By the same token, some of us can look a bow over with just an eye and see that it's fine (or maybe that something is amiss), while others of us look and see nothing. I have lost track of the number of deer that have given me the slip, and I know that I need help to see the truth of how my bow bends.

This is another lesson my bow has taught me: Sometimes, I see things the way they really are, and sometimes, I don't.

~Appendix C~

HOW TO MAKE A BLANK BALE
TARGET

As I think about the merits of making a blank bale target, I think about the old adage: Dress for success. The idea is that if we dress the part, then we are more likely to play the part. We are more likely to remain focused on our purpose and succeed.

I think this is a true principle, and it also applies to the sport of archery. When I see someone show up for an archery outing with gear that is out of whack, I know they are not committed to the sport.

If the brace height of their bow is obviously too low (or too high), or their arrows are eight inches too long and fly like drunken fish, or their bow is overly scuffed up, or their string is frayed beyond repair, I know to keep my distance when they shoot.

I think the same observations can be made of the places we practice our sport. If we are lucky enough to have a place to set up our private shooting area, but we neglect to give ourselves a dedicated blank target upon which to practice our form, then we have not dressed for success and are handicapping our progress.

If we must rely on a public shooting area in a club or park to practice our sport, and if no accommodation has been made for a blank bale target, it wouldn't hurt to offer to donate one for the cause.

Committed practice upon the blank bale with patience and without expectation is the foundation of good shooting. Having a target upon which to practice shows commitment.

Exercising that commitment on a daily (or at least regular) basis will wear a conventional target out, which gets expensive and inconvenient.

Thus, a customized target, designed and built to withstand the rigors of daily use for close-range practice while at the same time allowing the arrows to be easily pulled out, is necessary so that the practice is as painless as possible.

If our blank bale practice is made tedious by a target that is in constant need of repairs or that tires us out from pulling arrows, or that must be placed for each practice session and put away afterwards, we will probably not practice as much as we should.

I have found that having a blank bale target always ready and waiting for me can help motivate my practice. This is probably true for everyone.

CONSTRUCTING THE BALE TARGET

We don't all have a way to get a full sheet of plywood home to work with, so the dimensions of the target have been proportioned to allow it to be made from four pieces of two-foot by four-foot sheets available from home improvement stores and stowable in most cars.

It has also been proportioned to hold one bale of hay oriented so that the arrows are cast into the side of the bale without the string and in parallel alignment with the length of the hay grass.

While it might be tempting to use straw instead of hay for a target because it can be purchased for a fraction of the cost, this would be a mistake for several reasons. Hay is far denser than straw and, therefore, has far greater arrow-stopping power. Additionally, hay proves to be a much more durable material and will need far fewer replacements over time than straw. In the end, hay proves itself to be both the more economical and functional choice.

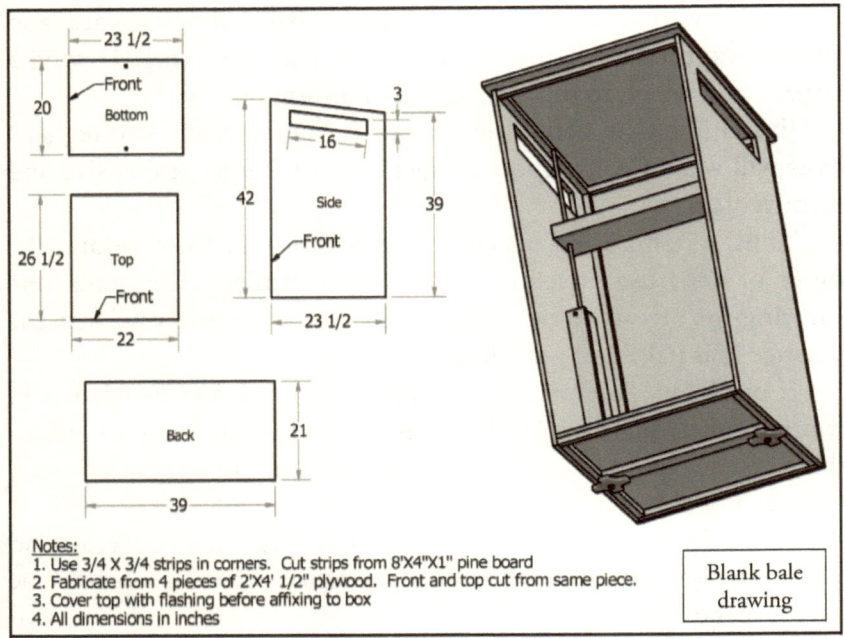

Notes:
1. Use 3/4 X 3/4 strips in corners. Cut strips from 8'X4"X1" pine board
2. Fabricate from 4 pieces of 2'X4' 1/2" plywood. Front and top cut from same piece.
3. Cover top with flashing before affixing to box
4. All dimensions in inches

Blank bale drawing

Once the choice has been made to purchase a hay bale, the individual bale must be chosen carefully. If a suitable bale cannot be found at the first place you shop, look elsewhere.

Look for a bale that is packed tightly. Loose bales are no good.

Look for a bale with straight and tight strings. A bale with loose string, or crooked strings that make the bale bulge out, is no good.

Look for a bale with clean fine grass. Hay quality is variable. The finest grass with the least burrs, twigs, stalks, or other impurities is the best.

Look for dry hay kept under a roof. Wet or moldy hay will not last long, will have poor arrow-stopping ability, and will permanently stain your arrows.

A clean, well-made, high-quality bale of hay is a valuable thing. Be ready to pay a fair price for it.

The last component of a durable blank-bale target of this design is a piece of rubber horse stall mat, available from most farm and garden stores. It should be affixed to the inside of the back wall of the target. While one piece is sufficient, I have two pieces layered in my target. They work well together to dissipate the energy of the arrow.

Blank bale target as viewed from shooting position

Once the rubber mat has been cut to size, it can be affixed with a deck screw at the top corner on each side of the mat. It should be affixed loosely with just a few screws at the top so that it can move and flex as it absorbs the energy of the arrows.

Every few years, the rubber mat may need to be replaced. Luckily, the horse stall mat, as purchased, will have plenty of material for several replacements, and thus, the extra mat not used for the initial installation can be stored for future use.

I add the new mat over the old shot-out mat. The shot-out mat still cushions the new mat and extends its life even further.

And while it's not necessary, I have found that adding a compression system to my blank bale target significantly increases the useful lifespan of the hay. As arrows are shot and pulled from the target, hay will inevitably be pulled from the bale. As the bale thins out, it can be compressed to restore its arrow-stopping ability.

COMPRESSION SYSTEM

Some 3/8" tie rods, knobs made from the plywood scraps left over from the blank bale construction, a piece of 2X6 pine board, and some threaded inserts are all that is needed to make a reliable compression system.

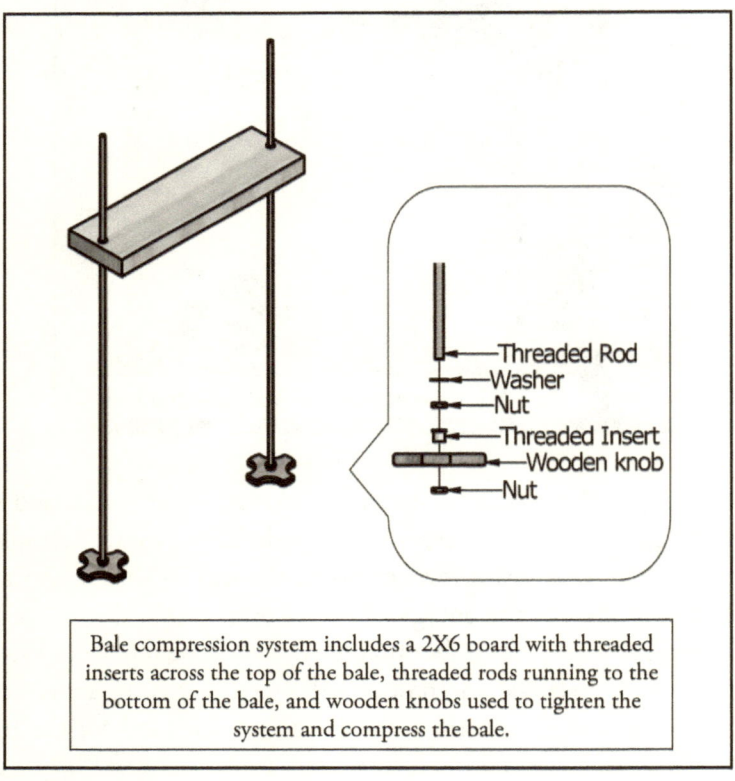

Threaded Rod
Washer
Nut
Threaded Insert
Wooden knob
Nut

Bale compression system includes a 2X6 board with threaded inserts across the top of the bale, threaded rods running to the bottom of the bale, and wooden knobs used to tighten the system and compress the bale.

Compression knobs shown at bottom of bale target

When the bale has been thoroughly shot out and no longer benefits from compression, it must be replaced. To do this, the threaded compression system must be relaxed so that the old bale can be removed and a new bale installed. I added a couple of angle brackets to the top of my target to hold the 2X6 compression board up in order to facilitate the removal and replacement process.

Angle bracket used to hold compress board up when replacing shot-out bale. Raise board up high enough that the angle bracket can be swung under it to keep it up.

One more handy little trick to extend the useful life of the blank bale target is to gently peen over the point of your blank bale practice arrow so that it is inclined to bounce off the rubber mat instead of stabbing into it.

I have a single arrow set aside for my blank bale practice for several reasons.

The first reason, already stated, is that I like to have the point rounded over. This keeps the arrow from damaging the rubber mat as much as a sharp point would. The trick is to round it over enough to prevent damage to the mat but not so much that it starts to smash through the hay like a blunt.

Another reason is that the arrows used for blank bale practice suffer more abuse than arrows used for regular shooting. They are repeatedly cast at close range into a target and suffer for it. Their feathers and finish show the wear. I don't mind using a beat-up arrow for my blank bale practice, but I like to keep my other arrows in better condition.

Tarp cut to size and secured to front of target with wood strip and screws

It's not uncommon for me to replace the feathers on my blank bale arrow three times before the arrow is lost, broken, or shot into the sky for one last glorious flight.

And finally, you must protect the hay within your target from the rain. I've used everything from plastic tablecloths to garbage bags stapled across my target to protect the hay. But the best and longest-lasting cover I have found is a piece of tarp. Affixing the tarp to the target using screws and a strip of wood keeps the tarp from pulling loose in high winds. Speaking of wind, a large binder clip holding the tarp to the bottom edge of the target keeps the tarp down when it blows.

A BETTER WAY

A friend who has embraced the swing-draw went so far as to ask me for my blank bale plans. He did this after seeing how much of a workout I had given mine and how well it had held up.

Naturally, I was happy to give him the plans, along with a good dose of pontification about how the plans had evolved through several iterations and that the design was based on vast and wise experience. I assured him that he could find no better, simpler, easier, or more durable design, no matter how hard or how far he looked.

Duncan (his real name is William, but that's another story) nodded at all the right times, said "yep" at all the right moments, and went home with the plans.

The next time I chanced to be in Duncan's backyard shooting hopelessly at his targets, I happened to notice his new blank bale target off to the side of his workshop. What luck! In order to distract him from where my arrows had ended up and in the hope that I could pull them without notice, I immediately congratulated Duncan on his fine blank bale target and asked how he liked the compression system.

"Oh, I didn't use it," Duncan said.

"What?!" I exclaimed. "Your bale won't last long without it," I warned him. I had forgotten all about my plan to pull my misguided arrows from his target.

"I just cut a couple of slots in the bottom and put a ratchet strap around the bale. The ratchet is under the bottom of the target. Works fine," Duncan said.

Yet again, my bow and arrows have come to my rescue, saving me from thinking that I had achieved perfection in thought or deed. There is always room for improvement if we take the time to think about it.

In this case, it is a simpler, easier, and likely cheaper way to compress the bale after it loosens up with use.

"Good job, Duncan!" I said, as I gave him a pat on the back. "What do you mean, you won that round? I just pulled all my arrows from the bullseye. You must have been distracted."

Duncan with his blank-bale target

"Nope," Duncan said.

As you mull over your need for a blank bale target, I would encourage you to do as Duncan did and look for ways to make it work better and better suit your fancy.

MAKING A STAND

If you have found a place to practice your blank-bale shooting that is level, dry, and durable, then you are in luck and good to go. But if you have not been so lucky, then you might consider adding a stand or platform to your construction plans.

Top view of platform showing deck boards.
Overall dimensions are 38 inches by 24 inches.

As discussed in the chapter on blank bale practice, whatever you can do to increase the consistency and ease of your practice will encourage you to shoot more and speed up your learning process. Having a level shooting platform that is unaffected by rain and snow helps in this regard.

I fabricated mine from pressure-treated decking lumber. The size of your platform will depend on your stance, but it doesn't need to be overly large. I am tall and have found that my platform, which is 38 inches long and 24 inches wide, works well. It has been a worthwhile addition to my blank bale setup.

Front view of platform showing 2X6 frame

~Appendix D~
GLOSSARY OF ARCHERY TERMS

<u>Archer's paradox</u> 1. The phenomenon of an arrow traveling in the direction in which it is pointed at full draw instead of off to the left, as it would be expected to do as it sits on a braced bow.

2. The flexing action of an arrow as it passes around the handle of a bow after the archer drops the bowstring. The flexing action is induced by the inertial forces created as the string pushes the fingers aside.

<u>Arrow shelf</u> – A step cut into the handle of a bow designed to accept an arrow laid upon it and hold it at the same level through the draw and loose of the bow.

<u>Back</u> – The surface of the bow that faces away from the archer and is under tension when the bow is drawn.

<u>Back set</u> – Used to describe the profile of a bow when the tips of the unstrung bow extend past the riser, away from the archer.

<u>Belly</u> – The surface of the bow that faces toward the archer and is under compression when the bow is drawn. Sometimes called the face of the bow.

<u>Bowyer</u>   1. A person who makes bows.

2. One who draws a longbow, a dealer in the marvelous, a teller of improbable stories, a liar (perhaps from the wonderful shots frequently boasted by archers). The word originated in the 12th century, according to Phil Cousineau, as recorded in *The Painted Word*.

<u>Brace</u> – To string the bow. A bow at brace is strung and ready to shoot.

<u>Brace height</u> – The measured perpendicular distance from the back of the bow to the inside of the bowstring when the bow is braced.

<u>Cast</u> – A measure of how well a bow can shoot an arrow with respect to its draw force and the arrow's mass weight.

<u>Centroid</u> – The geometric center of a two- or three-dimensional object. If the object is of uniform density, this point will also be the center of mass.

<u>Core</u> – The material, usually wood, in the center of a bow limb between the back and belly fiberglass.

<u>Fadeout</u> – The parts of the riser, located at the top and bottom of the riser, that form the transition between the grip and the limb.

<u>Fistmele</u> – The fist measure of the distance from the handle to the string of a braced bow, obtained by placing the base of the fist against the handle and extending the thumb to touch the inside of the string.

<u>Floor tiller</u> – The act of placing the lower limb of the bow on the floor while holding the upper limb in one hand and applying pressure to the grip with the other. Used to roughly judge the action of a bow.

<u>Grain</u> – Unit of measure for weight. One ounce equals 480 grains.

<u>Grip</u> – The part of the riser designed to accept the archer's hand. Usually located in the middle of the riser.

<u>Limb tip</u> – The far end of the limb, past the string nock.

<u>Mesomorph</u> – A body type characterized by large muscle and bone structure. This description was formed as part of a taxonomy of body types in 1940 by psychologist William Sheldon.

<u>Neutral plane</u> – The plane inside the limb that experiences neither compressive nor tensile stress, usually near the center of the limb between the back and belly surfaces.

<u>Nock set</u> – A bulge on the string, normally made of brass or string, designed to arrest the vertical motion of the arrow at the same point for every shot.

<u>Parasitic force</u> – Any force imparted by the archer into his bow and arrow that does not act along the draw force line.

<u>Parasitic torque</u> – Any torque imparted by the archer into his bow and arrow that acts around the draw force line.

<u>Pin nock</u> – An extremely narrow limb tip wrapped with cord or sinew that provides a lip to retain the string loop instead of notches.

<u>Riser</u> – The handle of the bow, located between the upper and lower limb.

<u>Sagittal plane</u> – In anatomy, the sagittal plane, or longitudinal plane, is an anatomical plane that divides the body into right and left sides. The plane may be in the center of the body and split the body into two halves or away from the midline and split the body into unequal parts.

<u>Self-bow</u> – A bow made from a stave of wood. Not laminated.

<u>Sight-picture</u> – The view an archer sees as they come to anchor, look past their drawn bow and arrow, and focus on the intended mark.

<u>Stack</u>   1. The thickness of all laminations of a bow, usually measured at the middle of the bow.

2. The sensation felt by the archer as the draw force begins to increase rapidly.

<u>Strain</u> – Material response to an applied force. When a force is applied to a bow, the material in the bow compresses (from compressive stress) or stretches (from tensile stress).

<u>Stave</u> – A block of wood roughly six feet long and two inches square from which a bowyer will make a self-bow.

<u>Stress</u> – An applied force. In the case of a bow, there are two principal stresses: compressive (push together) stress and tensile (pull apart) stress.

<u>String</u> – Flexible but inelastic cord connected at each end to the limb tips of the bow.

<u>String follow</u> – Used to describe the profile of a bow when the tips of the unstrung bow extend past the riser toward the archer.

<u>String nock</u> – Two opposing grooves near the limb tips designed to accept the string and hold it securely in place.

<u>String silencer</u> – Material added to the string to absorb noise and vibration after the shot.

<u>Tiller</u>   1. The act of shaping the bow limbs so that they bend together in harmony.

2. The shape of the bow limbs when the bow is at brace or drawn.

<u>Whip-ended</u> – Describes the profile of a bow limb in which the outer portion of the limb bends to a tighter radius than the middle or inner portions of the limb. Often associated with an elliptical curvature of the limb profile.

<u>Yips</u> – The yips is a colloquial term for a sudden and unexplained loss of skills in experienced athletes. Some credit the yips to a loss of fine motor skills; others consider the condition to be primarily psychological. However, it is poorly understood and has no known treatment or therapy. Otherwise known as target panic.

~Appendix E~
BIBLIOGRAPHY

The following books, articles, and studies include those that were quoted directly, as well as those that otherwise informed the writing of this book.

Abbey, Edward. *Desert Solitaire: A Season in the Wilderness*. New York, NY. Ballantine Books, 1968.

Ackerman, Jennifer. *The Genius of Birds*. New York, NY. Penguin Books, 2016.

Anderson, Fred. *Toxicated: A Treasury of Archery*. Grapeview, WA. Tox Press, 2010.

Aschem, Roger. *Toxophilus*. London, England, 1545

Axford, Ray. *Archery Anatomy*. London: Souvenir Press, 1995.

Bedau, Mark. *Weak Emergence, Philosophical Perspectives: Mind Causation and World* vol 11. Oxford. Blackwell Publishers, 1999.

Coche, J. *La Disciplina Del Tiro Instintivo Fluido Con L'arco*. Italy. Palutan, 1995.

Comstock, Paul. *The Bent Stick*. Delaware, OH. Self-published, 1988.

Duff, James. *Bows and Arrows - How to Make Them*. New York, NY. The Macmillan Company, 1946.

Eippert, Falk, et al. *Functional MRI, The Spinal Cord is Never at Rest.* eLife 2014;3:e03811 DOI: 10.7554/eLife.03811

Fields, Douglas. *The Brain Learns in Unexpected Ways.* New York, NY. Scientific American, March 2020.

Ferguson, Byron. *Become the Arrow.* Mequon, WI. Target Communications Corp, 1994.

Gladwell, Malcolm. *Outliers, The Story of Success.* New York, NY. Little, Brown and Company, 2008.

Goode, Erica. *No Dullard, Spinal Cord Proves It Can Learn.* New York Times. New York, NY. September 21, 1999.

Graf, Stephen. *The American Longbow.* Durango, CO. Raven's Eye Press, 2016.

Hamm, Jim, et al. *The Traditional Bowyers Bible.* Guilford, CT. Bois d'Arc Press, 1992.

Herrigel, Eugene. *Zen in the Art of Archery.* New York, NY. Random House, 1981.

Hickman, C.N., et al. *Archery: The Technical Side.* National Field Archery Association, 1947.

Hill, Howard. *Hunting the Hard Way.* Lanham, MD. Derrydale Press, 1953.

Johnstone, Ainslie. *The Amazing Phenomenon of Muscle Memory.* OxfordUniversity.com, December 14, 2017.

Kit, Wong. *The Art of Shaolin Kung Fu.* North Clarendon, VT. Tuttle Publishing, 2002.

Koch, Christof. *What is Consciousness?* Scientific American. New York, NY. Nature America, Inc.

Leopold, Aldo. *A Sand County Almanac and Sketches Here and There.* New York, NY: Oxford University Press, 1968.

Lewes, George. *Problems of Life and Mind: Third Series, The Study of Psychology, Its Object, Scope and Method.* London: Elibron Classics Series, 1999.

Ma, Justin and Tian, Jie. *The Way of Archery, A 1637 Chinese Military Training Manual*. Atglen, PA. Schiffer Publishing Ltd, 2014.

Madrigal, Alexis. *Scanning Dead Salmon in fMRI Machine Highlights Risk of Red Herrings*. Wired.com: 09.18.09 05:37 PM

Nagler, Forest. *Archery, An Engineering View*. Albany, OR. Frank Taylor and Son, Publishers, 1941.

Nelson, Richard. *The Island Within*. New York, NY. Vintage Books, 1991.

Pendry, J. H. *The Methods of George Phillips Bryant*. New York, NY. Forest and Stream Magazine, April 1913.

Petersen, David. *On the Wild Edge, In Search of a Natural Life*. New York, NY. Henry Holt, 2005.

Pope, Saxton. *Hunting with the Bow and Arrow*. Stilwell, KS. Digireads Publishing, 2007.

Sigurslid, Dave. *An Archer's Inner Life*. Lincoln, NE. Writers Club Press, 2001.

Schulz, John. *Straight Shooting*. Cody, WY. Self-Published, 2002.

Schulz, John. *Hitting Them Like Howard Hill*. Cody, WY. Self-Published, 1975.

Snyder, Gary. *The Practice of the Wild*. New York, NY. North Point Press,1990.

Thompson, Maurice. *The Witchery of Archery*. Memphis, TN. General Books, LLC, 2009.

Torges, Dean. *Hunting the Osage Bow, A Chronicle of Craft*. Winfield, KS. Central Plains Books, 1998.

Underwood, Emily. *Your Gut is Connected to Your Brain*. Science, American Association for the Advancement of Science, Sept 2018.

Vinding MC, Jensen M, Overgaard M. *The Time Between Intention and Action Affects the Experience of Action*. Front Hum

Neurosci. 2015;9:366. Published June 19, 2015. doi:10.3389/ fnhum.2015.00366.

Wernbom, Mathias & Augustsson, Jesper & Thomee, Roland. (2007). *The Influence of Frequency, Intensity, Volume and Mode of Strength Training on Whole Muscle Cross-Sectional Area in Humans*. Sports medicine (Auckland, N.Z.). 37. 225–64. 10.2165/00007256-200737030-00004.

ABOUT THE AUTHOR

One time NASA engineer having worked on some 50 Space Shuttle missions (the only evidence left is the stack of "rocket scientist" T-shirts in the drawer), and onetime semi-conductor engineer having worked on equipment and chemical processes used to produce some of the first submicron chips (now terribly obsolete), and one time entrepreneur having started an archery company based on a half dozen patents, Stephen now resides on his 50 acre subsistence farm with his family and spends his time farming with his son, building traditional archery gear, and roving the countryside as time will allow.